DIGITAL VISIONS FOR FASHION + TEXTILES

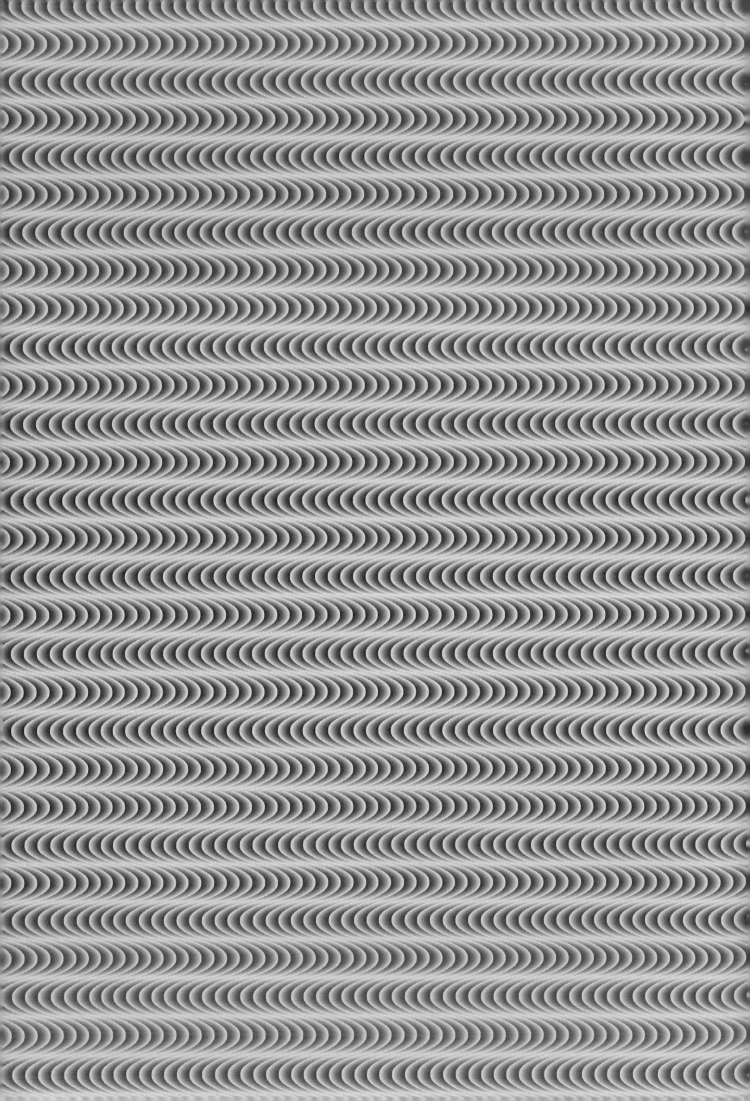

DIGITAL VISIONS FOR FASHION + TEXTILES

made in code

429 COLOR ILLUSTRATIONS

sarah e. braddock clarke and jane harris

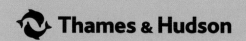
Thames & Hudson

We both very much appreciate the support and interest from all those who have contributed to the development of this publication, as well as the designers, artists, companies and organizations who have been generous in providing images and information. In addition, we would like to thank family and friends who have helped us navigate many a digital challenge.

On page 1
Bruce Mau Design, *L7*, carpet design for Shaw Contract, Shaw Industries, Inc., 2004

On page 2
Vibeke Riisberg, *Seashell*, 1997

On pages 6–7
Simon Schofield, *Plankton of the Ether*, 2008

First published in 2012 in hardback in the United States of America by Thames & Hudson Inc., 500 Fifth Avenue, New York, New York 10110

British Library Cataloguing-in-Publication Data
A catalogue record for this book is available from the British Library

thamesandhudsonusa.com

Library of Congress Catalog Card Number 2012931631

ISBN 978-0-500-51644-7

Printed and bound in China through Asia Pacific Offset Ltd

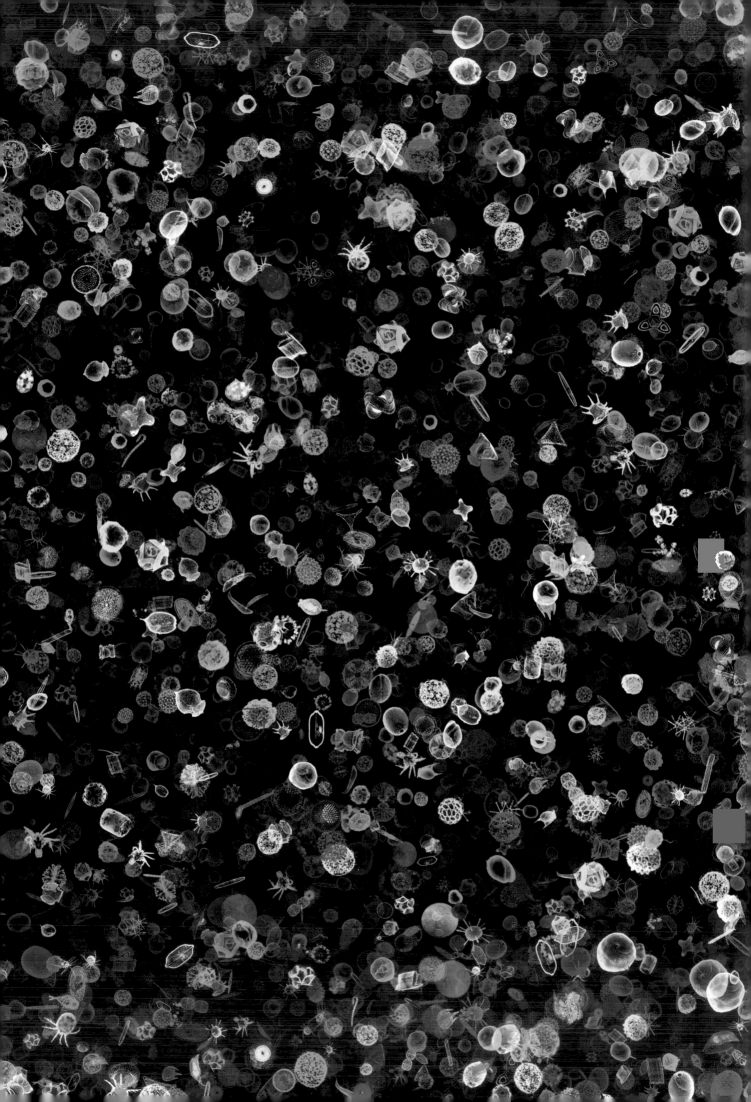

introduction: enigmatic machines

In just a few decades,
creative processes and material
approaches have undergone
a computing revolution that has
hybridized earlier traditional
working methods, defining new
codes of practice.

Ever since its inception in art and design education and the creative industries, digital media have generated new ideals, and continues to change experiential, visualized or processed information. Notions of space and time are constantly shifting and evolving, owing to successive emerging computing concepts that will continue to influence advances in technology for the unforeseeable future. Computer technology was adopted very early on by the product, engineering, automotive and architectural design sectors, the benefits to which seemed immediately apparent as digital methods of 2D and 3D computer-aided design increased capacity and experimentation, reduced costs and labour, and provided new tools with which to manage complex calculations.

The focus for this book stems from the digital arenas that meet with fashion, textiles and related industries. Computer-aided design and production processes have advanced textile construction/ embellishment, and enabled links between established art and design disciplines, including interior design, graphics, photography, film and gaming. Practitioners have responded to the arrival of digital media through collaborative necessity, and as a result, crossovers are extensive and ongoing. Fashion image-makers have developed a sophisticated use of digital special effects, using 2D, 3D and moving-image tools to fast-forward us to imagined lifestyles and future visions. Textile practitioners are combining digitized techniques with traditional 'analogue' versions, and using new materials to create pattern and form that are beyond the merely decorative.

Computing hardware developed throughout the twentieth and early twenty-first centuries with a consistent emphasis on speed and efficiency – a quest that has, to a certain extent, diminished, with scale, both macro and micro, becoming more prevalent. Widely acknowledged as one of the first forms of 'computer', the mechanized loom revolutionized the nineteenth-century workplace. The Jacquard loom, invented in 1801 by Joseph-Marie Jacquard, the son of a master weaver, allowed detailed and realistic imagery to be woven in material form through the use of a series of wooden cards, with punched holes, each row corresponding to one row of the design. The codification of the human weaver's actions was converted into binary information.

Inspired by the intricate weaving patterns achieved by the Jacquard loom, English inventor Charles Babbage developed a programmable machine, the Analytical Engine, in 1839. Owing to the incorporation of a calculation function, control flow and integrated memory, it was the first real precursor to the modern computer. Following the code-breaking work of Alan Turing and the development of Colossus, the first electronic computer, by Tommy Flowers, during World War II, one of the earliest designs for what became the recognizably modern computer was the ENIAC, or Electronic Numerical Integrator and Computer, invented in 1946 by J. Presper Eckert, Jr. and John W. Mauchly at the University of Pennsylvania. It weighed 30,000 kg and occupied 4,572 m^2 of floor space, and reduced computation from hours to seconds.

Early computers such as ENIAC were monolithic in appearance, installed in large, air-conditioned rooms to prevent overheating, and were often part of military-, space- and science-based units, rendering them inaccessible. Research programmes, driven in particular by the USA and Canada, hugely advanced computing in its efficiency, reliability of information transfer, and visualization of real-time scenarios. In the years following World War II, there were many breakthroughs in the research and development of digital technologies, including Univac I (Universal Automatic Computer I), the first American commercial computer, made and used by the US Census Bureau in 1951. Such government agencies and banks were among the first institutions to employ computing more widely, and on a consistent basis, during these early evolutionary decades.

It could be argued the emerging dominance of the computer facilitated an era of 'creative destruction'. Fascination with computing's potential drove its rapid growth and subsequent output, but this resulted in the breakdown of traditional artistic processes, only some of which the computer was intended to replace. The rules of realism could be easily broken using digital media, and the visual effects achieved by hand in, for example, the work of the Impressionists, Cubists and Futurists, could now be achieved through 2D imaging software. By the mid-1960s, while still accessible to very few, the computer had inspired astonishing feats of learning as artists built their own hardware, learnt complex code and developed working links with scientific communities. The

Basso & Brooke,
Sottsass,
Autumn/Winter 2006–7

Cutting-edge fashion duo Basso & Brooke are known for their illusory fabric designs (opposite), which are seemingly formed of broken-down computer pixels, adding to the painterly quality of their patterns.

resulting work, however, was not valued or considered as works of art would otherwise be because of the links with science, programming and technology.

Among the earliest proponents of computer animation, produced using machines of their own invention, were two brothers, John and James Whitney, of Pasadena, California. John Whitney was an animator, composer and inventor, who also created a form of analogue computer. Having begun collaborating with his brother in the early 1940s on a series of abstract film works, by the 1950s and '60s, their mechanical animation techniques were being employed to create short pieces for commercials, television and film, most famously the title sequence for Alfred Hitchcock's film *Vertigo* (1958), in collaboration with Saul Bass. Significantly, John Whitney was IBM's first artist-in-residence in 1966, and this access to emerging, fully digital tools ultimately resulted in a series of mesmerizing 2D motion graphic forms, most notably the film *Arabesque*, produced in 1975.

Another enduring and important figure in the emerging field of digital art was Harold Cohen, a painter and printmaker who both studied and taught at the Slade School of Fine Art, London. After a two-year scholarship at Stanford University's Artificial Intelligence Lab, he chose not to return to London, and instead joined the faculty at the University of California, San Diego, in 1973, where he began his authorship of the now infamous art-making software program, AARON. Cohen's key objective was that AARON would be able to simulate the cognitive process that is our ability to draw, using programming languages, and to create works of art that are entirely independent of human influence. The program has since evolved into a more sophisticated tool, and recent works have highlighted its capability to select and apply colours to produce exquisitely layered and patterned canvases – works that Cohen fully ascribes to AARON.

The value of these early challenges to art and design sectors is less apparent today, as the ease of current digital technology renders their truly groundbreaking work almost invisible. Crude effects and technical glitches were perceived at the time as sources of creative intrigue, rather than faults, and exploited for their unique application and for the visual qualities that could be achieved. Advances in computing hardware have designed out the facility to use the earliest and now incompatible software. Landmark digital facilities may be almost extinct, but the very basic capabilities of fledgling hardware and software renders the creative work produced – positioned between abstraction and digital craftsmanship, discernible by a specific time – no less sophisticated for that.

Many factors have determined the use and eventual integration of computing technology into the creative fields, particularly the fashion and textile industries. The science and design of the machine, early creative movements, the evolution of code and the chance interest in the potential of digital media from both artists and scientists have formed this extraordinary tool and the level of user-engagement that has followed. *Digital Visions for Fashion and Textiles: Made in Code* explores the realms of contemporary image, texture, surface, form and motion using 2D, 3D, 4D and interaction tools, as ingenious partnerships between creator and machine flourish in an established and openly evolving digital media culture.

Harold Cohen,
Coastal:1, 2008

For this work (opposite), the software program AARON was used to combine organic growth patterns with artificial ones. The finished artwork is both beautiful and sophisticated in its digital creation.

Me Company for Kenzo,
Genetic Politic I.I.,
Spring/Summer 2002

Genetic Politic I.I. (ill. overleaf) was created using early 3D computer modelling by digital-imaging studio Me Company. The artwork was produced for an advertising campaign for fashion company Kenzo's Spring/Summer 2002 collection.

1 digitally implicit

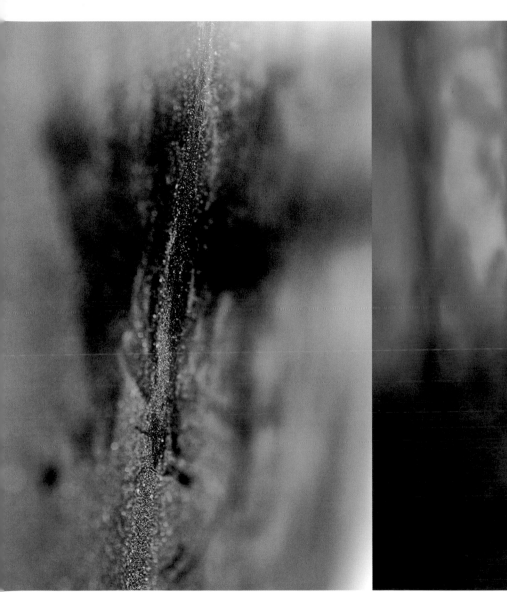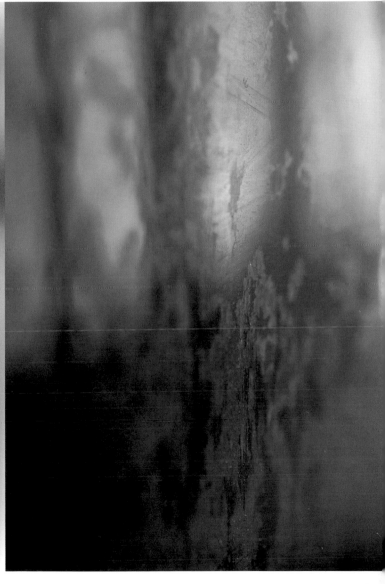

Nicola Naismith,
Enhanced Monitor
SG6383XW7Q6, 2007

Part of the *Everyday Obsolescence*
series, this work explores the
inner workings and metal-
and mineral-based materials
inside an abandoned computer
screen.

'We are, it seems, crossing the final technological frontier, where designers will be able to navigate a whimsical journey through the immaterial realities of our digitally disembodied age.'

Susannah Handley, *Nylon: The Manmade Fashion Revolution* (1999)

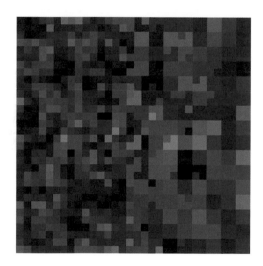

Gerhard Richter, *Woman Descending the Staircase*, 1965

At first glance, the painting appears to be a photograph or the product of computer-aided design. Its blurry quality alludes to long-exposure photography, yet is also evidence of the artist's hand. On closer inspection, tiny brushstrokes are visible. Photography © The Art Institute of Chicago

digitally implicit

the look of code

In the mid-1960s, the artist Gerhard Richter experimented with a combination of photographic realism and painterly brushstrokes to achieve figures that appeared apparitional and enigmatic, as if passing through a space in time. Influenced by Marcel Duchamp's *Nude Descending a Staircase No. 2* (1912), Richter's own *Woman Descending the Staircase* (ill. p. 17) also blurred the subject to create the impression of movement. The effect, which was achieved by hand, looked computer-generated years before such a process was possible. Other design sectors of the time anticipated the aesthetics of computers. Ultra-modern typefaces such as OCR-A and OCR-B, the latter designed by Adrian Frutiger, began to permeate design culture, appearing on record sleeves and magazines, along with futuristic fashions by the likes of Paco Rabanne, Pierre Cardin and André Courrèges. Textile designers, too, were exploring the new aesthetic, including Eddie Squires of Warner & Sons, who created a series of printed textiles (ill. below) with names that were inspired by the new technology in 1967, and Barbara Brown, who designed a print called *Frequency* for London department store Heal's in 1969.

Malcolm Cocks, from the *Fractal* series, 1997

This work (opposite) challenged traditional practice in the face of CAD/CAM use in textile design. Although the design started life on a monitor, digital printing was not yet capable of achieving such detail. Cocks hand-screenprinted the design using six hand-drawn devoré screens.

Eddie Squires for Warner & Sons, 'Univac', 1967

With this collection (left), Squires overhauled Warner's previously safe and traditional image. His futuristic textiles made use of psychedelic colours, inspired by the emerging digital world.

These pioneering attempts to capture the look of code influenced the designers of later decades, from Jean Paul Gaultier, whose 'High Tech' collection (Autumn/Winter 1980–81) combined punk couture with such digital references as hardware circuitry, safety-pinned onto leather garments, to Vivienne Westwood, whose 'Time Machine' collection (Autumn/Winter 1988–89), a nod to the H. G. Wells novel of 1895, referenced the idea of travelling back and forth through time by linking the Fair Isle jumper to computer-game patterns. With its characteristic use of two or more colours on a single row, the Fair Isle knitting technique perfectly captured the pixel imagery of early gaming.

At the time, computer technology was only just beginning to become affordable, but by the dawn of the following decade the computerized weaving loom became a relatively accessible tool, and was embraced by a new generation of textile designers. For their groundbreaking *Art and Industry* project, held at the Müller Zell weaving mill in Bavaria in 1991, the Textile Forum invited artists from across the globe to create computer-aided designs, which would then be interpreted on state-of-the-art electronic Jacquard looms. One such participant, Patricia Kinsella, experimented freely and created complex weave structures, shown in her works, *Jacquard I* and *II*. In 1991, she designed *Four Squares*, which achieved freer, more organic patterns by the stepping up of a type of pixellated imagery as the warp and weft threads interlaced. Kinsella went on to utilize digital technology throughout the decade to achieve accurate depictions of imagery with lavish colour and pattern abstractions.

But even as digital tools began to permeate the fashion and textile sectors, the cost of hardware and software remained prohibitive. Few practitioners were able to invest in computing, which still had technical limitations, and first-generation digital designers needed time to find an individual voice that would override the prevalent pixel aesthetic. For many new users, the concept of the machine and the abstract space within was overwhelming. The expectation of speed did not match the limited processing power available, and there was still a massive leap between onscreen design and the production of physical output. But the exciting potential of what might be achieved as the technology evolved overcame such frustrations, and some of the most experimental work of the time evolved from this crude yet fast-developing software and hardware.

In the early 1990s, Malcolm Cocks, a designer and senior lecturer at Central Saint Martins in London (access to computer equipment at the time was generally only available in a university environment), challenged both traditional and digital practice by developing the use of 2D imaging software in a way that would compose intricate and highly detailed designs on fabric. The designs were too complex for conventional hand-printing processes, and the printing technology needed to translate the imagery onto cloth was still very much at the development stage. Impatient to reproduce screen-based imagery in some form, Cocks devised laborious hand-printed techniques, specific to the production of his designs, which resulted in the near impossible materialization of incredible cloth imaging (ill. p. 18). At first glance, the fabrics look digitally produced, but, due to the multiple layers of image and surface pattern, it quickly becomes apparent that the cloth is in fact hand-printed. These highly accomplished designs could certainly challenge the output of modern textile manufacturing today.

Towards the end of the decade, digital printing slowly became more accessible. While still only able to process a limited range of substrates, digital print did offer an infinite palette using a four-colour process, much like a desktop printer. Silkscreen printing by hand required a separate screen for each colour, necessitating drying time between

In the late 1990s, Tang developed the use of the high-end 3D software Alias Wavefront to create wire-frame structures of floral imagery for 2D printed textiles. This was an unusual approach to developing imagery for textiles, and a contrast to the emerging use of Adobe Photoshop and Illustrator.

Hussein Chalayan,
'Airborne',
Autumn/Winter 2007–8

The video dresses
for 'Airborne' (right)
accompanied a catwalk
collection that consisted
of highly engineered
garment forms, displaying
sophisticated digital
animations that revisit
Eley Kishimoto's pixel-rose
theme from 1996.

Eley Kishimoto
for Hussein Chalayan,
'Nothing, Interscope',
Spring/Summer 1996

This striking design (above)
started life as a delicate,
hand-painted group of
flowers. The image was
digitally scanned and
enlarged to such an extent
that the individual pixels
became visible, exposing
the very foundations of the
digital image, and was then
manipulated to create
a design for a textile print,
in which the original flowers
can be deciphered by the
blocked shades of colour.
Chalayan used the design
on a stretch silk for a body-
conscious sleeveless, mid-
length dress (opposite).

the layers, but offered ink types, fabric ranges and techniques that digital printing could not. Today, combining the two offers a level of effect that is immensely rich, bringing new visual and tactile qualities to the field. One early proponent of CAD was Danish designer Vibeke Riisberg (see pp. 88–93), who was working between Copenhagen and Paris at the time. Another was Robert Mew, who had a background in television and film, and combined programming with fractal patterning systems that generated ongoing sequences of images, which in turn could be translated into pattern design, and then into garments produced on a circular knitting machine.

The next generation of designers, inspired by the look of computer gaming, explored 3D software packages as a means of creating 2D imaging designs, an approach now rarely seen in printed textiles. In the mid-1990s, high-end 3D computer-graphic animation software was complex and not easily accessible, and designers such as Eros Tang mastered these tools to define a new 2D/3D aesthetic that, while evidently digital, achieved a softer effect (ill. p. 21). Tang progressed to Rockstar Games, publishers of gaming titles such as *Grand Theft Auto*. Textile designer James Bullen, using 2D software, achieved stippled designs for printed surfaces that introduced an illusionary 3D quality that became associated with the sets of prime-time television shows. As computing technology became more available to both fashion and textile designers, the new digital aesthetic became the inspiration for visual commentary and new design ideas.

For fashion designer Hussein Chalayan's 'Nothing, Interscope' collection (Spring/ Summer 1996), Wakako Kishimoto of Eley Kishimoto hand-painted a conventional image of flowers that was then scanned and enlarged on the computer to such an extent that the image appeared broken down to its pixellated form (ill. opposite, above). Bright colours were selected to convey the

intensity of the backlit colours as viewed on a computer monitor. As computing evolved, the theme of pixellated flowers would be revisited, this time in animated form, by technical collaborator Moritz Waldemeyer in two 'video dresses' for Chalayan's 'Airborne' collection for Autumn/Winter 2007–8 (ill. p. 22, below). Rei Kawakubo of Comme des Garçons experimented with a similar pixel effect to create a print for their 'Optical Power' collection (Spring/Summer 2001), which played with illusion and camouflage pattern.

Camouflage was also picked up on by Hardy Blechman of Maharishi, who created a hard-edged and blocky design (in contrast to the typically smoother-edged, more fluid camouflage patterns for Autumn/ Winter 2004–5) called 'Mahapat', a reference to MARPAT, a digital pattern used by the US Marine Corps and a development from CADPAT, the first computer-generated camouflage, designed in the mid-1990s for Canadian troops. In another nod to early digital-design trends, Alexander McQueen looked to the luminescent bodysuits worn in the film *Tron* (ill. p. 209), released in 1982, for his Autumn/Winter 1999–2000 collection for Givenchy (ill. right and opposite). The circuitry patterning of the bodysuits, which caused the characters in the film to resemble human microchips, has had a major, if sporadic, influence on fashion collections; seventeen years after the film was made, McQueen sent models down the runway in body-conscious garments that featured photo-luminescent inks and battery-powered light-emitting diodes (LEDs) that glowed in the dark. Fashion designers, ever anticipating the future, clearly envisaged a move towards clothing that would merge with computer-operating systems.

Nearly a decade after McQueen's groundbreaking collection for Givenchy, Scandinavian design duo Maki Aminaka and Marcus Wilmont of London-based Aminaka Wilmont also echoed the circuitry and pale luminescent effects of *Tron* in their collection

**Alexander McQueen
for Givenchy,
Autumn/Winter 1999–2000**

This collection was all
about the fast-emerging
field of wearable electronics.
The look of computer
circuitry was printed in
photo-luminescent inks
on a number of different
substrates, while android-
like models (opposite)
recalled the 'replicants' of
the retro-futuristic science-
fiction film, *Blade Runner*
(1982). McQueen embedded
LEDs into a battery-powered
jacket (right), teamed with
trousers printed with
a computer circuit-board
design, which glowed in
a similar manner to thermal
imaging.

for Autumn/Winter 2008–9, 'Vector XXY'. 'Techno couture', a phrase coined by Rei Kawakubo's protégé, Junya Watanabe, to describe his work, now became part of the fashion mainstream. Watanabe's own 'Digital Modern Lighting for the Future' collection for Spring/Summer 2001 (ill. opposite) was a comment on the look of high-tech, and alluded to the emergence of an imagined digital aesthetic. The collection featured plain, white clothing with crushed minerals pressed into the surface of the fabric, which glowed as the lights dimmed – a futuristic spectacle that again referenced science-fiction films.

Other creative fields are also exploring the incorporation of LEDs into their work. Two sisters, Maria and Ekaterina Yaschuk, born in Russia but now based in London, who together form design company Meystyle, have been designing handmade wallpaper embedded with LEDs since 2004. In addition, they create digital prints for interiors, often incorporating light-catching Swarovski crystals, and are known for their bold, colourful designs that can be custom-made in any size on a range of substrates. Canadian artist Barbara Layne investigates the use of LEDs, microcomputers and sensors in hand-woven textiles, across which scrolling text and imagery are relayed wirelessly and in real time, as seen in *Jacket Antics* (ill. p. 29, top and middle). By embedding the technology within the cloth, patterns or messages are revealed when connected to a power source and triggered by sensors.

For Layne's wall-based work *Blue Code* (ill. p. 29, bottom), silver conductive threads were woven into black linen, and 384 LEDs were individually secured to the circuitry grid. An incorporated microcontroller was programmed with 256 different structures, responding to the actions of the viewer to create a variety of light effects. Following the same principle, Sydney-based Deuce Design, headed by Bruce Slorach and Sophie Tatlow, created *Slipstream*, a light sculpture

(ill. p. 28) that featured animated neon tubes with coded imagery, based on the rhythm and movement of the passing traffic in urban Melbourne.

As designers engage with material and environmental design, digital technology seems to both complement such initiatives and provide innovative decorative solutions. London-based design team Rachel Wingfield and Mathias Gmachl of Loop.pH deftly navigate between technology and nature to create works of poetic beauty for interior and exterior spaces. Their installation piece *Blumen* (2004) consists of a series of panels, which are composed of repeated cell-like sections with built-in electroluminescent technology and digital sensors that control how the pattern is illuminated. For another work, *Sonumbra* (2006), the pair combined textiles and interactive design to create a structure that responds to environmental needs. Functioning like an expansive architectural parasol, *Sonumbra* shades by day while collecting enough energy to provide light in the evening. Its filament is composed of a finely crafted lacework pattern, made from electroluminescent fibres. The piece responds to the interaction of people as movement or inactivity, effectively composing the corresponding sound and pattern that is emitted.

With digital output steadily increasing, designs began to lose that intangible, ethereal concept that the Japanese call *wabi-sabi* – the opposite of machine-perfect. *Wabi-sabi* celebrates the imperfect, the irregular and the asymmetrical, all of which are considered the essence of what is beautiful and the antithesis of overly slick computer-generated output. The machine-made product in its perfection removes evidence of the sensory relationship between maker and object, and the hand of the artist becomes less visible. Because imperfection does not naturally occur in computer-generated visuals, defects like ragged edges, loose threads and tears must

Junya Watanabe, 'Digital Modern Lighting for the Future', Spring/Summer 2001

With this collection (opposite), Watanabe was commenting on high-tech digital technologies, but in fact employed low-tech means to achieve the look. He used naturally glowing mineral powders, pressed into plain white clothing, that glowed in the dark to emit a spectacle of intense colour on the catwalk.

be consciously constructed (as evidenced by Comme des Garçons' famous 'lace' sweater of 1982). Wear and tear, disintegration and even self-destruction can be implemented by algorithmic means, and errors and flaws become effects in their own right.

At both the design and manufacturing stage, patterns can be programmed to randomly repeat, or to have such a long sequence of repeat that it is difficult to distinguish the pattern. But with the notion that digitally produced 2D and 3D forms can appear too perfect, and that the slight offsets and irregularities that occasionally occur can be intriguing, rogue or random elements can be intentionally planned. Faults that have often provided a tangential moment for the maker could be celebrated in the digital context, rather than controlled and corrected. Evidence of the unexpected, unpredictable and undone is becoming a welcome factor in the modern age of digital conviction.

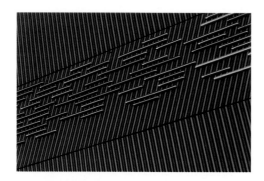

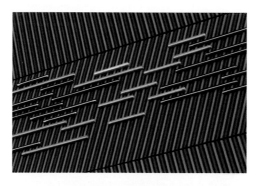

Deuce Design,
Slipstream, 2004
With McGregor Westlake
Architects

This light sculpture by Bruce Slorach, in the form of a visible code, scrolls across the façades of two tower blocks. It is interactive, responding to the beat of a winking car light and the ebb and flow of passing traffic. The pulsating colours and patterns evoke sound and water waves, creating a wonderful sensory experience and successful meeting of graphic design, public art and architecture.

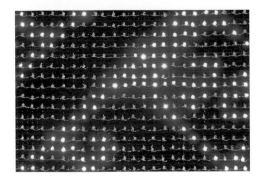

Barbara Layne,
Jacket Antics, 2007;
Blue Code, 2008

LEDs, microcontrollers and sensors were hand-woven onto the backs of two jackets (above and left, above). When the wearers are holding hands, a pattern scrolls from one garment to the other; when they let go, the pattern returns to the original design. The wall-based artwork *Blue Code* (left, below) is made of hand-woven linen with LEDs that interact with the viewer's movements.

'Much of life of the hands is a form of knowledge: not a linguistic or symbolic knowledge ... The knowledge is not only physical, but also experiential. The way of hands is personal, contextual and indescribable.'

Malcolm McCullough, *Abstracting Craft: The Practiced Digital Hand* (1996)

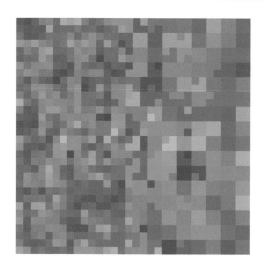

Deuce Design,
Psychedelic Engine,
2001

This wallpaper design (opposite) features an exploded drawing of a car engine, which was hand-drawn and manipulated in Adobe Illustrator before being prepared as a two-colour screenprint on silver Mylar. The engineering theme reflects the dual function of a cocktail bar-cum-automotive showroom.

Rupert Newman,
Flower Burst, 2008

Jonathan Fuller,
Computer-aided design
for fabric, 2008

A combination of painting,
collage, mono-printing and
computer-aided design
was utilized to create this
circular, radiating artwork
(above), which appears to
pulsate with life.

For this design (opposite,
left), Fuller made a series
of brushmarks by hand that
were then scanned into
the computer, and further
manipulated to obtain the
desired effect.

material code

In order to communicate something significant about the rapidly changing age we live in, artists and designers must frequently adopt new vocabularies, visual languages and codes. Digital media now provide a myriad of different expressions from imagined screen-based scenarios, incorporating abstract, hyper-real, macro, time-based, self-generating and fast-evolving imagery. Making material digitally tangible requires a connection with the real world. As contemporary design embraces both handmade and digital techniques, a touch of individuality is brought to industrial mass-production, and a new aesthetic is born: techno craft.

Rupert Newman,
Geo Circular, 2006

This explosive repeat design (below) combines hard-edged geometry with the softness of circular motifs. The overall effect is that of a dynamic space, turning and revolving backwards and forwards. A combination of painting, mono-printing and computer-aided design were utilized.

digitally implicit

Among the practitioners leading the way in this new field is Deuce Design. The firm originally combined hand-drawing with computer manipulation, and now create entirely digitally designed graphics for wall coverings (ill. p. 31). Other designers include Jonathan Fuller, who uses photography, painting and digital design to combine handcrafted idiosyncrasy with a more mechanized look in his textile designs (ill. p. 33, left), and fellow Brit Rupert Newman, who creates 'ambient patterns' through drawing, painting and mono-printing, which are then scanned, digitally manipulated and enhanced with Adobe Photoshop. Once the final design has been decided upon, Newman prints the result with Mimaki digital-printing technology (ill. pp. 32 and 33, right).

Glaswegian designer Jonathan Saunders (see pp. 162–65) also combines hand-drawing with computer-generated imagery to create his signature bold fashion prints, which carve up the body in colour-blocked areas to streamline and flatter. Saunders utilized the concept of 'engineered' print to fuse textile and garment design, transforming two dimensions into three. Another example of the engineered print emerged from the research work of Katherine Townsend, who by 2003 had designed a method of incorporating drape at the primary stage of the textile-print design process – an approach that challenged conventional practice.

Moving into the realms of interior design, Jo Pierce of the Textile Futures Research Centre at Central Saint Martins, creates textiles and wallpapers that have a digital signature, working with screen- and digital-print processes, stitch and graffiti stencil to achieve sophisticated surfaces that link found components and technology phenomena (ill. below). Paris-based artist and designer Florence Manlik similarly combines delicate hand-drawing with digital fine-tuning. Her trademark spiralling, organic compositions are mesmerizing and almost hypnotic as they defy notions of space, and form complex and beautiful visuals for both the fashion and interiors sectors (ill. opposite).

Even today there are ink types and materials that cannot yet be processed with a digital printer, so that layering and overprinting must still be done by hand. To develop print designs for sportswear, Kerri Wallace, Senior Lecturer at De Montfort University, combines a range of image-construction methods: drawing components

for each element by hand; scanning and digitally reworking the designs; and finally hand-silkscreen printing the results. She has experimented with heat-sensitive, thermo-chromic ink, which must be applied separately to the final garment, and intends to explore how different inks can be developed or altered to be compatible with digital-printing processes. The key objective of another designer, Marie Hill (now print and embroidery designer for fashion house Balmain, in Paris), when presenting her 2009 graduate collection of metallic and reflective body-conscious pieces (ill. below, left), was to create as textural a collection as possible. A combination of digital and silkscreen-printing techniques achieved a 3D effect, while intricate flocking and puff designs, on top of highly optical, linear digital imagery, provided the illusion of depth, and defied anyone to work out their construction.

The duo behind Glaswegian design company Timorous Beasties, Paul Simmons and Alistair McAuley, are well known for their interior and furnishing designs, which are generally realized by analogue silkscreen printing methods. Historic wallpaper patterns and botanical prints are key inspirations, which are occasionally given a contemporary digital twist (ill. below, right). Artist Kyu Jin Lee's designs also look

to the past for inspiration, and feature domestic objects and interiors that merge drawing, painting and mark-making with photographs and scans (ill. opposite). These strongly coloured and, in some cases, painterly interiorscapes might seem unlikely images for garment design, but the form of the body alters the context.

Illustrator and designer Rory Crichton, who creates printed textiles for fashion designers including Marc Jacobs, Marni and Giles Deacon, began experimenting on a newly acquired Apple Macintosh computer while studying painting at the Glasgow School of Art in the early 1990s. In the absence of scanning equipment, he recorded his drawings with a video camera and entered the data into a computer. The idea that this process enabled his work to be visible on screen, a connection to the world of video games, was exciting; thus liberated, he subsequently devised an entirely new approach to creating pattern for printed and woven textiles, informed by painting and illustration. Some of his distinctive 'image stories' for Giles Deacon are digitally printed to realize replication of line and texture (ill. pp. 38, 39), but often his designs are translated into a more lustrous or textured material form, using hand-printing processes.

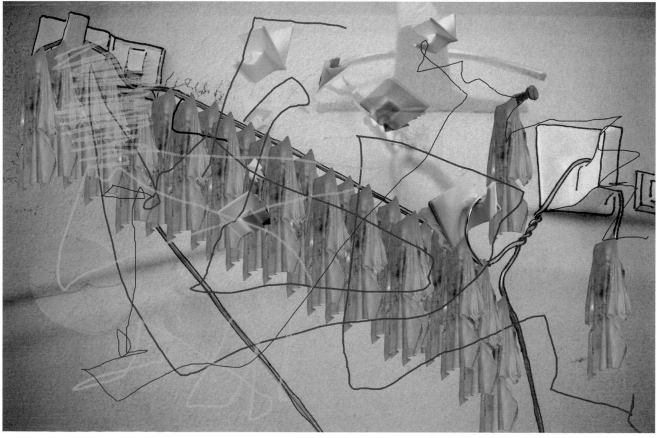

**Rory Crichton
for Giles Deacon,
Spring/Summer 2007**

Digital print assists
in creating the perfect
trompe-l'oeil effect for Giles
Deacon's Spring/Summer
2007 collection (right). The
play on scale to achieve this
simple outsize effect to fit
the length of the garment is
extremely effective.

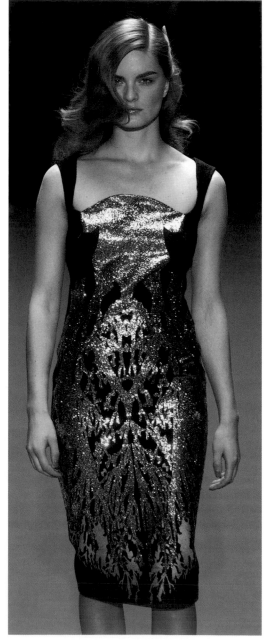

**Rory Crichton
for Giles Deacon,
Spring/Summer 2005**

Crichton's designs have
also been translated into
Jacquard weave, creating
a rich palette of material
components. The digitally
composited, wooden inlay
'gorilla' motif was recreated
in a silk print and weave,
manufactured for Giles
Deacon by Stephen Walters
(right).

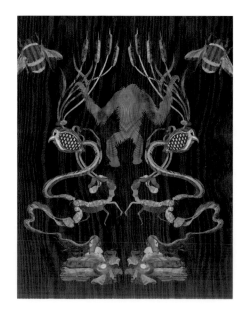

Rory Crichton
for Giles Deacon,
Autumn/Winter 2004–5

To bring Crichton's 2D
digital designs (right) to
life, fabric designer Fleet
Bigwood uses unlikely
materials and surfaces to
achieve effects that could
not otherwise be digitally
reproduced (opposite, right).

Karim Rashid
for Abet Laminati,
Kasa Digitalia, 2008
Triennale di Milano

Dubbed the 'poet of plastic'
by *Time* magazine, Rashid
designed this house in
plastic lamination (opposite,
left), characterized by bright
colours, for Italian interiors
company Abet Laminati,
for exhibition at the Milan
Triennale.

Peter Zuiderwijk
for Maxalot,
Dutch Eldorado, 2005

Zuiderwijk's wallpaper
design (left) combines
urban imagery with tightly
composed patterns of
natural forms. Nature
softens and complements
the visual impact of hard-
edged mechanical shapes.
The relationship between
the natural and the machine-
made is a recurring theme in
many digital works.

Along with fashion design, one-off and ambitious art projects are finally possible as technology becomes more widely available to individuals. Like Crichton, Scottish artist and designer Norma Starszakowna, whose work has applications in fashion and interior design, explores hand-processes alongside photographic and digital techniques, and incorporates digital media as part of her wide vocabulary of experimental print and dye techniques. In her desire to move away from flat 2D printing, and to communicate a sense of the passage of time, Starszakowna makes use of over-printing, embossing, glazing, oxidizing and patinating processes, heat-reactive inks and metallic finishing treatments, all in combination with digital printing, as seen in her large-scale, permanent installation *Hinterland* for the new Scottish Parliament building in Edinburgh (ill. above, right).

With ink-jet printing now being fully exploited by designers for a variety of applications, complex and hyper-realistic imagery can be transmitted from the computer screen onto an increasing range of materials, and engineered to fit both large- and small-scale material and structural outputs. Digital methods can facilitate a 'polymath' approach to design, in which a variety of applications can be explored. Dutch designer Hil Driessen (see pp. 120–25), for example, starts with digital photography, producing designs that are realized through the use of digital print or computer-controlled weave. As a result of this flexibility, designs for interiors – the pace and demand for which now seems almost as fast as for fashion – have radically altered. Trompe-l'oeil designs, combined with digital processes, have provided the ultimate in surface generation, and, in some cases,

Norma Starszakowna,
Hinterland, **2004**
Scottish Parliament,
Edinburgh

This installation (above) is formed of eighteen freely suspended panels, sited on a curved concrete wall outside the debating chamber. Photographs of the Scottish landscape were digitally printed onto a silk organza substrate, which was then screenprinted over and layers built up using heat-reactive inks to create embossed effects. Certain areas were glazed to halt oxidization processes, and sheen was added in the form of metal leaf.

almost entirely virtual-looking realms. One designer who fully exploits the possibilities is Markus Benesch. He ambitiously employs digital media at both the design and manufacture stages to create products, including wallpaper (ill. opposite, below), with 3D graphic effects. Benesch's expressive outsize imagery is breathtaking, and his large-scale interior and exterior spaces, produced for clients such as Italian laminate company Abet Laminati (ill. opposite, above), appear almost as alternative environments.

The new digital technology is also a freeing mechanism for graphic and communications designer Peter Zuiderwijk, whose passion lies in image analysis and construction. His approach in his wallpaper designs (ill. p. 40) is to incorporate an exacting analysis and execution of detail. Like a sheet of music, the composition incorporates variable scales of pattern; in this case, those found in nature, such as leaves and flowers. The result is highly polished: a form of visual sound. Fellow designer and digital practitioner Karim Rashid is also an enthusiastic advocate of all the tools that software and hardware have to offer, merging surface, fashion, interior and exterior design

(ill. p. 41, left). He works with a bold palette, and references lines and forms in nature, manipulating them to produce infinite pattern and form that encourage human engagement. An exterior for a food outlet in Singapore, for example, was covered in tiny chrome tiles to allow passers-by to see themselves reflected in pixel form. Another design, this one for an art centre in Pasadena, California, by graphic designer Bruce Mau, featured a series of dot-matrice decals, which were reproduced on panes of synthetic foil to dramatic effect (a variation on this graphic-dot theme was used for a woven fabric series for textile company Maharam). Mau's works have also been realized in the form of flooring, such as the *L7* design commissioned by Shaw Industries, in Dalton, Georgia (ill. pp. 1, 16, 30, 58). The immensity of scale that Mau engages with is impressive, creating a subtle yet effective patterning that helps to visually form space.

Photorealistic imaging has enabled artists to develop unlikely yet desirable propositions, in particular when exploring ambitious, large-scale ideas. Textile designer Hanna Palmgren has focused her interest in surfaces that define identity, interaction

Markus Benesch for Jannelli & Volpi, *Fantonia*, 2008

Patterns that reference swirling forms of the organic and mathematical hard-edged geometrics create an animated and fantastical world (opposite, below), where every possible surface is covered with digitally created designs.

Hanna Palmgren, *Set Nature Free*, 2004

Palmgren's *Set Nature Free* series depicts run-down housing, revamped. Wallpaper patterns more commonly used to bring nature into the living room have been subversively and effectively used to bring nature to a deteriorating urban and concrete environment.

Markus Benesch
for Abet Laminati,
Digital Sculptor Factory,
2003

For this project, Benesch
used laminates with
multicoloured stripes,
gradated colours, seascapes
and imitation wood-grain to
create a variety of effects.

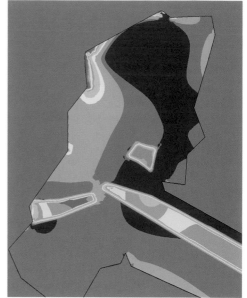

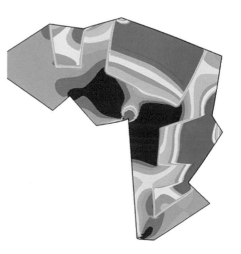

**Philip Delamore
for Hamish Morrow,
Spring/Summer 2004**

Delamore designed a series
of engineered prints for
fashion designer Hamish
Morrow (above). A nautical
theme inspired the Spring/
Summer 2004 collection.

**Philip Delamore
for Hamish Morrow,
Spring/Summer 2004**

Stress Print was a 2D imaging
concept informed by the
stress endured by a garment
when worn. Finite-element
analysis provided a distinct
pattern: the colour was then
altered and digitally printed
onto silk jersey (right).

and communication on the relationships between exterior spaces and domestic interiors. She applies motifs from nature that were originally incorporated into interior decoration (wallpaper, for example) to enhance the dilapidated exteriors of London's urban buildings (ill. p. 42). By digitally bringing an artificial nature designed for the inside to the outdoors, Palmgren proposes some fantastic solutions to the concrete jungle we have inherited from our architectural past, as well as providing solutions for future habitats.

Fashion giant Prada (see pp. 106–13) has also used the illusory effects of digital prints for several collections, to simulate textures or to play with the look of an entirely different surface or material, as have Eley Kishimoto, whose photorealistic textile designs use digital printing to create intricate and complex patterning that would be difficult to achieve manually (ill. p. 46, below). In the early days of digital print, it was only possible to print on certain weights of specially prepared cotton, but the pair have pursued printing on a range of materials, from textiles to ceramics and even plywood. Japanese designer Michiko Koshino (see pp. 170–75) has similarly applied her prints to non-textile substrates, such as footwear and motorcycle helmets. Also experimenting with a variety of surfaces, including metallics or tulle, is Swiss-based textile company Jakob Schlaepfer (see pp. 156–61), who pioneered the use of digital ink-jet printing in haute couture.

Another proponent of the sophisticated Japanese Mimaki technology is Cornwall-based artist and designer Simon A. Clarke, who combines photography, painting and digital printing (ill. right). Cultural references are taken from eastern Africa, as well as from his more immediate surroundings in southwest England, informing collage and print techniques that explore colour, texture and form. Textile designer Philip Delamore, Director of the Fashion Digital Studio, London College of Fashion, has combined the use of

digital 2D and 3D software to engineer images for print and surface decoration, including textiles for Hamish Morrow's Spring/Summer 2004 collection (ill. opposite).

Mary Katrantzou, a graduate of Central Saint Martins, has enthusiastically embraced digital print for fashion, and made it her own designing sympathetic garment forms for her bold engineered prints. She is also part of a new generation that is increasingly conscious of issues of sustainability, and is an advocate of the digital process, owing to the less toxic nature of the chemicals used and the reduction of waste. Her innovative work (ill. p. 46, top) acknowledges the strengths and limitations of imaging software, and the reproduction capability of the printing hardware. Alexander McQueen's Spring/Summer 2009 collection (ill. p. 47) was highly ambitious in its use of digital media, and was almost entirely composed of intricately designed engineered prints to fit structurally complex garments. With no limitations on design or production

Simon A. Clarke,
14 Falls, 2008

This virtually generated artwork is centred around a photograph taken by the artist of a waterfall in Kenya, near to where he was living at the time. The colours used reference the printed textiles worn throughout East Africa, as well as the abstract painting of 1950s Britain.

Mary Katrantzou,
Autumn/Winter 2009–10

While Katrantzou's first
collection featured hyper-
realistic representations
of outsize jewelry shapes
on simple shift dresses
in rich jewel tones, this
second collection (right)
saw 3D-constructed perfume
bottles recreated as striking
body-length imagery on
simple fashion silhouettes.

Eley Kishimoto,
'Another Place',
Autumn/Winter 2007–8

This print design, called
Galaxy (right, below)
featured haloed spots of
intense colour, making the
repeat difficult to identify.
The collection looked to
the twinkling stars of the
night sky for inspiration,
contemplating time and
imagining a future world.

Alexander McQueen,
'Natural Distinction,
Un-Natural Selection',
Spring/Summer 2009

McQueen's Spring/Summer
2009 collection (opposite)
was almost entirely
composed of intricately
designed, engineered prints
to fit structurally complex
garments.

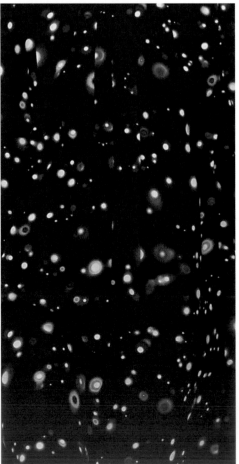

processes, speed or technology, the collection
employed sophisticated 2D designs on a
series of complex and powerful silhouettes.
Engineered-to-fit imagery was shaped to
the complex garment forms, achieving the
visually arresting effect of cleverly designed
dynamic pattern and colouration.

Digital weaving achieves otherwise
impossible imagery and complex structures,
examples of which are beginning to
incorporate smart, responsive components.
Both the Japanese company Nuno
(see pp. 84–87) and artist Sonja Weber
(see pp. 166–69) create woven designs on
a computer-controlled loom. Textile designer
Ismini Samanidou's design process
frequently begins with her own photographs,
which are then interpreted as woven
structures via computer-aided design
and manufacture (ill. p. 48). The ambitions
of designers can be digitally realized to
almost architectural scale, as Samanidou's
impressive work *Timeline* (ill. p. 49) illustrates;
at 16m long and 3m high, it is one of the
largest woven installations yet undertaken.
A site-specific commission for the Jerwood
Contemporary Makers exhibition, the work
consisted of a woven wall that wrapped
around itself, spiralling through the
gallery space.

Artist Mitsuko Akutsu likewise employs
image-manipulation tools before converting
her photographs to data for weaving on
a computer-assisted Jacquard loom. By being
able to control each individual thread, the
imagery is brought together to create
composites, as seen in her *Time* series (ill. p.
50). Woven textiles specialist Philippa Brock
(see p. 51) also explores finishing techniques
using CAD/CAM Jacquard looms. 'Fabrics of
Life: Nobel Textiles', a project directed by
designer Carole Collet, enabled scientists and
designers to work together to achieve a
dialogue between the two disciplines; Nobel
Prize-winner Sir Aaron Klug (in 1982, for
chemistry) and Brock were one of five
partnerships. A later collection, 'Self

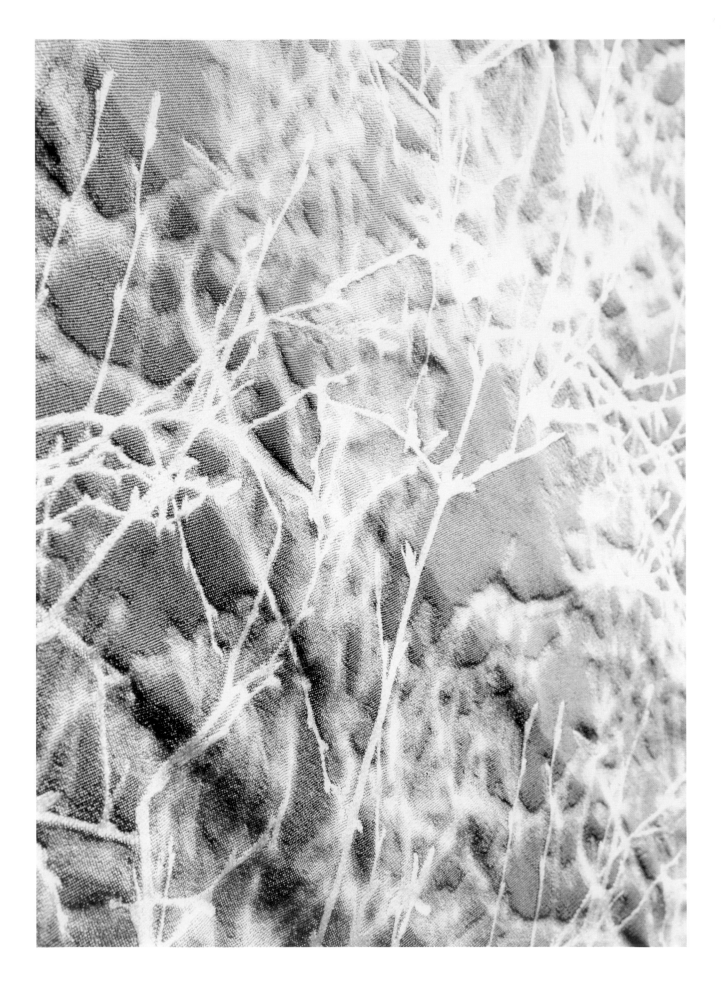

Assemble/Self Fold', was inspired by DNA and origami structures. Welsh artist Ainsley Hillard (see p. 52) uses digital print to transfer imagery to weft threads that are then woven with a transparent warp to create distorted effects. She incorporates sound into her works, using software such as Forge and Pro Tools to add another sensory level to her 'virtual sound cloth' installations.

Breakthroughs in software development have allowed explorations into new sensory dimensions that look beyond visual and tactile surface qualities in the material production of textiles. Textile artist Christy Matson's complex piece, *Soundw(e)ave* (2004), was composed of a series of spectrograms taken from different loom systems: a traditional hand-loom; a hand-operated Jacquard loom; and a fully automated industrial loom. The sounds from these operating systems were effectively translated into a woven visual form. In the work of

Janis Jefferies, photographic imagery is subtly fragmented, almost as if by digital interference, or white noise, once it has been realized in woven form. With scientist and computer expert Tim Blackwell, she explores the relationships between sound and woven fabric in generative artworks (ill. p. 53), which are also staged as live performances. At these events, the sound is woven in real time and appears as physical and sonic textures, ensuring that the link between visual and aural is closely maintained.

Three-dimensional forms are possible, a technique explored by Hawaii-based artist Emily DuBois (see p. 52), who combines digital ways of working with more ancient ones, including the textile resist techniques of *shibori* (a Japanese term for several methods of dyeing cloth with a pattern, like tie-dyeing) and *ikat* (a method of weaving that uses a resist dyeing process). DuBois employs the computer-controlled Jacquard

Ismini Samanidou,
Timeline, 2009
Jerwood Space, London

For this work (above), the artist incorporated details of maps, texts and other references to create a beautiful visual, composed of intricate surfaces.

Ismini Samanidou,
Forest, 2005

The sheen of the viscose and the glitter of the metallic yarns add to the magical quality of this prototype, made using a computerized Jacquard loom (opposite).

Mitsuko Akutsu,
Time J-07, 2007;
Time J-14, 2009

For this series, created at the Montreal Centre for Contemporary Textiles, photographic images were interpreted as digitally woven structures. In *Time J-07* (right), the artist's shadow is shown against a stone stairway. In *Time J-14* (below), two images are collaged: one taken near the city's Atwater Market; the other, showing graffiti, taken in a metro station. Brought together, one image is allowed to be slightly transparent to allow the reading of both simultaneously.

Philippa Brock,
Nobel Textiles,
2008

Brock's *Nobel Textiles* series (opposite) is a collection of woven lengths made from a variety of yarns with different behaviours that, once cut from the loom, take shape as 3D-responsive fabric forms. These forms are bold and conceptually unique, and appear intricate in their construction.

Ainsley Hillard,
Traces, 2008
Mission Gallery, Swansea

Created with the assistance
of sound engineer Paul
Knowles, this installation
(above) comprised a series
of twenty semi-transparent,
free-hanging vertical panels.
Computer-aided design
was used to enlarge and
'fragment' the images before
digitally printing them onto
heat-transfer paper, and then
onto translucent viscose
weft threads prior to being
hand-woven using a nylon
monofilament warp.

Emily DuBois,
Fig Leaf, 2007
Mingei International
Museum, San Diego

Fig Leaf (left) represents a
new direction for DuBois,
one that utilizes a shaped
and stiffened Jacquard weave
for a three-dimensional
unique piece. The computer-
controlled loom enables
such complex structures
where the interwoven warp
and weft threads achieve a
realistic effect of light falling
on an organic form.

loom to create complex weave structures that have evolved from 2D surfaces to become 3D forms. Vivienne Westwood's designs, too, typically take the form of complex sculptural silhouettes. Occasionally materials appear that have involved some level of digital intervention; when this occurs, the combination of textile and sculptural garment is very rich.

Knitted construction techniques have also undergone a sea change with digital tooling. Fashion visionary Issey Miyake (see pp. 94–99) first saw the potential of digital knit in the mid-1990s, when, together with Dai Fujiwara, he developed the A-POC range, which made use of customer participation and the latest in computer technology to create an entirely new way of making clothes. The other significant development in knit technology came via the Japanese company Shima Seiki, who have led the world in computerized knitting-machine innovation. Fashion designer Louise Goldin (see pp. 188–91) has also revolutionized knit design by combining digital and analogue techniques.

With laser technology becoming embedded in 2D and 3D design, we are now beginning to see a high level of innovation in fashion and interiors applications, and more recently in the field of sustainable textile design, in which the deconstructive and reconstructive properties of laser-cutting, etching, sintering and welding enhances material that would otherwise be on the way to landfill. Fashion designers who have made the use of the new technology include Prada, Tom Gallant (see pp. 192–97), in his

designs for the collections of Marios Schwab, and Savrithi Bartlett (see pp. 136–39), who has investigated the use of the laser for her PhD thesis, as well as creating laser-etched designs for fashion label Boudicca. Laser-cutting has also become the signature of Daniel Herman, who uses the technology for both construction and decoration, employing a CNC drilling machine to create a mould shape for forming lace (using latex as the material). The laser allows a particular relationship between the fabric and the underlying body: when a surface is cut, it drapes, producing folds that can be hard-edged or fluid in character. Herman has collaborated with Jakob Schlaepfer to realize his laser-cut designs (ill. p. 54, bottom). Fellow designer Eunsuk Hur devised an interchangeable modular system that enables users to build their own small or large-scale textile constructions, which can transform an interior space or surface, or be built around the body to create uniquely fashioned garments (ill. p. 54, top).

Dutch textile designer Eugène van Veldhoven has used computer-controlled engraving and cutting for two decades, often making use of the laser equipment at the Netherlands Textile Museum in Tilburg, and carefully considers the inherent properties of his substrate and response to the unpredictable. Interested in a variety of finishing techniques, he combines cutting-edge methods with traditional processes, including devoré, or 'burn out', in which the finished design is achieved through the chemical removal of cloth. Expanding on

Janis Jefferies and Tim Blackwell, *Woven Sound*, 2006 Dana Centre, London Science Museum

Live sound was interpreted into computer-controlled Jacquard woven images, with the incoming sound digitized and linked to the fabric. During performances, the sound was woven in real time. Each image represents several seconds of music, emerging as 'visual' and 'sonic' textures.

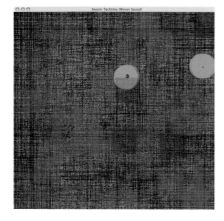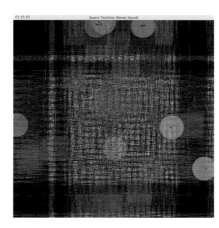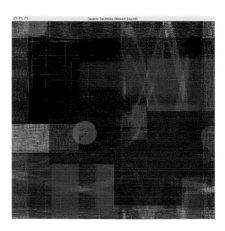

This modular textile system
is devised from hundreds
of interlocking laser-cut
sections. Using a variety of
materials (leather, felt and
wood), Hur emphasizes
how individual pieces
can be reconstructed into
numerous forms to create a
sustainable product (right).

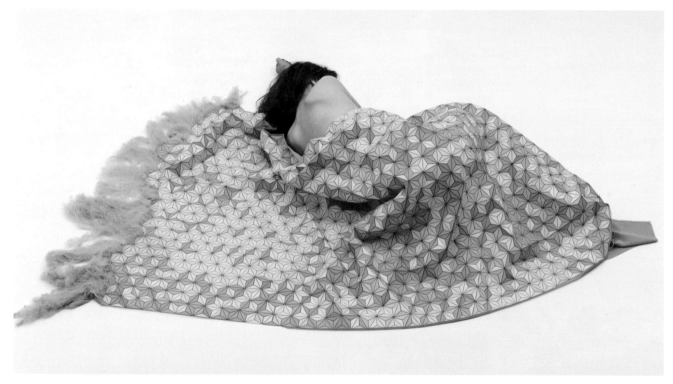

Daniel Herman,
Laser-cut cape, 2002

This cape (left) was made
from laser-cutting a circular
piece of polyester to create
a dramatic form that
drapes around the body. No
material was removed; the
slits reveal flesh and allow
for maximum movement.

Elisa Strozyk,
Wooden Textiles,
2009

Stroyzk's wooden textiles
(above) present fluidity
evident in a solid material,
achieved through laser-
cutting and crafted
precision. The hybrid
qualities of the final pieces
are both playful and poetic.

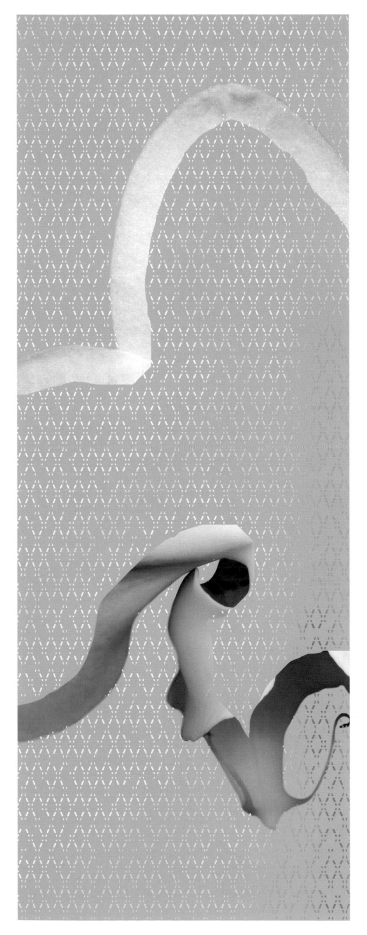

Eugène van Veldhoven,
Orchid 1, 2006;
Orchid 5, 2006

Eugène van Veldhoven,
Serpentines, 2008
Museum of Art, Rhode
Island School of Design

This fabric (left) was digitally printed onto cotton satin, and subjected to a devoré treatment in a diamond pattern, which allows light to filter through the cloth when it is suspended in space. For another version (below), hand-pleated polyamide satin was laser-cut with the motif.

For this design (bottom), hand-painted and laser-cut strips of cotton were heat-set onto cotton tulle. This design illustrates a different appliqué approach by using the laser to add to the substrate rather than remove from it, as is more usually done.

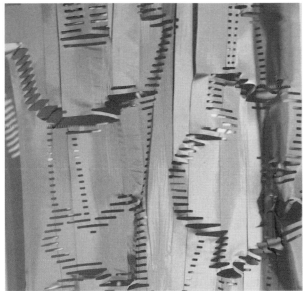

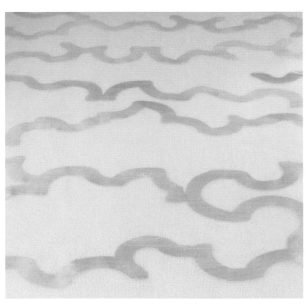

Kate Goldsworthy,
MultiSheer 1, 2006

This series was 'designed
for disassembly' as a way of
producing interim textiles
using digital manufacturing
methods and the recycling
of packaging waste.

the idea of removing material to create a
design, van Veldhoven turned his attentions
from the chemical to the digital to work with
computer-controlled laser-cutting. For his
design *Serpentines* (ill. p. 55, below right), the
technique was cleverly subverted to a method
involving appliqué, in which laser-cut strips
were collaged onto a substrate. The result is
a fusion of technology and craft, ensuring
both visual and tactile appeal.

Computer-controlled laser-cutting can
also be used for large-scale works. In 2005,
Eley Kishimoto teamed up with 6a Architects
to create the plywood-clad installation
Hairywood (ill. opposite), which demonstrated
complex patterning systems and lace-like
effects. Wood also becomes a poetic fabric
in the work of Elisa Strozyk, who devised a
meticulous process of laser-cutting fine wood
veneer, which she then applies to material
surfaces (ill. p. 54, middle). In so doing, she
achieves a fluid, articulated 'wooden textile'
that challenges our perception of materials
and how they are used. The pioneering
research of textile designer Kate Goldsworthy
challenges the capability of industrial laser
tools to achieve sustainable design methods,
particularly when applied to polyesters.
Having worked with recycling processes since
2000, she is currently exploring laser-cutting,
welding and etching technologies, with the
aim of elevating waste materials to objects
of beauty and value (ill. left).

The computer is generally considered
a tool for mass-production, yet the appeal
of bespoke crafted goods in the digital
era is expanding approaches to computer
use in relation to imaging, design and
construction. Knowledge of materials has
achieved new relevance in the learning and
application of emerging technology, helping
to drive discerning decision-making. As
traditional and advanced media converge,
new vocabularies and future aesthetics
of computer-generated design are being
composed of both analogue and digital
techniques.

Eley Kishimoto,
Hairywood, **2005**
Old Street, London

Originally built in 2005
for the Architecture
Foundation's new gallery
in Old Street (this page),
Hairywood was rebuilt in
Covent Garden's piazza in
2008 as part of the London
Festival of Architecture.
Computer-controlled
laser-cut plywood was
used to clad the structure.
The intricate forms are a
reference to the tumble
of Rapunzel's hair as it
fell from her tower in the
fairytale by the Brothers
Grimm.

'For the digital image can turn the clock back, scramble time, fast forward, reverse and then cut to the chase. It can impose a riot on a fashion scenario or a fashion scenario on a riot. Digitalization reduces the image to a scrapyard, a jumble of shards and fragments to be cannibalized and made into new forms.'

Caroline Evans, *Fashion at the Edge: Spectacle, Modernity and Deathliness* (2003)

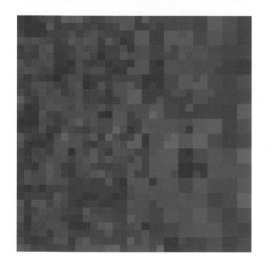

**Me Company
for *Big Magazine*,
'Horror' issue,
2000**

Imagery by Me Company
for *Big Magazine*'s 'Horror'
issue (opposite) featured
Pandora opening her box
and releasing evil into the
world.

digital imaginings

By the late 1970s, the appearance of digital colour graphics, drawing and painting packages had radically changed the image-based industries in a range of sectors. While 3D modelling and moving-image tools made inroads into film and commercial sectors, computing entered the realm of gaming. Over the next few decades, media developers ensured that imaging software such as Adobe Photoshop, Illustrator and After Effects would become as common as the pencil, and that still and moving-image design and manipulation processes would be accessible to everyone. Added to this was the formidable Internet, which has become an indispensable creative medium and platform for visual and interactive design, communication, publishing and entertainment. During the early 1990s, digital and analogue image-making converged, and the computerized wizardry of post-production was duly established as a genre.

Mike Thomas
and Lost in Space,
The Difference is Clear,
1998

Collaboration was key to early digital image-making. This groundbreaking visual (opposite), photographed by Mike Thomas, computer-graphically reworked by Lost in Space and published by *Dazed & Confused*, showed a distinct advance in digital fashion imaging.

Me Company for Kenzo,
Autumn/Winter 2001–2

These images presented a digitally conceived 'alternative exploration of the autumn garden' (left), created to form part of a fashion advertising campaign for Kenzo.

The computer began to make a particularly significant contribution to fashion-related communication during this meteoric rise of digital technology. One of the earliest ventures to emerge in this field was Me Company, founded in 1985, which combined a modern aesthetic with technical image innovation for art and fashion. Image-making, or 'contemplative metamedia', was seen as a subtle deviation from a norm that achieved a level of believability. Provocative and complex fantasy visuals were devised for clients that included online publication *Big Magazine* (ill. p. 59), fashion designers Kenzo (ill. p. 61), Lanvin (ill. below) and Hussein Chalayan (ill. pp. 70, 71), and the singer Björk.

Visual special effects had by this time exploded as an industry. Images were morphed together to create backdrops that would otherwise be unachievable, and fashion models, shown with scanned or 3D-constructed props, were digitally composed in the unlikeliest of settings – inhospitable deserts and scenes from the past suddenly became inhabited by the impossibly beautiful. Larger post-production houses that were able to afford vast super-computers cite the 1990s as a particularly surreal time for creativity. Hardware and software, together with the man hours necessary to run them (in almost exclusively male environments), became valuable commercial commodities but led to a high turnover, due to burnout of both man and machine. Hardware was slow to run and yet evolving quickly, posing yet more logistical challenges. Music companies were known to underwrite tens of thousands of pounds to allow for the purchase of hardware that would create the slickest music videos and special effects possible.

With most specialist high-level hardware made in the US, access to the wider international sphere was limited. Necessity opened the door to collaboration, bringing

Me Company for Lanvin, Computer-animated studies of birds, 2003

These images were created as part of a series of 3D-modelled and computer-animated studies on the movement of caged birds in motion, developed for Paris fashion house Lanvin.

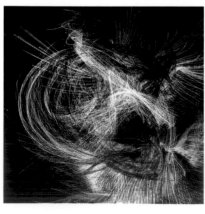

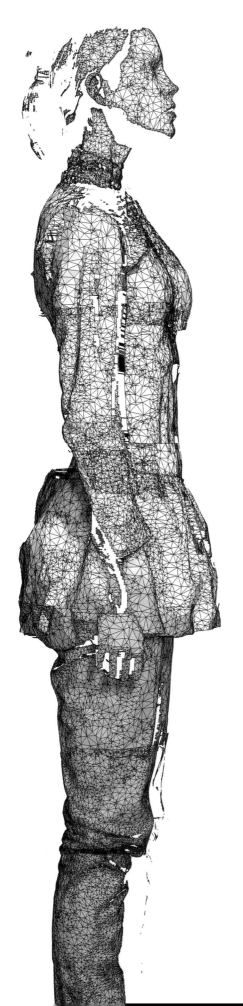

together digital artists, including Christian Hogue of Lost in Space, and experimental photographers such as Mike Thomas and Sølve Sundsbø, the artist behind the iconic cover for Coldplay's *A Rush of Blood to the Head* album. *The Difference is Clear* (ill. p. 60), a well-known image by Thomas, with digital artwork by Hogue, features a model in a coat by Hussein Chalayan that appears to take the form of distorted glass. The viewer is caught between the form of the coat and the urbanscape of concrete buildings that its fractured transparency reveals. The image was timely in its commentary on the rise of technology, as architecture and computing engendered both excitement and unease as the pace of life was set to radically change. With the use of digital gimmickry beginning to permeate imagery, certain software filters also became easily recognizable; the trick was to make their use believable.

Inspired by Yves Klein's exclamation 'Long live the immaterial!', fashion duo Viktor & Rolf designed the immaterial element of their Autumn/Winter 2002–3 catwalk show as a series of transient images that appeared as if part of the actual fabric of the collection (ill. p. 65). Bluescreen technology, borrowed from the film industry, was used to digitally merge landscapes of skyline and desert with the garment silhouettes. The catwalk collection of entirely chroma-key blue pieces was filmed live and projected onto two large screens either side of the runway, while linked to a digital feed of software filters that altered the degree to which the landscape imagery and garment details were visibly merged, phasing between a series of infinite variables.

Another boundary-testing fashion designer, Alexander McQueen, teamed up with photographer Nick Knight to produce some of the most provocative visual experiences of the 1990s. The image of a model gazing vacantly from the depths of a pale-pink Japonaise dress from McQueen's Spring/Summer 1997 collection was innocent enough, would it not be for the startling

Lost in Space and Sølve Sundsbø, *Wired*, 1998

As few organizations in London had experience in 3D scanning, Lost in Space collaborated with Sundsbø to devise a technique for this wire-frame CG image, which was later applied to the cover design of music group Coldplay's 2002 album, *A Rush of Blood to the Head.*

realization that one of her eyes is milk-white and that two pins have been pierced through the skin of her forehead. Another collaborative effort depicts McQueen himself in an arresting portrait for the April 1998 cover of *The Face* magazine. The designer's bald head is encircled with fine plaits of hair, like a halo, and the piercing red eyes complete a look that was suggestive of McQueen's growing reputation as both genius and enfant terrible. At the time, imaging software was commercially available but not readily accessible, so its effect was arresting. This kind of imagery was most successful in its subtlest form: beguiling, mystical, and a little menacing. Highly crafted visuals began to challenge notions of identity and representation that belied perceived digital imaging capability.

As computer engineering evolved, artists and designers subverted the tools to create new kinds of image-based propositions. The visual gimmickry written into new software was overlooked or ignored, as it was quickly deemed creatively inadequate to simply apply a new imaging filter. Nick Knight's own experimental work, including a fashion shoot that depicted a series of beautiful but distorted heads in 3D (ill. p. 66), exploited computing technology from the start. In preparation, Knight's collaborator Jane How applied sweet wrappers to the upper bodies of the models to create a surface of refracted, broken, highly coloured light effects. Early scanning technology was used like a camera to capture the models' heads in the round. Such digital tools were new at the time, and generated unintentional yet stunning 'flaws' during the capture process. As imperfections in the technology were designed out, such intriguing imagery became more difficult to achieve.

Having established their design partnership in 1998 to combine art direction, photography, image creation and post-production to achieve implausible visualization processes, Warren du Preez

and Nick Thornton Jones collaborated with designer and fashion futurist Suzanne Lee eight years later to describe a fusion of science and fashion that was yet to appear in tangible form. Still and moving imagery responded to a series of far-reaching, wearable concepts that would evolve, in material terms, in the laboratory and studio. The resulting collection was a seductive fashion fantasy that combined analogue styling and digital trickery.

Now that it was possible to control each pixel – sharpening, adjusting, softening and streamlining to perfect skin blemishes, smooth wrinkles and plump lips – such editing has become an extension of design, with the conventional elements of fashion photography (model, lighting, styling and location) accompanied by the choreography of digital retouching. Believability is the new reality. Peter Allen and Carla Ross Allen of KnoWear took the concept further by using 2D and 3D visualization techniques to digitally, and subversively, 'tattoo' logos of iconic brands such as Chanel (ill. p. 67, left) and Fendi (right) onto images of the human body. The idea is to question the new commercial relationship between fashion and the body, and to highlight the perceived value of branded fashion products and how consumers have come to rely on them to define their own value and identity.

Having exploited imaging possibilities in paper form, fashion magazines are now doing the same with online versions. In 2000, SHOWstudio, a non-profit art and fashion web publication, was launched by Nick Knight and graphic designer Peter Saville. This distinctive space for experimental projects, film and live performances appeared at a time when broadband was just emerging. Still thriving over a decade later, SHOWstudio retains its collaborative formula as a key fashion conduit for artists and designers. Predating SHOWstudio by ten years and founded by the photographer Rankin and publisher Jefferson Hack, the print magazine *Dazed &*

Blommers/Schumm for Viktor & Rolf, 'Long Live the Immaterial', Autumn/Winter 2002–3

Anuschka Blommers and Neils Schumm assisted fashion designers Viktor & Rolf to realize their collection, 'Long Live the Immaterial', achieved by a bluescreen imaging technique. The chroma-key blue in the background and garments was digitally selected, and phased in and out to expose footage of nature and cityscapes in transition with the model and clothing.

Confused has been a standard-bearer for the altered, illusionary image. The magazine's format also included social and political debate, and covered such controversial issues as the perception of beauty and disability, but it was the provocative photography that was the key to its success. Additions to the business portfolio include Dazed Film & TV, luxury biannual publication *AnOther Magazine* and an online presence, DazedDigital. While the basis for the last is, like SHOWstudio, magazine-orientated, DazedDigital offers a network of ideas, web-based events and collaboration opportunities in fashion, film, art and music.

It is only recently that such a format could provide a genuine shift from the printed page. New generations of techno-journalists are now making their mark via blogs, unhindered by the technical and financial concerns that accompanied early computing. Fashion companies, however, have yet to fully engage with the potential that an online presence offers. Luxury brands rely on simple website formats to promote their wares, despite being creatively well placed to develop web content and new mechanisms for consumption that could set them apart and free up revenue that is currently spent on traditional print advertising. Now that online shopping is competing successfully with the high street, and consumers are spending more and more

time online, film and interactive media have much to offer the luxury sector.

Hollywood and Silicon Valley have been profitable bedfellows since the early 1980s, with software innovation and related special effects becoming particularly lucrative for post-production companies. Towards the end of the 1990s, computer-graphic imaging achieved new levels of composition and image construction, with companies like Industrial Light and Magic making 3D CGI their own. *Toy Story* (1995), with CGI animation provided by Pixar (originally part of the Lucasfilm group), proved that with sufficient processing power, a feature-length 3D animated film was possible – but only just. The equivalent of an aircraft hangar-full of computers, connected and operating as one unit, was necessary to provide the requisite rendering power; today, it is not beyond the realms of possibility that all of that power could be supplied by one desktop computer. Following the success of *Toy Story*, the race was on to create a CGI film that used entirely digitally conceived actors. *Final Fantasy*, a series of interactive video games produced by Square Enix in 1987, was hugely influential in terms of CGI developments, and eventually led to the feature film *Final Fantasy: The Spirits Within* (2001; ill. p. 68). The next step in the filmic journey was the digitization of human form and movement using motion capture.

Nick Knight and Jane How/ SHOWstudio, *Sweets*, 2000
With Dominic Wright, Createc London

Stylist Jane How's application of shiny sweet wrappers enhanced Knight's intriguing 3D scanned, interactive online work *Sweets* (opposite).

KnoWear, *Skinthetic Redux*, 2009; *BrandX*, 2007

Skinthetic Redux (below, left) digitally merges the look of Chanel's iconic quilting, used on leather bags, onto human skin, provoking ideas about the power and pervasiveness of twenty-first-century branding through consumerism. In the series *BrandX* (below, right), Fendi's logo appears to be growing on, or branded into, the skin of the mannequin, a potential consequence of brand addiction, according to the designers.

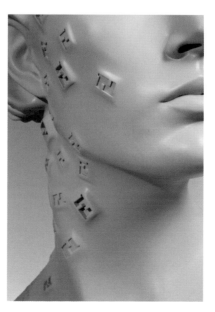

One of the most successful characters created using this new technology was Gollum from the *Lord of the Rings* trilogy (2001–3), played by Andy Serkis, an extraordinarily believable character in computer-graphic form.

Film's ability to describe fabric in relation to the body, and the newly emerging methods of computer-graphically visualizing textiles and dress, have been explored by Jane Harris (see pp. 126–31), Professor of Digital Imaging Design at Kingston University, who combines 3D CG animation and motion-capture technology to create virtual garment forms. In her work, the wearer has so far maintained an invisible guise; there is no visible virtual human or avatar, merely a suggestion of the form, thus emphasizing the characteristics of the textile and its behaviour, and the kinetic relationship between fabric and body. Collaborations with fashion designer Shelley Fox and CG operator Mike Dawson have achieved digital models of fabric and clothing that appear very believable, belying their computer-graphic origin. But the increasing sophistication of CGI simulation has improved the ability to model 'soft' forms, including skin, hair, clothing, fur, feathers and scales. The use of photorealistic computer-graphic effects, however, is a much debated and complex issue. There is a particular discomfort in viewing realistic representations of human forms, and real and virtual perceptions do not always meet expectations. For many, the digital double of our human selves is an impossibly eerie image.

At the time when they were grappling with the complexities of computer-graphic cloth modelling, large firms like Square Enix were supported by substantial teams of programmers and processing power. The fashion and textile sectors, however, owing to the high cost of hardware for image capture, editing and manipulation, were restricted to working on a much more modest level. Industry-standard software and hardware slowly filtered through to more general use, although access remained an issue until the mid-2000s. Despite these challenges, young designers were choosing to navigate this new dialogue as an integral part of their practice. Measured in their use of digital media, and bypassing the trappings of special effects, filmic works began to evolve that suspended the viewer between real and virtual space.

In 2001 Me Company produced an animation entitled *Ventriloquy* (ill. pp. 70, 71), which opened Hussein Chalayan's Spring/Summer 2001 show of the same name. The video was formed of a virtual space, which hosted a group of scribbled figures that broke up into digitally fragmented dust. The live fashion show mirrored this virtual aesthetic, featuring garments with drawn doodles incorporated into their surface design, and culminated with three live models wearing

Hamish Morrow,
'Beauty of Technology',
Spring/Summer 2004
With Warren du Preez, Nick Thornton Jones and UVA

The show culminated in a virtual print display (opposite), where sequential 3D moments of imagery were created in digital code and then projected onto the 'blank canvas' of the dresses. The idea was to create a print that was not fixed in time, but rather virtual and ever changing.

Hironobu Sakaguchi (director),
Final Fantasy: The Spirits Within, 2001

This film was celebrated for the algorithm employed to depict moving hair, which enabled the improved portrayal of digital 'actors', an amazing feat of creativity and engineering for the time. Having received mixed reviews upon release, the film has achieved cult status.

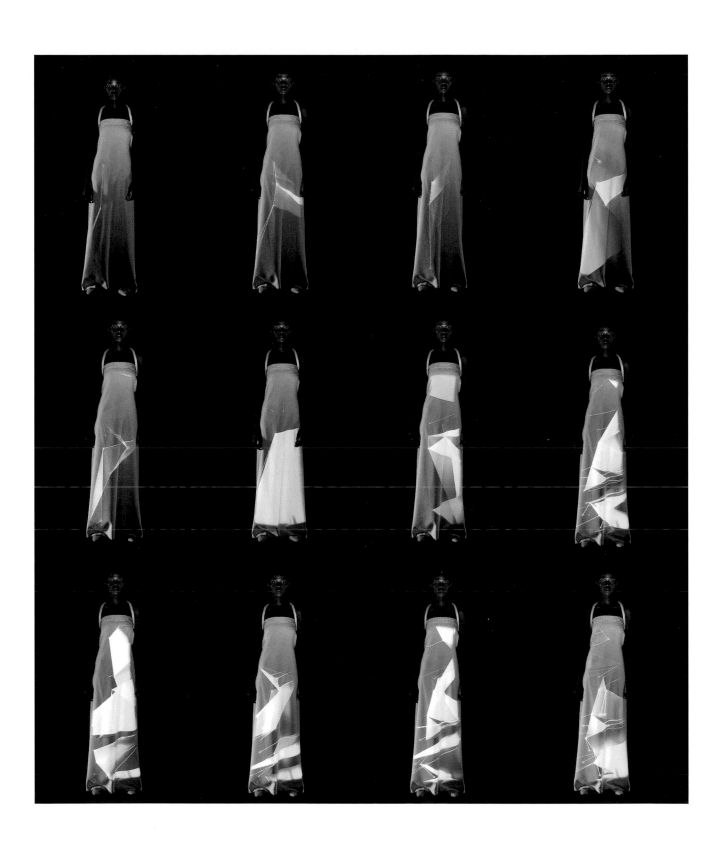

**Me Company
for Hussein Chalayan,**
Ventriloquy,
Spring/Summer 2001

In this animation (ill. pp. 70, 71), the virtual space is defined by a computer-grid aesthetic, which hosts a group of intricately drawn figures. The fragility of these characters is highlighted as the figures eventually break each other up into digitally fragmented dust.

Nicola Naismith,
Video Triptych,
2003

Video Triptych depicts recognizable tools (needles and thread) that are mechanized through their digital composition. It examines our relationship to everyday tasks, which today are often associated with computer use.

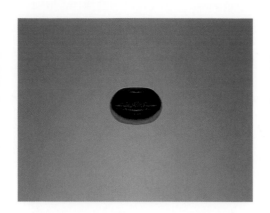
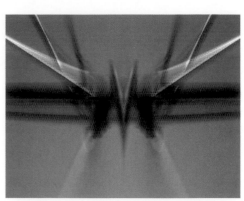

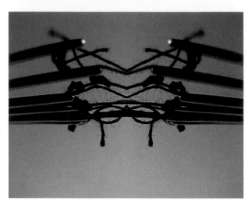
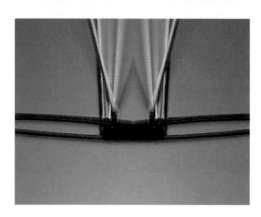
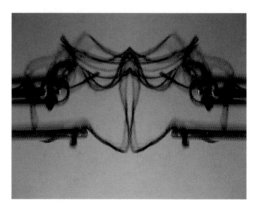
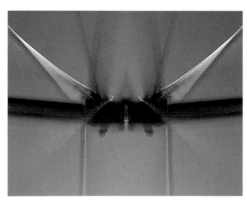
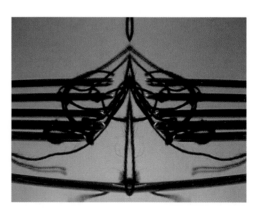

spun-sugar glass dresses, partnered by virtual models that proceeded to destroy the delicate garments with a hammer. The intrigue of this type of virtual layer, despite the notoriously unpredictable nature of live media, became ever more tempting. For his own collection three years later (ill. p. 69), fashion designer Hamish Morrow also chose to introduce a virtual dimension. One of several collaborations with Warren du Preez, Nick Thornton Jones and multimedia artists UVA, the show used a digital feed of live imagery of each model as she entered the catwalk. The captured data was reworked to produce a series of alternating forms that preceded and shadowed each model. In an additional technical feat, integrated into the show was a live installation work, composed of four distinct garment shapes. These blank canvases became luminous and three-dimensional, as a series of infinite virtual prints were projected onto the forms.

Equally groundbreaking was *Trembled Blossoms*, a digital animation directed by visual-effects artist James Lima for Prada's Spring/Summer 2008 catwalk show (ill. p. 111). The narrative frame is an exquisite visual, which leads viewers into a magical environment of flowers and forest that is sensual and rich in colour and motion, with compelling imagery that combined hand-drawn and painterly aesthetics, the antithesis of commercial CGI animation. This wonderland was inhabited by pale elfin beings, created with motion-capture technology, with the main character adorned in Prada clothes and accessories. The ingenious beauty of the film was that it reached beyond the web, and could be imagined as an exhibition piece or a collectible download for mobile phones and music media.

The psychological complexities of the human–computer relationship are only just beginning to be understood; we spend much of our time working with computers and yet rarely stop to consider the connection. Textile

artist Nicola Naismith examines this evolving computerized society from the perspective of textile-making. In *Video Triptych* (ill. opposite), she uses digital media to highlight an important yet almost invisible working textile tool: the sewing needle. Using large-scale projection, the viewer is brought uncomfortably close to this otherwise tiny, apparently insignificant object. A series of needles are linked together digitally by their threads, which never seem to tangle, despite the seemingly anarchic and menacing choreography of the movement. It is difficult not to wince at the effect of the swinging needles, as if near vulnerable eyes. In *Enhanced Monitor* (ill. p. 15), Naismith explores the hidden world inside an abandoned computer. When in use, the monitor was viewed solely in terms of its exterior – sterile, modern, functional – but once inside, Naismith sees evidence of the handmade in the machine's manufacture, and reveals the iridescent, crystal-like qualities of the now-precious mineral components.

For his own installation work, *Timeless* (ill. p. 75), Naoki Hamaguchi also uses a familiar, everyday object: a traditional kimono, specially woven by Setsuko Kawahara using silk and phosphorescent yarn that stores light and 'glows' in the dark. In this piece, the distinctive sounds and imagery from the techno-frenzy of 24/7 Tokyo are portrayed on an entirely still analogue backdrop – the kimono – an intentional

Nicola Naismith,
Two Prosthetics,
2003

For this piece, a multiple of hand-stitched prosthetic forms are linked by a series of threads, which, like thimbles, are fitted to fingers that type on a computer keyboard. The mechanical links between hand, eye, brain and machine become very apparent.

contrasting of culturally opposing and iconic reference points that together create an artwork of exquisite connection.

Low-resolution 'bitmap' textures defined the computer-graphic aesthetic in its early commercial contexts, and in particular during the cultural boom of computer gaming in the 1990s. The economic drive towards software development at the time was such that the plots of films and computer games were often determined by triumphs in coded special effects and 3D CG modelling and animation. Real-time imaging technology filtered down from sectors, including the military, which invested heavily in simulating live-environment scenarios. 'Virtual reality' offered worlds that were infinite, defied gravity, and could be programmed to operate in ways that differed from our own experience. These environments, however, still had to visually succeed in creating spaces that people wanted to inhabit, along with desirable fantasy formats that broke from cartoon-like representation. Constructed solely from code, gaming realms consumed processing power voraciously in conveying that imagery. The speed of a machine runs according to the user's ability to consider and implement tasks; as hardware has improved, so has the complexity of the graphics to meet human capability and a boom in 3D gaming.

The 1990s witnessed the arrival of several landmark icons in the world of computer games, including the character Lara Croft of the *Tomb Raider* video-game series, created by graphic artist Toby Gard of Core Design. For gaming enthusiasts, it seemed that years of reliable but clunky 2D graphics were superseded almost overnight by a fantastic 3D visual realm. Infamously dressed in made-to-measure adventure gear, accessorized by strategically positioned weapons, Lara drew the attention of both male and female gamers. Her appearance was timely for Sony, who had invested $500 million into the development of their early PlayStation consoles at a time when other parts of their business were floundering. This seismic shift in hardware could support the thousands of polygons required to build and run 3D characters and environments in real time. Lara Croft became a uniquely prominent digital celebrity, and, during the Cool Britannia era in 1997, was elevated to virtual-icon status as the cover girl of *The Face* magazine, complete with digital 'couture' supplied by Alexander McQueen.

It was surely only a matter of time before fashion felt the full impact of these digital film and gaming characters. One such creation, Babelle (ill. p. 76), the brainchild of Roland Maas and Maurits Brands, is cleverly positioned between the real and virtual worlds; gamers are openly invited to design her digital wardrobe, an activity that has caught the imagination of numerous teenagers. Babelle has become prolific in trend reports for the fashion trade, and is routinely 'booked' by manufacturers and designers to model collections; such is her appeal that she was showcased in SHOWstudio's *Future Tense* film series.

This series of imagery for *Numéro* magazine (below, left and right) was based on the Japanese concept of *kawaisa*, or cuteness, the child-like qualities found in manga and anime. The work on the left is titled *Little Gun*; on the right is *Action Gun*.

Naoki Hamaguchi
Timeless, 2006
With Setsuko Kawahara

Timeless (opposite) is an analogue and digital collaboration. Hamaguchi's vibrant imagery and sound, portraying Tokyo's noise and bustle, is digitally mastered and projected onto a Jacquard-woven kimono by Setsuko Kawahara. The reflective nature of the light-sensitive yarn adds an unexpected 3D quality.

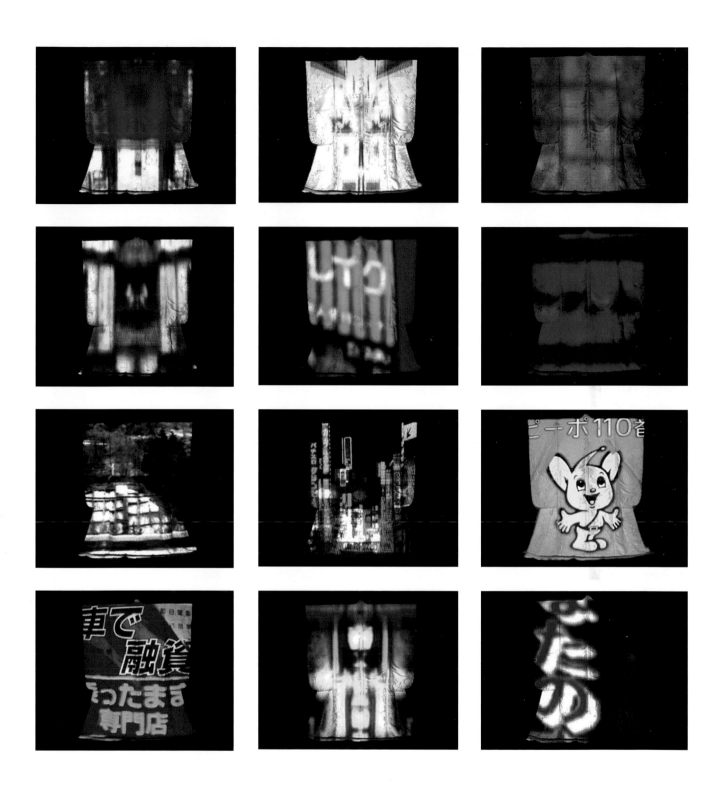

Roland Maas
and Romy Smits,
Babelle, 2008

Described as embodying
'the ultimate elegance of
genetic perfection', the
toonmodel Babelle presents
Romy Smits's 'art couture',
showcased in SHOWstudio's
Future Tense film series.

This form of 'toonmodel', or avatar-like
representation, offers new ways for the
commercial sector to connect with the high
street, and particularly with young audiences.

Following in the footsteps of simulation
gaming designers (particularly Will Wright,
the designer behind *SimCity*, released in 1989,
followed by *The Sims* in 2000) is Berlin-based
eBoy, whose work depicts the essence of
what is digital, using a distinctive pixel
aesthetic as the building blocks for their
graphic environments. The resulting eCity
imagery has been applied to a wide range
of products, including fashion and textiles.
For his Spring/Summer 2005 collection,
fashion designer Paul Smith commissioned
a digital view of London as an addition to
eBoy's roster of cityscapes (ill. below). Also
making use of alternative environments was
David Jones, who created *Grand Theft Auto* in
1997, an award-winning series of video games
set in hyper-real fictional cities around the
world. Raising the virtual-environment bar
even higher was Nick Phillips, with *To End
All Wars*, a video game based on World War I.
Having specialized in interactive games,
Phillips, a trained sculptor, used his practical
knowledge of materials to create hyper-
realistic portrayals of hair, skin and clothing.

Underlying all digital imagining is,
of course, code. Benoît Mandelbrot, the
mathematician behind fractal geometry, saw
the generative potential of code as a means
of realizing the structural components

eBoy for Paul Smith,
London Cityscape,
Spring/Summer 2005

After visiting their Berlin
studio, Paul Smith
commissioned eBoy to
apply their characteristic
pixellated imagery to this
cityscape of London, as
part of their *Pixorama* series.
Smith applied the resulting
print throughout his Spring/
Summer 2005 collection on
a variety of substrates for
clothing and accessories.

of natural forms (clouds, snowflakes, lightning). In design terms, code has become a means of creating interactive imagery, conceptual objects and architectural forms that challenge conventional 2D, 3D and 4D software approaches. A key principle of generative software systems is that they can be designed with in-built strategies to populate surface and space in an infinitely evolving manner. An algorithm may be constant until otherwise determined; practitioners who make use of these tools, such as artist, researcher and software developer Simon Schofield (ill. pp. 6–7; 79, top), can opt to implement control through mathematical parameters, or surrender control to the machine.

The influential work of designer and computer scientist John Maeda radically altered the perception of code as a graphic visualization tool. His experiments have expanded the potential of programming and are responsible for much of today's web-based interaction graphics. In the early 1990s, there was a propensity to view the computer as a replacement for traditional media, including painting and drawing, but Maeda passionately maintained that computing should be accepted as a medium in its own right. He brought together engineers, artists and designers to allow different spheres of practice to engage and inform one another, thus freeing the connection between technology and creativity.

The incentive to explore programming was initially driven by frustration, as crudely designed interfaces and graphics dominated the digital market in the late 1990s and into the new century. There was a passion to create and control something individual and new; as a palette of algorithms that operated outside the constraints of the vast commercial mainframes, code showed untapped potential. One of the advantages of code was the ease with which collaboration could be achieved via digital networks. Generative designers Casey Reas (see

pp. 150–55) and Ben Fry, who studied under Maeda at the MIT Media Lab, together authored the versatile open-source programming environment, Processing. The software was revolutionary in that it opened up the world of programming to beginners, using the Internet as a distribution tool.

Initially, the integrity of generative artworks came under scrutiny; in question was the computer's role in the making process. But designers like Reas, Daniel Brown (see pp. 146–49) and Joshua Davis (see pp. 182–87) have taken command of the medium, authoring their own software imaging systems to produce art and design work that has been used in fashion, textile,

Rainer Stolle,
Counterfeit Couture,
2004

Inspired by the open-source software Processing, Stolle explores how digital technology may be translated into a twenty-first-century surfacing aesthetic.

interiors, art and design contexts. Just as with other computer-generated forms, 3D output from code may be made physically manifest through the use of computer modelling and rendering technology, rapid prototyping and 3D printable technology. While programming offers new ways of conceptualizing ideas, this alone does not guarantee them to be physically workable; the tangible experience of working with material and construction processes still determines the best outcomes.

Among this new generation of code pioneers are Vicky Isley and Paul Smith of Boredom Research, who combine genetic and computational algorithms with rules from nature to create poetic digital systems. Mesmerizing, large-scale projected works, such as *System 1.6* (ill. opposite, bottom), create powerful surfaces and resonate with a richness of colour. Otherwise calm spaces are interrupted by 'biome machines', the twenty-first-century equivalent of PacMan. Each microscopic form is intricately designed and programmed with sophisticated behavioural mechanisms to randomly swim, flit or explode, shifting from gentle to aggressive character traits. The duo's work appears to uncover what science could not see or find in its own systems. Recent works have included small, highly designed framed

portals, including *Ornamental Bug Garden* (ill. below, left and right), which alter while viewing – much like watching cells grow and change in a biologically controlled Petri dish. This format serves to contain or frame the space, within which their unpredictable, generative animations play out.

A number of artists have used code as an inspiration for surface pattern and form, including Chicago-based textile artist Christy Matson, who takes contemporary digital culture as her source material and creates artworks that combine weave with other media. Borrowing imagery from the computer game *LOOM* (1990) by LucasArts, Matson designed *LOOMscapes* (ill. p. 80), a tapestry woven on a Jacquard loom for precision and realism. Her 'loomscapes' offer highly detailed, if slightly surreal scenes that visually cross gaming with traditional panoramas.

German designer Rainer Stolle, who has a background in film production, is similarly fascinated by code, and has recently begun working with Processing software to create unique surface patterns for textiles (ill. p. 77). The idea of misusing GPS data to detect city crime scenes as a game concept led to the development of *Geohacktile* (2007), a composition of impossible maps of non-

Simon Schofield,
Tokyo Flowers, 2007

Schofield has written a semi-automated software tool that builds imagescapes from drawn visual elements. In this work (opposite, top), 'constellations' of texture and pattern illustrate vibrant, highly naturalistic recreations of landscape and nature.

Boredom Research,
Ornamental Bug Garden 001, 2004; *Ornamental Bug Garden* 002, 2007; *System 1.6*, 2001

These two works (below, left and right) are part of a series that, along with *System 1.6* (opposite, bottom), combines gaming techniques with artificial life modelling.

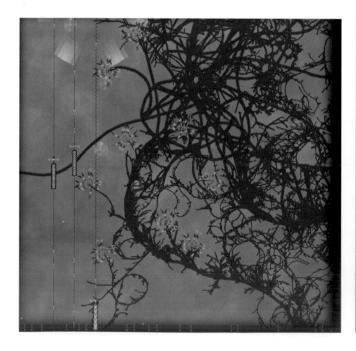

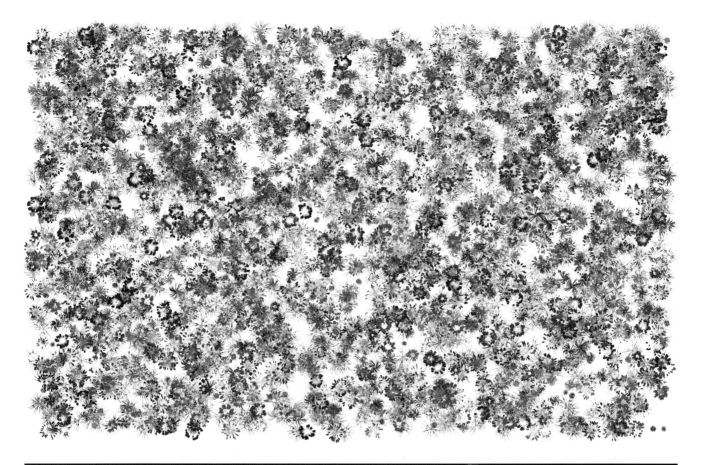

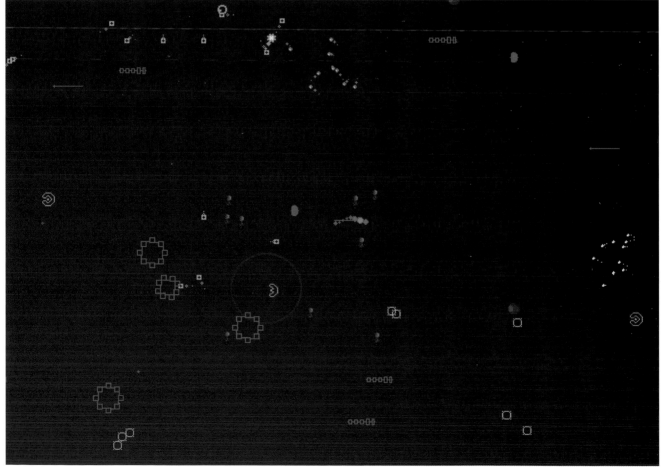

existing landscapes that incorporates map graphics to create digitally printed fashion fabrics. Avant-garde fashion designer Shelley Fox also turned to code for her inspiration. As part of her research for her Spring/Summer 2000 collection, Fox visited Bletchley Park to understand how information is decoded, and then interpreted the dots and dashes of Morse code as prints on garments. Some of the symbols were lightly burned into the fabric so as not to be readily visible, and thus remain secret.

It is unlikely that a computer will ever have the sensory understanding experienced by humans. Even if it were possible to translate such subjective information into code and install it onto a hard drive, it is doubtful that a machine would be capable of making aesthetic decisions, which by their nature are unpredictable. Can a computer program design fashion? Computer scientist Ben Maron thinks not, although it is possible that

software could be devised to develop many different versions of one design concept. Having investigated the role that generative design principles could play in fashion, while working with IBM's supercomputers, Maron was able to determine an approach to developing code that could aid the creative process. His initial experiments included plotting random arcs and circles, and allowing the computer to play with a series of intersecting components. The final geometry was then refined to realize a form that could be replicated as a pattern (ill. opposite).

Maron then explored iterations of the garment form, and developed a series of algorithms based on the lines and motion of Futurism. The resulting application drew variable forms of abstract lines and shapes around a body image. An infinite range of image data led to the more complex decision of knowing how to select designs that could be worked further; many possibilities

Christy Matson,
LOOMscapes, 2007
Oriole Mill, North Carolina

Each of the three works of this Jacquard-woven series was composed of screen shots taken from the computer game, *LOOM* (1990). Adobe Photoshop software was used to manipulate and paste together the screen shots to create the effect of a timeline and a virtual panorama.

emerged from the early stages of this project. Perhaps in the future it will be possible to personalize algorithms using body data or DNA as source information, combined with information on an individual's favourite art form or fashion style, to realize a bespoke fashion-design system.

Initially, few creative practitioners had regular access to computing tools, and for those who did, the technology was disappointingly slow. But for those who persisted, the results were exciting. Software and hardware developments have tended to be commercially ambitious in order to justify investment, and consequently less engaged with the requirements of artists and designers, who have ultimately intercepted technical developments at various stages, challenging their intended purpose and subverting their course. Almost every creative discipline has been re-engineered and rethought, with practitioners shifting between the various art and design worlds,

combining computing and analogue processes. Aesthetic and conceptual qualities have emerged, at times expressing thinking that was beyond the vision of most. Digital media have dramatically altered capabilities in 2D, 3D and 4D image, form and motion-making, while gaming and interactive tools have defined alternative and now established kinds of narrative. Expectations of digital capability have dramatically shifted, and the medium itself has transformed, somewhere between the threshold of the known and the unknown – a liminal state.

Ben Maron,
Computational Fashion,
2008

Maron's final-year collection at Central Saint Martins consisted of a series of algorithms. Geometries based on Futurist principles are a component part of a generative-drawing tool created by Maron, to inform new processes of fashion design. The same geometries were also used to develop patterns for printed textiles.

2 designers in code

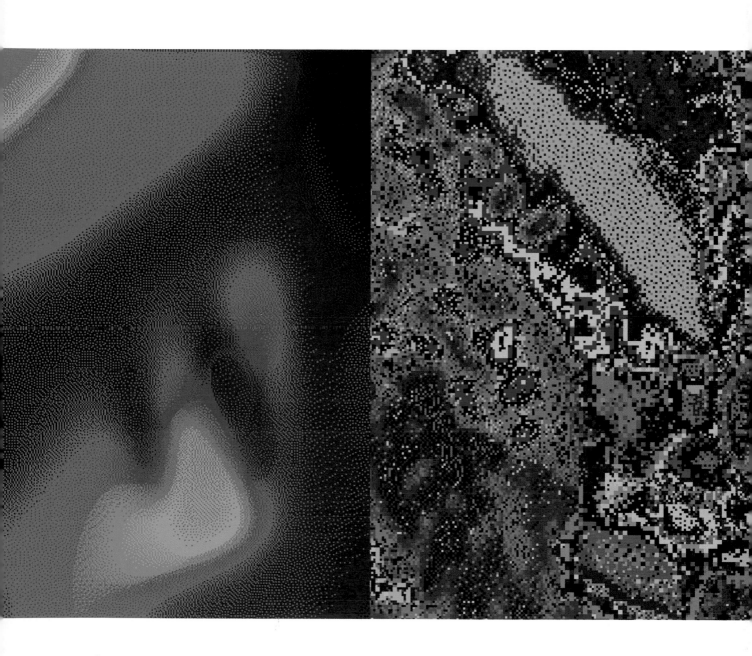

**Peter Struycken,
Computer-controlled
Jacquard weaves (details),
2002 and 2004–5**

This design (above) was
one of a series of wall-based
works that explored the
interplay between colours.
The design on the right is
a detail of *Entoptic Perception*
(ill. pp. 102, 103). By zooming
in close, the warp and weft
appear as pixels.

nuno

Japanese textile company Nuno (*nuno* is the Japanese word for fabric) was founded in 1984 by Jun'ichi Arai and Reiko Sudo, and is renowned for its woven fabrics, which combine tradition with the latest technologies. Nuno's designs are practical as well as beautiful, having applications for both fashion and interiors, and from the company's earliest days were the result of using digital equipment as important design tools, largely as a result of the early experimental work of Jun'ichi Arai.

Bridging the gulf between art and science, Arai has pioneered new techniques throughout his career, from the use of metallic yarns to advanced finishing treatments. He began experimenting with computer programs in the 1970s, to create and vary patterns, and to thoroughly test the properties of different yarns and their combinations, and how durable or flexible a particular yarn combination might be. It was Arai who suggested scanning Reiko Sudo's hand-woven structures, thus allowing the designs to be industrially produced. Jun'ichi Arai was also the first innovator to revive ancient Japanese weaving techniques, using a computerized loom and adapting them to industrial methods of production. In the early 1980s, Arai was using scanners, computer-assisted and direct Jacquard machines to create textiles with an entirely new aesthetic; many of the Nuno fabrics from this period look like one-offs, but were in fact mass-produced on industrial Jacquard looms. Occasionally, random generators were used to ensure that built-in flaws would occur in the weaving process to give the 'look of the hand'.

Continuing the traditional role of layered cloth in Japanese textiles and fashion, Arai and Sudo, now Nuno's main designer, create multi-layered textiles with amazingly complex patterns and intricate structures, which are digitally woven. Three-dimensional effects can also be achieved, along with cloth that is fully reversible to reveal different patterns on each face. The incredible forays that Japan has made into textile research and development over the past few decades has brought science and technology closer to ancient, rural handicrafts to create a totally new aesthetic. Formerly labour-intensive crafts can be kept alive as their manufacture is speeded up, and historic textiles preserved by digitally rendering and recreating the pattern on a computer-assisted loom. New techniques such as these can enable much faster production, freeing up the design process and allowing more time for experimentation.

Designs by Reiko Sudo and Jun'ichi Arai have been included in many international exhibitions, and are held in the permanent collections of museums around the world, including the Victoria & Albert Museum in London, the Cooper-Hewitt National Design Museum in New York and the National Museum of Modern Art in Tokyo.

Basket Weave Big Pocket, 1985
Designed by Jun'ichi Arai

For this design, based on the geometric patterning found in ancient bamboo basketry, a complex double-weave structure with two warps was used: flat machine-knitted ribbon and plain yarn (a technical innovation for which Arai holds the industry rights in Japan). Plain weave, herringbone and basket-weave patterns were morphed together to create a fabric that is different on both sides – a good example of how computers were used before the introduction of direct (non-punch card) Jacquard looms to Japan.

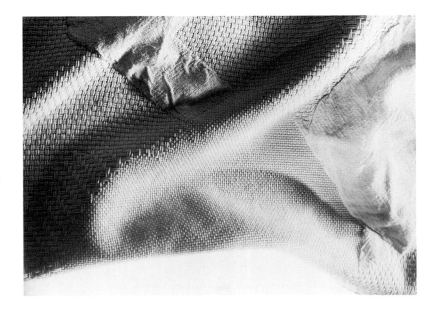

Woven Structure Pattern,
1984
Designed by Jun'ichi Arai

A traditional African
kente cloth was repeatedly
photocopied until the
imagery became pixellated.
The photocopy was then
scanned, and the resulting
design woven on a
computer-driven Jacquard
loom. A double-weave
structure produces a fabric
with two distinct faces; the
texture of the final cloth is
further enhanced by cotton
yarns that are tightly twisted
in opposite directions to
create a surface that is elastic
yet not bulky.

Deckle-Edged, 1993
Designed by Reiko Sudo

The inspiration for this
design came from the
distinctive 'deckle' edges
of the handmade paper
of an antique book.
A photograph of the paper's
ragged edges was scanned
into a computer program
to create the design, which
was then linked to
a computer-assisted
Jacquard loom to interpret
it as a monochrome
double-weave in 100 per cent
cotton. Two warps were
woven independently with
inter-layer 'bridges' to
connect and strengthen
the cloth in specific places.
The choice of black and
white serves to emphasize
the graphic quality of the
design.

***Bark*, 1986**
Designed by Jun'ichi Arai

This Jacquard double-faced weave (left) recreated the look and texture of tree bark using a mix of cotton, wool and Spandex. After scanning, the images were translated into a binary pattern by hand-drawing onto graph paper, and using the drawings to make the punch cards that drove the loom. Cotton and wool layers were interlaced in an irregular pattern of elastic yarns to create a relief effect.

Prairie, 2007
Designed by Reiko Sudo;
furniture by Gwenael
Nicolas; produced by
Arti, Inc.

For this quadruple-layered
design (opposite, above),
two sets of two layers of
fabric were independently
constructed, coming
together at strategic points
to create an integrated
textile. The result is a fabric
with completely distinct
patterns on each side. The
application of computers
in textile design and
production has enabled
complex structures such
as double, triple, even
quadruple-layered weavings
to be achieved more easily.

A subtly toned drawing
of a windswept prairie
was scanned and sent to a
weaving mill to create this
upholstery fabric – seen here
used for seating (left) and for
a sofa (below) – where it was
woven using a computer-
controlled Jacquard loom.
Working digitally, rather
than manually, created a
particular aesthetic in which
the lines were rendered
more deeply. Cotton slub
yarns were used for texture,
together with linen and
cotton threads. The result
conjures up a vast, open
landscape with limitless
horizons.

vibeke riisberg

Textile designer Vibeke Riisberg, now Associate Professor at Kolding School of Art and Design in Denmark, was an early and enthusiastic embracer of the possibilities of computer imaging, and has faithfully kept each computer purchased over the years, as well as the work created on each one, some of which is impossible to view on anything other than the original processor. In 1987, Riisberg received a grant to attend the School of Visual Arts in New York, and found herself in a computer lab from nine in the morning to eleven at night, hooked by the new media. Despite the low resolution of imaging programs of the time, Riisberg recognized the potential of the emerging media.

The tools may have been simple and slow, but they were efficient and suited to textile design: with limitations came an intuitive focus. That same year Riisberg purchased her first computer – the first Apple Macintosh with a colour screen, a considerable investment – which produced about ten years of work. Very few of the major graphic-design studios would have had even one or two Macintosh computers, and Riisberg was the first textile designer in Denmark to own one. She used Superpaint, followed by Studio Eight, which enabled her to take a section of an image and effectively make it into a brush, a concept she later explored using the open-source programming software, Processing. In the early 1990s, she beta tested Symmetry Studio, a vector-based program written by the School of Visual Arts' Timothy Binkley, in which a drawing could be automatically repeated with seventeen symmetries.

Riisberg took pleasure in the simplest of computing actions, such as being able to delete or erase. Not being committed to a mark or a pattern was liberating and very different to working manually (with paper,

for example). She devised masking and layering techniques, implemented in a primitive but workable way by working on top of images and erasing what went before. Modern tools such as Photoshop's History and Layers, which retain past actions, perhaps make things too easy; without these memory banks, one had to work harder at making design decisions. By saving variations of a design along the way, Riisberg gradually built up an image into its more complex format. In the early 1990s Malcolm Cocks (see p. 18), a designer and lecturer at Central Saint Martins, was similarly passionate about the imaging revolution and its impact on textile design, and produced highly complex digital imagery, using multiple layers of colour and pattern, which were then laboriously translated into fabric form by using a range of hand-screenprinting techniques, including devoré, flocking, discharge and resist. This involved lengthy processes that few would contemplate today.

From her design base in Paris, Riisberg adopted a parallel approach to her work, conscious that a digital aesthetic was not yet commercially viable. She created simple designs for commercial printed and woven textiles, while at the same time developing a visionary approach by creating futuristic imagery that explored the illusion of 3D, convinced that a common aesthetic language would evolve in which these two methods would somehow fit together. *Vibration*, designed in 1991 for the Charlottenborg Autumn Exhibition in Copenhagen, was put in production by Danish textile firm Kvadrat in 1992, along with two other designs (*Refleksion* and *Impression*) for their interiors collection. All three were included in the exhibition *Textiles and New Technology: 2010* (1994–96).

Neither Nor, Both And,
2004
Crafts and Design Biennale

For this installation (opposite, above and below), held at the Trapholt Art Museum and North Jutland Art Museum, both in Denmark, Riisberg worked in a more narrative way with the imagery. Transparency and reflection are important qualities that the designer brings to the exhibition of her work as part of this narrative.

Terezzo Perl, 1995;
Kalejdoskop, 1995

These designs (overleaf), along with *Seashell* (ill. p. 2) and *Plastik* (1998), were among Riisberg's first complex computer images to be sold for commercial production.

As digital fabric-printing did not become available in Denmark until 2000, Riisberg gradually learned how to get her more creative work off the screen, using the limited four-colour separation print processes and devising her own colour palettes. Eventually, computerized fabric-printers became more accessible in Europe, and design schools began to invest in their own digital facilities. With two major exhibitions behind her using the fabric-printer, Riisberg still considers digital print (as opposed to digital design) a process that she is very much in the early days of exploring. She continues to be intrigued by details and characteristics that cannot be achieved with four-colour separation, along with rough, low-resolution effects that achieve a sensuous surface in a printed fabric. Early digital experiences seem particularly poignant to us now, as our use of digital media has become so fluid, unquestioned and seamless.

Vibration, 1991
Curtain fabric for Kvadrat

With the first version of this early work (right), designed and hand-screenprinted for the Charlottenborg Autumn Exhibition in Copenhagen, Riisberg began to achieve a 3D visual effect. The complexity and limitations of the medium in its early form spurred her to create imagery that has become both timeless and iconic.

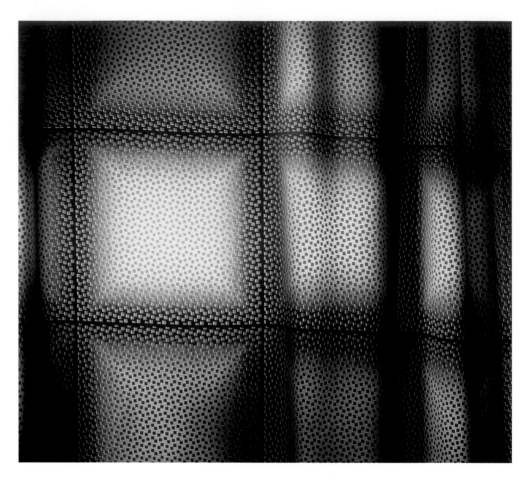

7 Illusions, 1993
Danish Arts & Crafts Museum, Copenhagen

Alongside more commercially viable designs, Riisberg created futuristic imagery that explored 3D effects, resulting in a series of works called *Illusions*. The piece illustrated here (left) was first exhibited at the Danish Arts & Crafts Museum, and later at the Danish Architecture Centre, also in Copenhagen.

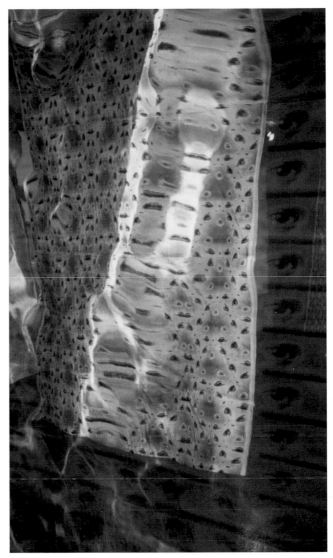

Digital Files, 2001
Hordaland Art Centre,
Norway

This installation for the
exhibition *Digital Files* at the
Hordaland Art Centre in
Bergen, Norway, was entirely
digitally printed. Riisberg
experimented with the
presentation of the textile
collection using reflection
and multiples, which
responded conceptually
to some of the effects that
could be achieved using the
current 2D software.

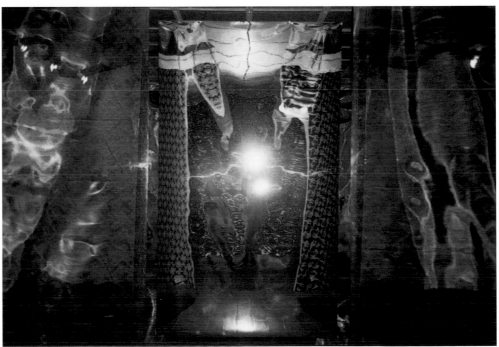

issey miyake

Passionate about technology, curious about research and ever the experimenter, it is not surprising that Japanese designer Issey Miyake turned to digital technology to realize A-POC, a groundbreaking DIY system of clothing that exploits the very latest computer capabilities and confronts issues of waste and sustainability. Having already established the Miyake Design Studio in 1970 with textile designer Makiko Minagawa, Miyake set up a collaborative venture with textile engineer Dai Fujiwara in 1997. Miyake had previously shown collections that, with hindsight, could be seen as a prelude to A-POC: 'Just Before' (Spring/Summer 1998), in which a range of clothes emerged from a continuous knitted tube; and 'Tube Knit' (Autumn/Winter 1998–99), which featured garments fashioned on a computerized knitting machine.

The concept behind A-POC ('a piece of cloth') dates back to the 1970s, when Miyake began experimenting with clothing made from single lengths of fabric. Unlike that of other designers, Miyake's work evolves in themes that are rethought, reinterpreted and reworked. A-POC begins with the thread itself, and uses industrial knitting machines from the 1930s and '40s, together with weaving looms that are connected to state-of-the-art computers. The wearer purchases a roll of fabric, which contains a variety of outfits, complete with accessories, and then chooses the cutting line that will influence the final design. Earlier versions of A-POC encouraged this element of interactivity, but the latest versions no longer require cutting, and are instead merely separated. Miyake and Fujiwara continually explore new territories, including a braiding technique (using one of Japan's two remaining braiding companies), with a mathematical construction concept

developed by an American university. Also under further investigation is double-structure, in which the front and the back of the cloth have different threads, construction, colour and texture, fully testing the computer software with its intricate data.

A-POC's modular and seamless system displays resourcefulness and economy of means, as each design is carefully worked out to minimize waste of fabric. Because no sewing is necessary, the processes needed for production are greatly reduced. At the beginning of the catwalk show for A-POC's Spring/Summer 1999 collection, staff cut out the design *King & Queen* from a single piece of cloth laid out on the floor, and assembled the clothes and accessories on model Alek Wek directly in front of the audience. The finale, which received a standing ovation, showed another design, *Le Feu*, for which twenty-three models came out onto the catwalk connected by a continuous line of cloth, all wearing bright-red dresses of slightly varying permutations.

Issey Miyake for A-POC,
King & Queen,
Spring/Summer 1999

King & Queen (opposite) demonstrated how one roll of fabric could produce an entire wardrobe. Through cutting, a one-piece dress, socks, underwear, a hat and a bag are released – an extremely inventive process that does away with traditional methods of manufacture.

Issey Miyake for A-POC,
Le Feu,
Spring/Summer 1999

Le Feu (left) showed a procession of models walking down the catwalk, each wearing a different permutation of a dress that was still connected and linked. A piece of cloth (opposite, left) was placed on the catwalk and cut to release pattern pieces for garments and accessories.

Miyake is a born collaborator. Warren du Preez and Nick Thornton Jones provided digital imagery and art direction for advertisements, while artist Pascal Roulin created photographs, illustrations, videos, digital animations and the evolving logo. In collaboration with Habitat, Miyake used the A-POC system to create a kitchen apron with a double-weave technique, which allowed the design to ingeniously lengthen when cut along the indicated line. Miyake has also worked with inventor James Dyson to create a collection using a silk/polyester fabric that incorporated woven imagery of Dyson's blueprints for a retro science-fiction look. Other collaborations included the *Ripple* chair, with experimental furniture designer Ron Arad, for Italian firm Moroso, and the design of Miyake's flagship store in New York with avant-garde architect Frank Gehry.

Ever since the Industrial Revolution, technology has played a huge role in the design and manufacture of textiles and clothing. Miyake has become a part of that tradition, fusing material and garment by utilizing today's advanced computing technology. With its binary language, the on/off of digital is ripe for connection with textiles that utilize code in their construction.

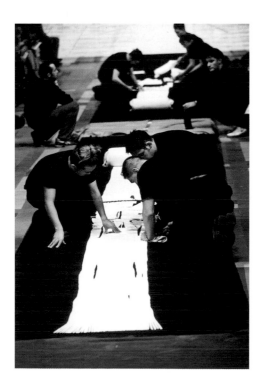

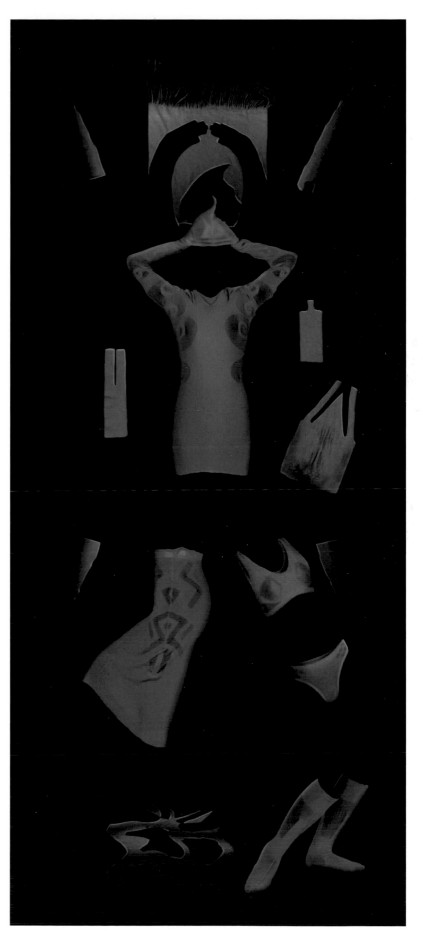

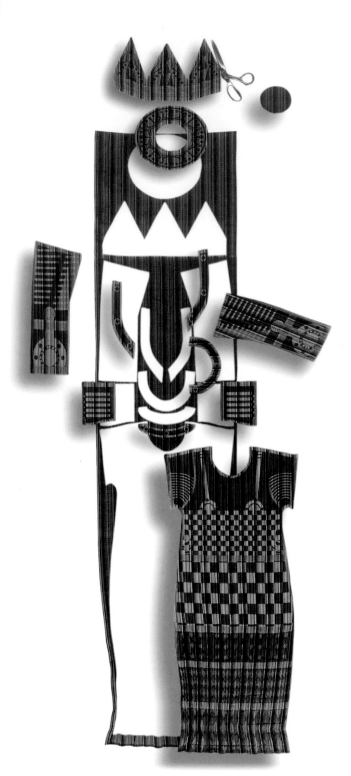

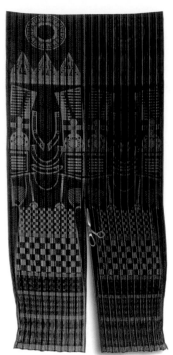

Issey Miyake for A-POC,
Berlin District,
Autumn/Winter 2001–2

Miyake finds Berlin, once a symbol of East and West, a very exciting city and paid homage to it with *Berlin District*. By varying knit patterns and shape, a collection of wearable forms can emerge from one roll of cloth.

Miyake is always seeking to create the 'perfect' design, prime examples of which are the simple white T-shirt and a pair of jeans. This environmentally friendly design, *Flat Jeans* (left), cleverly got the most out of a single roll of fabric, creating little waste.

**Dai Fujiwara
for Issey Miyake,
'Rondo No. 2',
Autumn/Winter 2011–12**

Dai Fujiwara's last show as Creative Director for Issey Miyake used both low and high technologies by combining manual paper-folding with 3D digital printing. Design staff created a range of garments on the catwalk by folding and stapling paper (opposite, below), thus removing the mystery of making, as Miyake did for Spring/ Summer 1999 (ill. pp. 94, 95). The resulting paper forms were then interpreted in fabric for geometric but wearable designs (right). This collection built on Miyake's '132.5' collection (2010), in which clothing worked with computer algorithms as patterns.

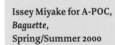

Issey Miyake for A-POC,
Baguette,
Spring/Summer 2000

Some of the A-POC designs, including *Baguette* (above and left) – a reference to the French loaf of bread, which can be sliced thick or thin, straight across or diagonally – can be cut anywhere, not just along set 'cutting' lines. The design was manufactured at a Japanese fishing-net factory, whose equipment was linked to a sophisticated computer programming system. Both the sleeves and neckline can be adjusted, according to the owner's whim. When a scoop-neck is chosen, the fabric left behind cleverly becomes a balaclava or cuffs.

Issey Miyake for A-POC,
'Zoo',
Autumn/Winter 2001–2

The playful *Turtle* design
(left, above and below)
allows the wearer to put her
arms or legs through any
of the openings at the top,
bottom or in the middle,
while *Octopus* (above) has
a wavy texture and relief
areas that recall the eight
arms of this sea creature.

peter struycken

The work of artist Peter Struycken encompasses architecture and textile design, as well as dynamic, real-time 'colourscapes' that accompany music and theatre performances. In 2006, his *Beatrix* postage stamp (first issued in 1982) was named as one of the twenty-five best Dutch designs of the past one hundred years.

Having studied both painting and computer programming in the 1960s, Struycken's abstract paintings began to evolve into 'systems' in which colour and shape were precisely calculated. Instead of a mathematical approach, it was the visual-based proportion of one colour or shape relative to another that informed his work. Struycken was considered a pioneer in forging links between the abstract and the digital; while at the Delft University of Technology in the 1970s, a computer-controlled colour monitor that enabled real-time operations was built especially for him. Computer codes were converted into punched tapes, which were linked to a light box fitted with an electronic switching system. In 1974 Struycken began to write his own graphic programs, and while at MIT from 1978–79, he collaborated with Professor Walter Lewin and Nicholas Negroponte's Architecture Machine Group to write computer programs that led to new aesthetics. Since then, Struycken's work has involved constantly changing colour-based spaces.

These early forays into the digital eventually led to the transformative colour sequences that would become Struycken's signature. He is particularly interested in the connection between the visual and the audible in the performing arts, visually interpreting both the music and the atmosphere evoked, and has created colour works to accompany the music of, among others, Johann Sebastian Bach, Iannis Xenakis and Pierre Boulez (see ...*explosante-fixe*...; ill. p. 104). The time-based works show an infinite number of pictures, while specifically chosen stills represent a pause, a moment captured. In 1997, the Netherlands Broadcasting Company commissioned Struycken to create a dynamic colour space for a television production of Russian composer Alexander Scriabin's symphony, *Prometheus: The Poem of Fire* (ill. p. 105), which featured two 'voices' for changing coloured light and five hundred colour changes, with a 'jarring' colour score and a 'harmonious' one. Scriabin's symphony, written in 1910, was first performed with coloured lighting using a 'colour organ' in 1915, but because of the lack of available technology, the composition had never been fully realized. To do so, Struycken collaborated with Dutch computer-graphics company cThrough and software specialist Daniel Dekkers.

Struycken was also commissioned by the Netherlands Textile Museum in Tilburg to create a large piece, woven on a computer-controlled Jacquard loom, called *Esman-1"88'* (1988), followed by *Ambaum* (1989) and *Millennium Damask* (1999), the last produced on the museum's newly acquired Dornier weaving machine. Taking this work further, Struycken used the Jacquard loom again to create an enormous (about 50 m²) wall-based work for the Achmea Insurance building, in the Dutch city of Groningen, in 2001–2. Made of various pieces of fabric, it shows stills of an ever-changing series of images created by Modules software (a program written by Dekkers). The choice of a particular still out of an unlimited number of possible pictures was based on its ability to offer visual interest up close, from a distance, and from a variety of angles.

Between 2004 and 2007 Struycken created a series of colour works to accompany Boulez's musical composition, ...*explosante-fixe*... . First published in 1971, it was rewritten twenty years later using live electronics; it is this version that was Struycken's inspiration. Following the composer's use of serial techniques and controlled chance elements, Struycken used Modules software to arrange five screens in a given space, which showed dynamic, three-dimensional, computer-generated colour works. Five computers projected onto the screens, while an additional computer relayed instructions and played the music. The multiple-screen output showed different imagery working together in harmony, with the viewer experiencing the inter-relationships between the visuals and the music as he or she enters and moves through the space.

Continuing his exploration of the computer-controlled Jacquard weave, Struycken created a series of nineteen wall-based works called *Entoptic Perception* (ill. pp. 83, 102, 103) with the Panorama computer program, digitally manipulating the imagery with PaintShopPro. These were vertically orientated pieces, designed to work in a space from ceiling to floor. Eight colours were used, allowing a palette of 256 colours to be created through optical mixing. Each 'pixel' in the piece is made up of two or more coloured threads, with alternating black and white warp threads used for diversity and control. Viewed up close, the works have a fragmented look, but from a distance the geometry dissipates to suggest a state of continual flux. The viewer can imagine ephemeral and shifting forms found in nature, such as patterns of growth, thermal imaging and embryonic scans. The title refers to a phenomenon of sight, in which images can be 'seen' with closed eyes, due to still-tingling nerves.

Struycken's work clearly demonstrates the great variety of creative applications that can be afforded by using digital technology. By tracing his work from the pioneering days of the 1960s to the present, the upward trajectory of the capabilities and potential of the digital can be observed.

Computer-controlled Jacquard weaves, 2002

By using the Modules software program, Struycken was able to produce a stunning array of decorative effects. Close up, the pixellated construction is visible; but seen from a distance, the colours morph and blend to create the appearance of an image in constant flux. The viewer becomes immersed in the abstract images, which suggest, imply and provoke.

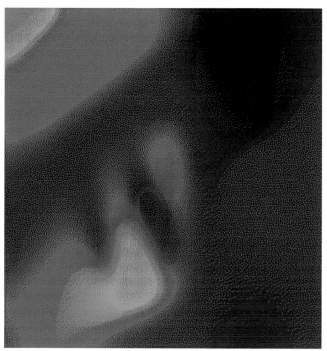

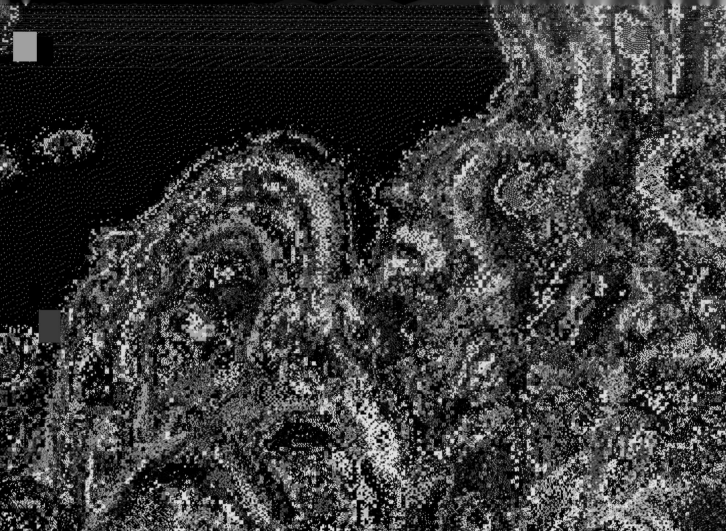

In this series of nineteen
Jacquard-woven wall-based
works, inspired by entoptic
visual experiences, colours
merge and patterns collide,
and have no distinct
definition or form. The
woven works are designed
to be viewed from several
distances to achieve
different experiences.

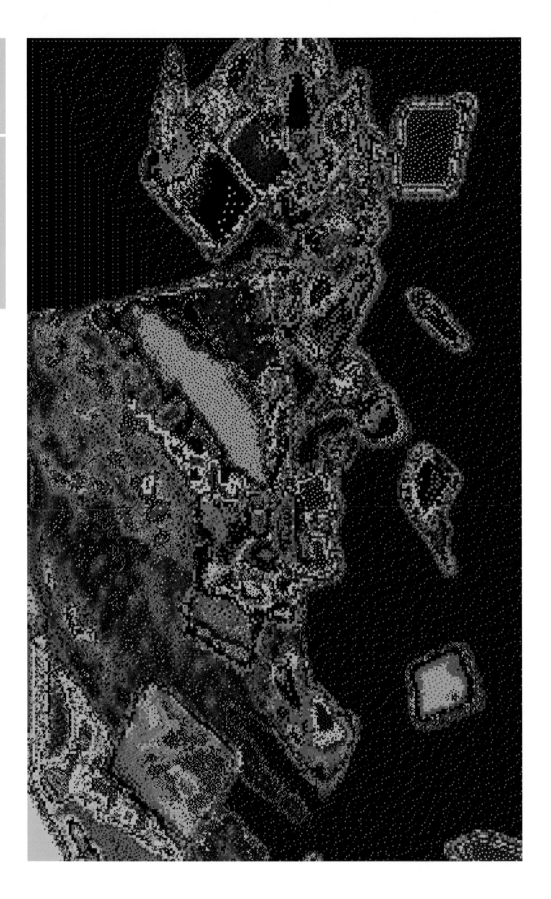

Dynamic colour space for *...explosante-fixe...*, 2004–7

Scriabin's Vision, 1997–99

Layers of colour and imagery respond to the tonal layers found in this piece of music by the French composer, Pierre Boulez (below). Quieter passages are suggested by calm, peaceful transitions in colour and form, while more 'explosive' ones are implied with dramatic imagery. The computer-generated visuals were a commission for the Pierre Boulez Foundation and the Groninger Museum, Netherlands.

Commissioned by the Netherlands Broadcasting Company, this dynamic colour space (opposite) is based on Alexander Scriabin's symphonic work, *Prometheus: The Poem of Fire* (1910), which includes two 'voices' for changing colour. The colour space heightens the experience of the music with its constantly changing visuals.

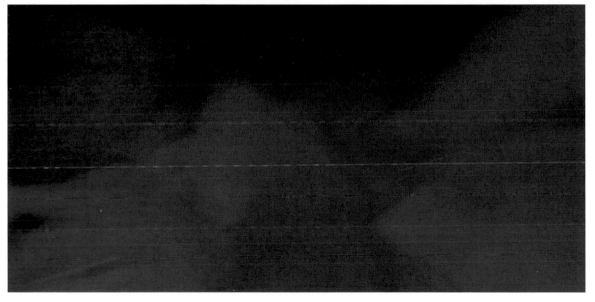

prada

For their internationally renowned collections, fashion label Prada makes use of the illusory effects of digital print along with computer-controlled lasers to create provocative imagery and compelling tactile effects. Their crisp, clean garment shapes, often with a strong 1960s vibe, give full attention to the prints or surface treatments – a pared-down, modern look that says 'less is more'. In digital print, the reproduction of textures, relief surfaces or three-dimensional forms can be used to create illusionary effects to trick the eye and allow visual play.

For the Prada Woman Autumn/Winter 2004–5 collection (ill. opposite), the look of a pleated surface was digitally printed for a wrap-over dress, in which the physical folds and trompe-l'oeil pleats work together convincingly. At the hem of the dress, the edge of the print could be seen, making apparent the representation of folded cloth. For the same collection, the wrinkles and creases of the female body were digitally printed onto semi-transparent fabric and made up into garments, which in turn are worn – a fascinating concept.

This idea was taken further for Spring/Summer 2005 (ill. p. 108), where digital prints portrayed different types of feathers, printed on a large scale for a variety of garments. Feathers are lightweight yet create volume, possessing a dynamic movement that softens and animates the body, and feminine fabrics including silk faille and chiffon were used to reflect their inherent softness, delicacy and fluidity. For the collection, actual feathers were also used, both for garments (skirts covered in peacock feathers) and accessories (such as hats), to produce a collision of the physical and its digitalized depiction.

Prada Woman's Spring/Summer 2008 collection (ill. p. 110) had an organic and painterly aesthetic with folkloric, fairytale imagery. The very crafted element of hand-drawn, hand-painted and hand-stitched layered and bonded silk chiffons and organzas was combined with digital animation in a short film directed by visual-effects artist James Lima, which encapsulated a poetic aspect with its title, *Trembled Blossoms* (ill. p. 111). Another short film, *Fallen Shadows* (ill. p. 112), was also directed by Lima; both films featured a female model, moving through a rural idyll and an urban environment, respectively, and presented a new way of looking at fashion.

'Design by deconstruction' – the precision removal of fabric by computer-controlled lasers to create a type of contemporary lace – was the idea behind the Miu Miu Autumn/Winter 2008–9 collection (ill. p. 109). Square blocks of grey or black woollen fabric were removed

Prada Woman, Spring/Summer 1998

On this early example of digital print, a large border challenges the usual method of repeat printing. Placement and scale have been adjusted to create a playful yet sophisticated image. The print conjures up an idyllic image of a wheat field, transfigured by the computer.

to create large-scale, open-worked structures, with repeating forms reminiscent of Modernist architecture. The intricate, geometric 'lozenge', 'diamond' or 'arrow' shapes created a 'techno lattice' – a contemporary version of lace. These laser-cut garments were worn layered over sleek bodysuits or knee-length leggings to allow glimpses of colour to show through. Close-fitting skullcaps with functional chin straps completed the sporty yet sophisticated look. The dark colours typical of autumn/winter collections were used, enriched with electric, jewel-like colours such as bright orange and emerald green, and there was a strong emphasis on texture, with evening satins juxtaposed against more utilitarian felts or cotton blends.

Layers of laser-cut fabrics were also in evidence in the Prada Woman Autumn/Winter 2008–9 collection, for which lace and mesh-like textiles in perforated shift shapes were worn over colour-blocked areas or,

alternatively, allowed skin to be glimpsed through the cut-outs to sensual effect. A play on the look of animal skins was seen in the Prada Woman Spring/Summer 2009 collection (ill. p. 108), where digitalized python prints adorned sleeveless, below-the-knee dresses. The snake is both decorative and deadly, and its associations with sexual power and rebirth create strong imagery. Its lavish patterns are enlarged and broken down into a pixellated effect, which blends a futuristic look with the primal quality of wearing a snakeskin. Other trompe-l'oeil effects were also evidenced, including a digital *ikat* print that was beautifully blurry on silk faille for a simple shift dress.

Prada makes full use of the aesthetic afforded by digital printing, in which colours and textures can be expertly fused together to create patterns that are incredibly sophisticated, and where the traditional and the technological converge to create a new sense of what is beautiful and sensual.

Prada Woman, Autumn/Winter 2004–5

An image of the ruins of a temple was digitally printed onto an empire-line silk faille dress (below, left), giving a traditional and romantic look a more contemporary edge. The same print was used for a silk/wool-mix coat (below, right).

**Prada Woman,
Spring/Summer 2005**

**Prada Woman,
Spring/Summer 2009**

For Spring/Summer 2005
(above), digital prints were
used to create trompe-l'oeil
effects that played with the
traditional use of feathers
to embellish clothing. The
distinctive patterns were
taken from the feathers of
parrots, swans and birds-of-
paradise.

For the Spring/Summer
2009 collection, a digitalized
python pattern (above,
right) and a large-scale 'wave
pixel patch' aesthetic in red,
grey, black and white (right)
were digitally printed onto
duchesse silk for asymmetric
shift dresses.

Miu Miu,
Autumn/Winter 2008–9

For this collection,
laser-cutting was used
to create decoration by
deconstruction. Graphic
areas of fabric were removed
to create a new type of lace,
while dark matt wools were
contrasted with shiny,
intensely coloured satins.

In this collection, an
alternative, almost folkloric
theme is in evidence, with
pixies and fairies given a
contemporary edge through
computer animation.
A digital print on silk twill
displays a hand-drawn, fluid
aesthetic (far left), while
the 'pixel' effect of another
digitally printed dress (left)
is a comment on the fact
that everything today is
viewed through a computer
screen. The square 'pixels'
are distorted by the shaping
of the garment, especially
around the bust.

Prada with James Lima,
Trembled Blossoms,
for Spring/Summer 2008

Stunning visuals with
animation by Sight Effects,
music by CocoRosie and the
work of concept artist James
Jean conveyed a sense of
beauty in a fantasy world in
this digitally animated short
film (opposite). The blue
and red-checked dress from
the Prada Woman Spring/
Summer 2008 collection
(left) features strongly
throughout. Imagery from
the atmospheric film was
also used for a line of
wallpaper designs, show
spaces and fabrics.

This glamorous, mysterious film (opposite) is set in an urban landscape reminiscent of the paintings of Giorgio de Chirico, and features an elegant woman who gazes out of a window as her 'shadow' sets out to explore the city. The woman's black lace dress echoes the 'techno' latticework achieved by the laser-cutting showcased in the Miu Miu Autumn/Winter 2008–9 collection, and in the lace and mesh textiles used for the Prada Woman Autumn/Winter 2008–9 collection.

A wonderful shimmering quality was created for this below-the-knee dress (right), which was achieved by using an ottoman fabric that was given a gradated digital print to create a futuristic look.

hussein chalayan

The design work of Hussein Chalayan, the winner of two back-to-back British Fashion Designer of the Year awards (1999 and 2000), is infused with cultural references, and a consideration of futures in the context of the past and our relationship with technology. 'Panoramic' (Autumn/Winter 1998–99; ill. below) explored the broken image, with mirrors generating a visual confusion as the models gradually merged with their reflections, and culminated in giant 3D pixel forms being carried forth, a representation of the emerging digital building blocks of contemporary image-making.

Following this early reference to new computer-imaging media, Chalayan continues to challenge the notion of 'fashion' as interface, with digital technology providing the tools to facilitate the realization of his unique design thinking, particularly in the form of stunning film and interactive artworks. Opening his show 'Ventriloquy' (Spring/Summer 2001; ill. p. 117) was one such film, a computer-graphic animation of wire-frame characters in the perspective space of an infinite 3D realm, developed in collaboration with the pioneering digital-imaging team, Me Company.

Another of his film works, *Place to Passage* (ill. p. 116), was Chalayan's most technically ambitious. It comprised a surreal, six-screen 3D soundscape by Jean-Paul Dessy, and was created in collaboration with design and visualization group Neutral and sponsored by Lucky Strike and BAR Honda F1. Touching on Chalayan's own passion for travel and flight, the film depicts an androgynous figure, travelling at speed in a futuristic pod, who is self-sufficient and contained within a calm, quiet and protective interface, surrounded by scenes that allude to a futuristic, virtual world. Using CAD visualization and 3D

computer-graphic animation techniques, the film begins in an underground car park and travels across urban, post-industrial landscapes, exploring notions of speed, technology, memory, exile and displacement along the way.

An ongoing collaboration with the designer and engineer Moritz Waldemeyer has produced some of Chalayan's most challenging garment pieces. The metamorphosis of fashion that has taken place over the last century was the subject of 'One Hundred and Eleven' (ill. opposite), Chalayan's collection for Spring/Summer 2007. Waldemeyer was commissioned to develop six costumes, which would magically evolve over a period covering the years from 1900 to 2007. Fashion pasts were animated through a subtle range of apparently effortless mechanical interventions, each period of dress making way for the next; an embellished flapper dress would appear from within the folds of a Victorian gown, hemlines retreating without a hitch. Multiple layers with hidden compartments and numerous electrical mechanisms operated like automatons, elegantly gliding through a series of fluid movements.

'Panoramic',
Autumn/Winter 1998–99

The huge 3D 'pixel' shapes carried by models towards the end of the catwalk show served to represent the contributions that digital media have yet to make in altering our perception of image and form.

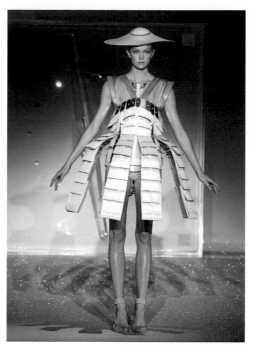

'One Hundred and Eleven',
Spring/Summer 2007
With Moritz Waldemeyer

Moritz Waldemeyer has
been instrumental in
the technical realization
of Chalayan's futuristic
ambition. For this collection,
a group of six garments
mechanically executed
a seamless metamorphosis
from one structure to
another, through a series
of implied design periods.

Garment components and fabric sections parted, split, unzipped and unfolded, like origami performed by invisible hands, each transformation taking just a few minutes.

Waldemeyer, when describing the feat required for assimilating the cumbersome mechanics with the needs of design and tailoring, says: 'The different effects in the show were achieved through six months of experimenting with servo-driven motors, pulleys and wires, which were fed through hollow tubes sewn into the dresses. The real challenge lay in keeping the integrated technology lightweight yet strong enough to manoeuvre different fabrics and material.'

For 'Airborne' (Autumn/Winter 2007–8; ill. pp. 118, 119), Chalayan and Waldemeyer produced two mechanical dresses with full video capabilities. Hazy silhouettes of water and sharks were depicted on one dress, with a time-lapse sequence of a rose blooming on the other. Fifteen thousand LEDs were embedded into the fabric of each garment form, over which a loose, white fabric covering softened the overall effect and disguised the appearance of the technology. The result appeared like a live, digitally animated print design, producing an

effect that was both beautiful and beguiling. With only four weeks' production time, methods had to be simple, using off-the-shelf technology, rather than anything bespoke. The analogue catwalk collection was also distinctive in its use of digital print. Geometric and linear fabric pieces were digitally designed and engineered to fit each highly structured and corseted garment.

Another collaboration with Waldemeyer, the installation 'Readings' (Spring/Summer 2008; ill. p. 118) was inspired by themes of ancient gods and sun worship, and the obsession with celebrity culture. Chalayan designed a series of highly structured dresses, heavily embellished with Swarovski crystals. Attached to moving mechanical hinges, hundreds of lasers were incorporated into each garment, which the crystals reflected and deflected, with the result of constantly animating the space between the garment, wearer and audience. As a result of their partnership, Chalayan and Waldemeyer have merged digital technology and fashion design in an unprecedented way. Conceptual thinking, enhanced by an innate aesthetic prerequisite, drives the use of technology away from potential gimmickry.

Place to Passage, 2003
With Neutral

Me Company
for Hussein Chalayan,
'Ventriloquy',
Spring/Summer 2001

The production of this
film (below), a Tribe Art
commission, involved a
large technical team in the
CAD design fabrication
and animation of a
futuristic pod. The digitally
constructed journey was
filmed in a bluescreen
studio, and composited
using a combination of
CG environments and real
analogue 16mm footage as
a background. The entire
computer-animated film
took six thousand hours of
rendering time.

The catwalk show for
'Ventriloquy' (opposite)
began with a technically
complex and visually
intricate CG animation by
Me Company. In contrast
to Chalayan's more filmic
works, this abstract narrative
set a stark scene within a
virtual wire-frame realm.

**'Readings',
Spring/Summer 2008**
With Moritz Waldemeyer

This collection (right) was presented in the form of an installation, which consisted of static garments, with built-in, mechanically controlled lasers that operated in constant motion. Swarovski crystals, embedded into the garment structure, reflected the intensely coloured light and created a spectacular, animated strobe effect around the body.

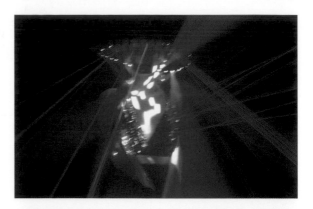

**'Airborne',
Autumn/Winter 2007–8**
With Moritz Waldemeyer

Chalayan's video dresses were brought to life for the 'Airborne' collection by Waldemeyer, who developed a tapestry of LEDs that were integrated into the garment form (left). With only four weeks' production time available, the construction process devised was simple but labour-intensive. As intended, the highly structured dress came ethereally to life on the catwalk (opposite).

hil driessen

Designer Hil Driessen employs digital technologies at the design and production stages, combining evidence of the hand, with all its imperfections, with a digital slickness. The results demonstrate a high level of technical expertise, illustrating fully the power of illusion, communicated through the medium of textile. She works across many different techniques to create a range of sensual experiences. Driessen established her studio *De Textielkamer* (The Textile Room) in 1998, and frequently collaborates with spatial designer Toon van Deijne, who creates scale models of her designs to show how they would work in a particular environment.

It was while undertaking a residency at the European Ceramic Work Centre that Driessen first dipped cotton crochet into clay slip. She discovered that, when fired, it burned away to leave behind the impression of the construction, and used this technique to create a porcelain bowl design, *Lia*. Intrigued by the surface imperfections, Driessen photographed the bowl's relief textures,

enlarged them and digitally printed the imagery on fabric and laminate substrates. In collaboration with the Netherlands Textile Museum, in Tilburg, the design was digitally printed and also taken into a computer-controlled woven textile for interior use.

For *Drift 23* (ill. p. 124), a listed building and part of the University of Utrecht, Driessen used digital technology to combine the historic with the futuristic. The original wallpaper, dating from 1859, had deteriorated beyond repair, and Driessen was commissioned to create something new. Inspired by Dutch Baroque interiors, with their illusions of depth and volume, she began stitching and folding vinyl to make the silhouette of a tree in winter, photographing this in the shadow of a real tree. The resulting image was digitally printed on Trevira CS, a robust fabric ideally suited to public spaces, and mounted on the wall. Another project, *Tactility for Architecture* (ill. p. 125), was a vehicle for Driessen and van Deijne's desire to communicate the temporal quality of the

Scale model with fabrics, 1998–99
Model by Toon van Deijne; *Square*, 1998–99

Driessen's first digitally printed collection was inspired by the landscape photographer Toshio Shibata and by New York's skyscrapers, with their repetitive forms and interesting shadow effects. Her *Square* design (left) is from this collection, a digital print on silk. All of the fabrics were produced by Print Unlimited.

play of sunlight on the surface of water through something more tangible. For IJburg 52 a/b, a large apartment complex in Amsterdam designed by Jan Bakers Architects, photographs were shot of decorative ironwork and reflections in the water, and the ideas taken further by using a mirror and digitally photographing samples created by manipulating silver material. The resulting imagery was then translated into screenprints on 750 glass sheets for balcony fences, giving the illusion of a surface that appears to be constantly capturing and holding watery reflections.

Having been commissioned by Dutch property firm Dudok Wonen to create an interior for Dudok Hall (ill. p. 123), in Hilversum, Driessen and van Deijne began by taking photographs of terraces, rolling hills and folds in the land, and researching the work of Willem Marinus Dudok, city architect for Hilversum in 1928, and the landscape designer Charles Jencks. With the aim of introducing tranquillity and a tactile quality to an otherwise stark environment, Driessen folded and layered green velvet and silk/metal organza to create rippling forms that were digitally photographed. Van Deijne then created a scale model to visualize the

design. Photoshop was used, along with Stork Colour Management software to create the eight-colour print. The end result was a digital print on Trevira CS, produced by Print Unlimited, which meanders horizontally around the room, with the drapery's vertical folds enhancing the undulating appearance.

In 2008 Driessen and van Deijne designed wall panels for eight interior corridors at the De Brug courthouse (ill. p. 122), again designed by Jan Bakers Architects, in Amsterdam. The brief was to provide a work of art, while at the same time offering acoustic insulation. They began by creating images that depict the way fabric responds as people move past, or when doors and windows are opened and shut. Cotton, satin and a non-woven material were hand-coloured using Ecoline inks in blues and yellows, and then layered and folded before being photographed in the studio. In order to capture a sense of movement, the fabrics were placed on a turning platform and photographed, with the resulting images manipulated in Photoshop before forming the basis for digitally printed Trevira CS by Print Unlimited. The fabrics were then backed with a sound-absorbent and flame-retardant non-woven textile and mounted onto frames.

Lace from the 'Into Focus' collection, 2002
Gallery Legio, Tilburg

The impressions left behind when crochet is dipped in porcelain were photographed, and the imagery realized as digital prints using a Stork ink-jet printer owned by the Netherlands Textile Museum (below, left) The relief texture was used to create digital prints and computer-controlled weaves in this conceptual dining room (below, right), exhibited in 2006–7.

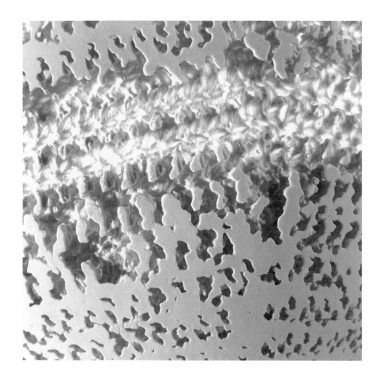

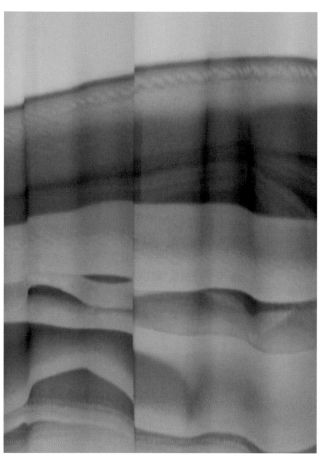

De Brug courthouse, 2008
Amsterdam, Netherlands
With Toon van Deijne

Dudok Hall, 2007–8
Hilversum, Netherlands
With Toon van Deijne

The art budget for this commercial and industrial building in Amsterdam was used to commission wall panels that were made from digitally printed textiles (opposite), which not only embellished the eight interior corridor walls, but also provided improved acoustics by absorbing and thus reducing the sound.

Inspired by the work of architect Willem Marinus Dudok, this design (left and below) stemmed from Driessen's manipulation of different fabrics by layering and folding, the results of which were then photographed. The imagery was digitally printed onto Trevira CS, which was draped in the form of curtains.

Drift 23, 2005
Utrecht, Netherlands

Driessen created digitally printed trompe-l'oeil wall panels of high-relief forms for two rooms in this historic house owned by the University of Utrecht. Imagery taken from manipulated vinyl was digitally printed on Trevira CS, and mounted onto the walls. Although the wall panels appear soft and crumpled, they are in fact hard to the touch.

Tactility for Architecture, 2007
Amsterdam, Netherlands
With Toon van Deijne

After reproducing digital
photographs onto glass
sheets, enamel was
deposited onto the glass
using a screenprinting
process that was then
vitrified using heat at
600° C to leave one side of
the building – the IJburg
52 a/b apartment block
by Jan Bakers Architects –
permanently decorated.
A Stopsol mirror-effect was
used between the glass
layers to create reflective
glazing.

jane harris

As Professor of Design at Kingston University, Jane Harris conducts research into computer-graphic animation and real-time dress representation, 3D CG modelling and animation tools, body scanning and optical motion capture. Her work is underpinned by a background in textiles, and reflects her belief that there is something intrinsically valuable in understanding the material process, which she applies to the relatively new sector of digital-imaging media.

In the 1990s it was evident that computing capability was still quite limited in terms of aesthetic expression, and that CG rendering and the animation of malleable forms (cloth, skin and hair) was still a few decades away. Unable to realize her ideas through 3D CG modelling, Harris employed a range of early computer-imaging techniques, augmenting bluescreen, motion capture and 2D compositing processes, to express digitally ideas that could not be achieved in physical form. The advances in computing towards the end of the decade made film-industry tooling more capable, enabling some of these ideas to be more fully realized.

Harris's research has led to an area of development with many applications, from the examination and interpretation of historical textiles to the depiction of 'future' fashion for e-commerce, museums, film and gaming. In 2004, she staged *The Empress's New Clothes* (ill. p. 128), an installation at the Museum of London in which an eighteenth-century silk dress was recreated, using 3D CGI technologies to envisage how it would appear when worn at the time it was made. These sophisticated tools emulated the virtual motion and characteristics of the fabric, and interpreted each minute change as it interacted with the body. To create a hyper-realistic impression, consideration was given to the way each material layer mathematically responded to the other. The project demonstrated how fragile garments that cannot otherwise be exhibited might emerge from storage by way of digital media. The technique was subsequently employed at the Whitworth Art Gallery, in Manchester, to contextualize a series of rare and decaying fragments of fourth-century Egyptian textiles.

Harris has also collaborated with fashion designer Shelley Fox, who is known for her conceptual approach and complex 3D designs. One of Fox's signature pieces was digitally modelled, using three slightly different fabrics, to visually describe their shift from 2D to 3D form (ill. below). The flat pattern pieces rose up to fit the mould of an invisible presence, or spectre. In a series of short animations, this work exhibited a particularly complex construction, the relationship between the fabric and the wearer. The familiar activity of taking a hanging, limp

Balloon Top, 2003–4
With Shelley Fox
and Mike Dawson

This piece, from Shelley Fox's 'Collection 7' (Autumn/Winter 1999–2000), was based on a hollow, spherical form. Using 3D CG animation, the bodiless sequence of imagery simulates the morphing of a drawstring-backed top from a flat, circular surface, which revolves to create a fully three-dimensional garment.

or folded garment and putting it on was shown in all its detail and beauty, paralleling Fox's own practical investigations into the direct physicality of cloth. The work reveals the process of fashion from the inanimate to the animate.

Along with alternatives to the traditional catwalk show and the process of designing garments, insights into the portrayal of clothing in the computer-generated realms of film, gaming and real-time commercial and leisure applications are being explored. Moving-image narratives demand descriptions of fabric in relation to the body in a particular way, and it is these ideas, together with aesthetic concerns pertaining to animated and real-time forms, which interest Harris. Her attention has turned to the complex aesthetic challenge of live computer-generated representations, alongside augmented visualization systems that provide new technical demands, as well as new levels of digital engagement.

Harris's practice is concerned with the subtle characteristics inherent in a fabric or design of complex material form, and how these may be conveyed believably, taking the physical into the virtual. She transfers the nuances of a rich, haptic and yet tacit textile knowledge of texture, surface interest, touch and handle, including the wrinkling, creasing and folding of cloth, the effect of environment on a fabric and movement, and the visualization of a worn garment in time and space. Acknowledging the youth of digital media, Harris recognizes the potential of the technology and how it may yet be crafted to define digital spaces and experiences for consumers that could enhance culture, communication, entertainment and commerce – where the physical and the virtual amicably converge.

Digital wire-frame 3D form, 2006
With Mike Dawson and Elli Garnett

Motion-capture technology was used here to create a believable body form. The person being 'captured' wears a black body-con suit with reflective markers, which the infrared cameras detect and relay to the computer software to convert into an animated skeletal form. The person's movements become the digital data used to drive a wire-frame form, which 'liaises' with the subsequent virtual textile and animates the computer-generated virtual garment.

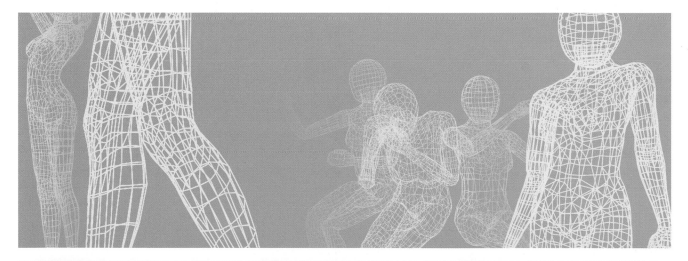

The Empress's New Clothes,
2004
Museum of London,
with Mike Dawson and
Ruth Gibson

For this project (above and
right), Harris created
a realistic illusion of the way
a period costume would
have appeared, both static
and in motion. The complete
ensemble, consisting of a
dress, corset and crinoline,
was digitally recreated from
an existing garment in
the museum's collection.
Mike Dawson devised the
3D form, and dancer Ruth
Gibson performed the
choreographic motion,
developed in conjunction
with Harris. At the time,
processing power was
limited. Subsequent to
construction, the two-
minute animation took
six months to render.

Potential Beauty,
2002–3
With Mike Dawson
and Ruth Gibson

Harris observes and
develops relationships
between fabric, garment
and the presence of the
human body, as shown in
this digital simulation of
a garment twisting and
turning in space (opposite).
The asymmetric, long-
sleeved dress demonstrates
both drape and a body-
conscious fit, achieved
by digitally constructing
the form, followed by the
application of digitally
'painted' textile surfaces.

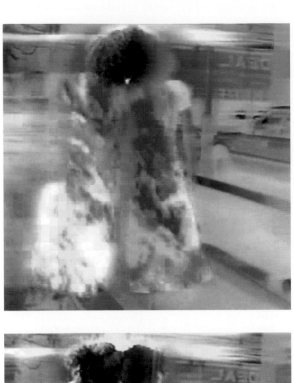

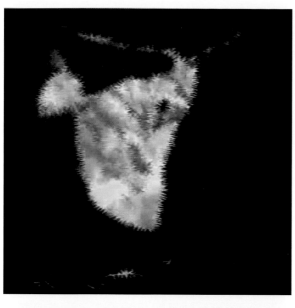

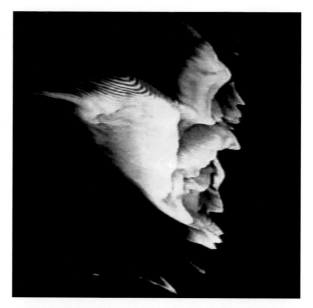

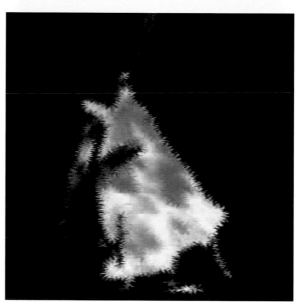

A Dressing,
1996–98

Metamorphosis,
1996–98

In the absence of CG
cloth-simulation software,
Harris devised a digital
masking process to create
the illusion of a virtual
cloth, never to be physically
realized. The technique was
applied to the moving dress
of performer Emily Bruni, to
create a metamorphosing
surfacing effect in motion
over time (opposite).

Harris applied the use
of high-end digital
compositing tools at
post-production house
Mill Film, in London,
to develop stunning
transforming effects in
motion to choreographic
work and costume,
originated by Johanne
Mills (above and left).

simon thorogood

Simon Thorogood graduated from Central Saint Martins in 1992, a year that marked the end of a recession and the beginning of a period of innovation and growth. It was also the point at which fashion design began to look beyond the actual garments. Just as with music and the fine arts, conceptual ideas were beginning to be explored, and Thorogood and his contemporaries were questioning conventional methods of design and presentation. A series of exhibition projects was developed in conjunction with Spore, a collective of artists and designers with a common interest in digital media, whose key members included Suzanne Lee, Benedict Sheehan, Stephen Wolff, Emma Quinn and Julie Freeman.

Thorogood launched his design practice in 1998 with the multimedia installation *White Noise* (ill. opposite), in which couture garments were displayed among forty-four discarded Apple Mac II computers. Sketchbook drawings were translated into digital animations and shown on a bank of computer monitors, while live, improvised sound (from the electronic group Barbed) responded to visual prompts. After the show, the software was sold, and the buyer received a free computer; commissions for a garment from the collection would similarly be accompanied by a computer and its inherent artwork, which, in effect, became the item's label. *Digital Sketchbook* (ill. p. 134), from the same year, further explored some of these ideas. For this piece, pressure-sensitive flooring located the position of individuals in the audience, triggering the appearance of stored visual images on multiple screens. The user's movements and changing location influenced the image selection and composition, thus inviting a form of co-authorship.

Thorogood describes his fashion style as simple yet bold, incorporating elements of Modernism and minimalism. He is fascinated by the beauty of dynamic machines such as stealth aircraft, and by the fact that they were the products of the early computer-aided design and manufacture of the 1970s. With similar exactitude and a sharp, calculated aesthetic, Thorogood designs 'demi-couture' collections that are halfway between ready-to-wear and couture. His capsule collection 'C4i' (ill. below), which combined distinctive geometric lines with his trademark blocks of colour, was commissioned by the Judith Clark Costume Gallery in 1998 and named after the computer-guidance system used for the stealth aircraft of the time. The theme of

Vane coat, 'C4i', 1998

Commissioned by the Judith Clark Costume Gallery, this demi-couture capsule collection in duchesse satin was accompanied by a series of dynamic wall-mounted relief works and bespoke mannequins to complement the garments.

flight continued four years later with *Digital Runway* (ill. p. 135). A 15m-long catwalk, designed to look like an airport runway, was embedded with twenty-five pressure-sensitive mats, each of which would trigger an image that would appear on both the garment and on a screen as the model strode down the runway. Blends of these images would be achieved by running, generating random design or patterning. Members of the audience were encouraged to partake in the experience and use the catwalk themselves, effectively DJ-ing the event visually.

As computing evolved, it became less physically evident as a facilitator of Thorogood's output. His engagement with programming garnered a series of interactive works that broadened consideration of design and how it could be approached. Projects such as *Projextiles* and *Soundforms* incorporated co-design principles, using a range of visual material and sound. Created in collaboration with composer Stephen Wolff, *Soundforms* (ill. p. 135) was a software-imaging program that linked sound with Thorogood's shapes, colours and forms, which then assembled or dressed themselves around the linear image of a female model. As the sound is amplified, sketchbook components from Thorogood's archive arrange themselves in different ways – the louder the sound, the bolder and brighter the forms that evolve.

Soundforms led to the ongoing concept *SoundWear*, in which single-instrument works of music by composers such as John Cage and Eric Satie were realized through colour, layering and shape by applying synaesthetic principles. *SoundWear* is intended as an interactive design tool for use online or in a live installation setting, in which the user could blend or design fashion forms using sound, and to open up the design process and develop new methods of creative engagement. The musical compositions of Icelandic band Sigur Rós were also realized, but were difficult to illustrate due to their multi-layered construction.

Thorogood was working with digital media tools at a time when they were fast-evolving and particularly challenging. In this respect, he has been instrumental in broadening our understanding of what digital media are capable of in the broader context of fashion. Thorogood's approach to design is expanding into a hybrid practice of product and fashion within architectural realms. As digital capability continues to become less visible and more powerful, further collaborations will inevitably be sought to continue determining new ways of engaging with this sector by design.

White Noise,
1998

For this collaboration with digital art group Spore, abandoned Apple Mac II computers relayed a programmed narrative of visuals, creating an immersive setting for a series of couture designs that were suspended in the exhibition space (below).

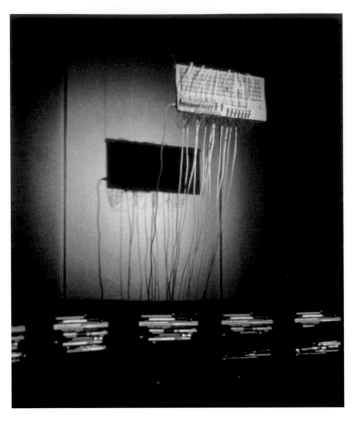

**Digital Sketchbook,
1998**

This interactive work – illustrated are 'Keyboard' (left) and 'Monitors' (below) – was determined by audience engagement. The movement of each person within the installation space would trigger visual compositions and contribute to the design narrative.

**Soundforms,
2004
With Stephen Wolff**

Soundforms (opposite, top) was driven by a selection of musical works that activated an archive of drawings and photographs to create original digital sketches. Sound levels altered the brightness, colouration and structural patterning of the designs.

Digital Runway,
2002

This project (right) challenged the idea of the catwalk as a concept. A series of sketches and images by Thorogood, stored in a computer, appeared on a screen in real time, triggered by audience participants as they walked up and down the digitally connected runway.

savithri bartlett

Designer Savithri Bartlett investigates the methods and processes of using a computer-controlled laser on various substrates to achieve a range of effects. Her research work has demonstrated that by exposing fibres to specific wavelengths of laser radiation, their molecular structure changes and can degrade, indicated by the fraying and singeing of the fabric. Some of her experiments explored tonal laser-marking on woven textiles by using industrial laser equipment, manufactured by CadCam Technology and designed in conjunction with Levi Strauss for use on denim. The speed at which the scanning beam travels across the cloth, the specific power output and the marking resolution can all be adjusted by the software to work with the different tonal values in each pixel. Subsequent settings will affect the depth of laser-etch or laser-cut, and the visual definition of the resulting image.

The digital, binary-coded format produced when original artwork is scanned is crucial to the process, as the image can then be read by a computer-controlled laser. The software translates a full-colour image into shades of grey, which in turn are reduced to four predominant areas. In preparation for laser-marking, the various light and dark areas are then translated into a series of black-dot patterns to determine the resolution of the 'scan lines'. The black-and-white pixels are subsequently read by the laser beam as 1 or 0 (if the laser beam is instructed to be 'on' or 'off' during the marking process). For her doctoral research, Bartlett tested a range of substrates – from natural cottons and silks to lightweight paper nylon, a glazed Polyamide 6.6 woven fabric – to see where surface charring might occur. (This tends to happen on areas of darker shades of grey, or at the edge of a motif where the laser moves both forwards and backwards.) In this case, an interesting 'halo' effect is often achieved, almost like a solarized photograph. Charring can cause a point of weakness in the cloth, which might then tear or wear out easily, but the laser settings can be controlled to ensure charring is kept to a minimum. Access to an electron microscope allowed Bartlett to examine each fibre's internal construction, and to set the laser controls accordingly.

Bartlett has often collaborated with avant-garde fashion company Boudicca, a 'conceptual couture' partnership founded by Zowie Broach and Brian Kirkby, and used her knowledge of digital laser technology

Savithri Bartlett for Boudicca, 'The Beautiful and the Insane', Spring/Summer 2005

This pair of trousers (left) was placed on a purpose-built mannequin and marked using a laser machine. The trousers rotated while the laser beam embellished the surface of the fabric in specific places. The front, neck and lapels of the jacket (opposite, top) – both inside and out – were laser-marked, while scrolling across the 'secret' folds of the sleeve cuffs (opposite, below) were the lyrics of the song 'Hand in Glove', written by Morrissey of The Smiths.

for their 'Immortality' collection (Spring/ Summer 1999; ill. p. 138), which featured ethereal, often multi-layered garments. The title referred to the outpouring of grief after Princess Diana's death in 1997, and to Milan Kundera's novel (1990) of the same name, in which he observed: 'Immortality is when people remember you who don't know you.' In this case, 'immortality' referred to the memory, or history, of clothes; each garment was sold with a notebook, in which the wearer could record when and where it was worn. Words taken from gravestones and poetry, even the scrawled handwriting of suicide notes, were laser-marked on a variety of fabrics, including black leather, tissue-like white or baby-blue cotton organdie, polyamide, polyester and silk organza/ taffeta. Because the laser can be controlled to either gently etch or cut through a substrate completely, it is ideal for imparting a message with words or picking up on subtle textures.

In 2001 an exhibition staged by the British Design Council at New York's Grand Central Station showcased the work of innovative British designers. Included was a dress that Bartlett made, together with haute-couture designer Deborah Milner and textile embellisher Karen Spurgin, in which fabrics were superimposed to create a moiré effect. Inspired by the paintings of Bridget Riley, Bartlett researched the areas of kinetics and illusion, and worked closely with a 3D software graphic designer to create holes, lines and spaces in a series of layers that, when overlapped and offset by less than 30°, gave an optical illusion of depth and volume. The fabrics were dyed, cut with a digitally controlled laser, embellished with sequins, and then multi-layered.

For Boudicca's 'Performance' collection (Spring/Summer 2004), Bartlett laser-cut leather with text to create belts. White-on-white, they showed intricate cutting, made possible by the digitally controlled laser; achieving the same level of detail using traditional leather-tooling techniques would

be prohibitively labour-intensive. Boudicca's 'The Beautiful and the Insane' collection, presented one year later, included laser-marked clothing in specific areas with words and graffiti by Baudelaire, Giacometti and Morrissey of The Smiths (ill. opposite and below). The designs were created with Maino International's Sky laser-scribing machine, and the completed clothing put onto a mannequin that inflated to the size required, and rotated while laser-marking took place.

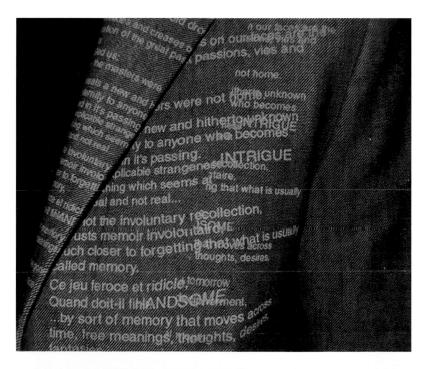

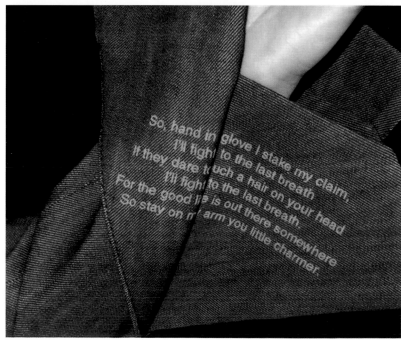

Savithri Bartlett for Boudicca, 'Immortality', Spring/Summer 1999

Savithri Bartlett for Boudicca, 'We Sell Disguises', Autumn/Winter 2003–4

The skirt (below and right), entitled *Life Descended Upon Her*, featured layers of polyester and cotton organdie, which were laser-marked with messages. Laser-etching and -cutting creates an ethereal impression of the text where slight charring of the edges adds a further fragility.

The top two layers of fabric of this asymmetric dress (opposite) were laser-cut with holes, while the bottom, bright-pink layer featured both a panel of laser-cut holes and a plain area that functioned as a backdrop for the layers above. These open and solid layers created an effect of depth and dimension, animated still further when the model moved.

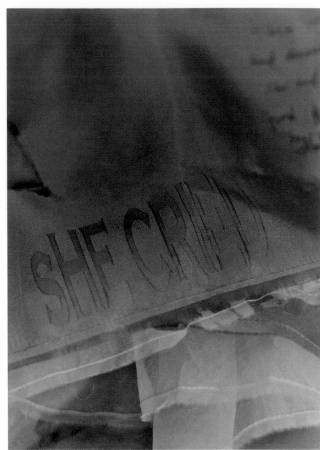

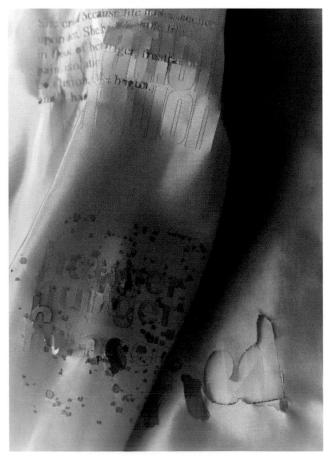

nancy tilbury

Fashion designer Nancy Tilbury set out from the start to challenge and subvert the field by integrating technology-driven concepts into clothing. Inspired by the early wearable computing produced by MIT, she focused on how digital media might be integrated into clothing and the body while a student at the Royal College of Art. Her graduate show in 1997 signalled a new approach to fashion's potential role, and determined how it could be the catalyst for future ideas if technology, design, communication and commerce could be brought together.

Soon after, Tilbury joined Philips Design as part of a new wearable technology group, where she was able to develop approaches to what fashion might become as design begins to infiltrate the worlds of technology and science. Unimaginable materials, forms and functions were digitally crafted to enable the visualization of beautiful but as yet unattainable fashion futures. This early design work evolved into a series of projects that explored futuristic rituals of dress, body area networks and the potential of conductive–active textiles, and led initially to the publication *New Nomads: An Exploration of Wearable Electronics by Philips* (2010), which set out conceptual blueprints for wearable technology.

Emotional computing became a key topic during the early years of the twenty-first century, led by research from the MIT Media Lab. In 2006 Philips Design launched the *Skin Probes* series, taking the best from intelligent materials and programming soft-sensing technology with interactive and ambient outputs that linked to the body, resulting in the much-publicized *Bubbelle* (ill. p. 143) and *Frisson* (ill. p. 142, top) dresses. The design hypothesis was that they would express and subvert the emotion of the wearer, whether happy, sad or angry. Two years later, the team reconvened to produce *Fractal Living Jewelry* (ill. pp. 144, 145). Tilbury designed a series of virtual concepts that portrayed crystalline forms, frozen to the body, which were documented growing in irregular yet formulated ways, exhibiting the health and emotional state of the host. The idea behind this evolving 'living jewelry' – part body, part functional adornment – took inspiration from computer science and mathematics, specifically Benoît Mandelbrot's definition of the fractal, relocating fractal geometry in relation to the body.

In 2009 Tilbury devised *Digital Draping* (below and opposite), a design tool that

Digital Draping,
2009

This process was devised by Tilbury to enable a form of design 'visioneering', which challenges modes of garment craft and construction in relation to future fashion narratives.

projects still and moving imagery onto the skin, enabling the conceptualization of body-related designs, and informing related ideas about sensory devices and how they will be powered and used on and inside the body. *Digital Draping* was introduced as a digital teaching tool on the MA course at Kingston University, the operative of which is more akin to a fashion laboratory, as it challenges modes of future design, science and craft narratives. Tilbury encouraged use of the technique in examining the body's relationship to media, exploring new ways to cut, drape and fabricate form by designing with light, rather than cloth toiles. The next generation of fashion practitioners are envisioning a symbiosis between fashion and science, with the computer used to visualize related narratives that will craft as yet unknown worlds.

Digital Skins Body Atmospheres (ill. p. 142), a film set in the year 2050, is an ongoing project developed by Tilbury in conjunction with 125 Creative. Analogue and digital techniques are combined to express biological shifts and experiences that illustrate fluid and permeable body interfaces. Couture gowns are assembled by gas and nano-electronic particles, with tailoring and cosmetics constructed by 3D liquid formations. This is a time when couture will be cultured and farmed as fashion facets of human flesh: skin is the material interface, engaging with almost invisible technology.

Tilbury's passion for persistently probing design thinking and engaging with the potential of couture is likely to continue, formed by a peripheral scientific vision. As she challenges our perception of fashion and the body, her practice interfaces with digital media to portray a vital and imperative language that both imagineers and informs the creative, science and industry sectors, which will inevitably realize some of these extraordinary concepts in the future.

Digital Skins
Body Atmospheres,
2009–present
With 125 Creative

For this ongoing project
(below, left and right),
Tilbury used imaging media
to demonstrate conceptual
technology interfaces, which
may, in time, be realized
as human and scientific
environments converge.

Philips Design,
Bubbelle and *Frisson*
dresses, 2006

Forming part of Philips
Design's *Skin Probes* series,
Bubbelle (left) and *Frisson*
(opposite, top) explore
emotional sensing
technology, conceiving
dresses that blush and
shiver, conveyed through
colour and pattern changes.
© Philips.

Philips Design,
Fractal Living Jewelry,
2008

This project, part of Philips Design's *Design Probes* series, was inspired by Benoît Mandelbrot's investigations into fractal geometry and related computational behaviour. 'By incorporating sensors that measure movement, excitement levels and the proximity of other people, and using this input to alter the intensity of its integrated lighting,' say the design team, 'fractal essentially becomes an extension of the body.' © Philips.

daniel brown

Artist and designer Daniel Brown's earliest memories are related to computers and computer graphics; his father, Paul Brown, founded the UK's first computer-graphics company, Digital Pictures, in 1981. Captivated by the possibilities of computing from a very early age, the younger Brown, aged five, took ownership of a coveted cast-off from his brother, a Commodore Vic-20 with 3k of memory (later, aged ten, he would progress to a Spectrum PC and an Atari ST). Since the computer games available at the time were as primitive as those one could program oneself, the notion of programming – to Brown, at least – was an accessible one. His skills were honed by experimenting with the code published at the back of computer manuals that accompanied early hardware. Following the long, complex, often-misprinted numerical text necessitated a laborious process of undo and redo – a beneficial learning curve.

Today, Brown pursues the making of beautiful things with what could be considered unwieldy and incongruous components: zeros and ones. He introduced a considered aesthetic to commercial programming, and was one of the first designers to appreciate the importance of the user-experience in relation to Internet and mobile interface systems. The portfolio of companies he has worked with – Sony, Volkswagen, *Dazed & Confused*, to name a few – illustrates the range of his approach to interaction design, which he has also taken out of the computer realm and into public spaces. For Conran & Partners' Park Hotel

in Delhi, Brown created an installation of never-repeating kinetic forms, a generative design that over time, is replaced by another coded landscape. The early generative flower work from the evolving series *Play-Create* (ill. p. 148) is also constructed entirely from code, referencing nature, both structurally and aesthetically. As the code evolved, Brown incorporated a visual depth into the imagery by programming in layers of shadow and form. His work occasionally employs a greyscale palette, bringing a refreshing and rarely explored aesthetic to computer-graphic imaging.

The multi-faceted installation *Angel* was composed of moving image, sound and interaction works commissioned for the Avignon Festival of Beauty in 2001 (ill. below). Created by Alexander McQueen and Nick Knight, *Angel* was set in an atmospheric chapel, accompanied by a sound piece by Björk. The outline of the angel's head and its simplified features was formed by the construction of an intricate, two-dimensional linear frame of fine steel sections. The frame's component parts, positioned atop a 1.8m-high metal cylindrical plinth, were then shaded with living dyed maggots. The vision, only viewable in a 6m-high mirror reflection, appeared like a painting; close up, the real and more sinister composition became apparent. Brown captured the spatial depth, hollowness and mysterious light of the chapel at the beginning of his interactive. Initially, the unfocused visual of the Rococo gilt ceiling is unable to be still, rocking and bowing gently; the view changes as the cursor

Daniel Brown
for SHOWstudio,
Dress Me Up, Dress Me Down,
2005–9

Created in collaboration with Nick Knight, Peter Saville, Liberty Ross and Jonathan Kaye, the fashion scenarios illustrated (opposite, top to bottom) are: 'Silhouetted', 'Military', 'Veiled', 'Fringed' and 'Biker'. Taking inspiration from live pornographic video chats, SHOWstudio explored the idea of control in fashion image-making. Brown designed a series of fashion film interactives, the creation of which was in fact determined by the online audience and the model (Liberty Ross) herself.

Daniel Brown
for SHOWstudio,
Angel, 2001
With Nick Knight, Alexander McQueen and Björk

Angel (below) was an interactive work for SHOWstudio, set in a Rococo chapel. The cursor only momentarily reveals the image of a mystical head.

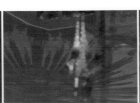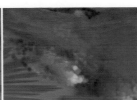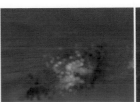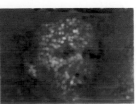

moves, revealing traces of another image. An angel's face enigmatically takes form the faster the mouse interacts with the image, but retains an element of mystique by never appearing in its entirety.

In another work, *V_A* (ill. p. 149), or *Virtual Accessories*, Brown reflected on fashion branding and the consumer's desire for expensive accessories, the seduction of ownership, and our emotional relationship with the process of acquisition. Brown worked with key pieces from the Spring/Summer 2002 collections of Balenciaga, Marc Jacobs, Missoni and Prada to devise a series of abstract interactives that explored the material and aesthetic qualities associated with these brands. Logos are absent from the four virtual experiences, which aim to seduce the viewer's cursor, rather than his or her purse. Brown created a series of online graphic interactive surfaces for the SHOWstudio project *Dress Me Up, Dress Me Down* in 2005, which reveal, through the cursor, the deconstruction of outfits disassembled by model Liberty Ross. Composed of nine key looks – 'Silhouetted', 'Biker', 'Volume', 'Military', 'Tomboy', 'Ecclesiastical', 'Fringed', 'Victorian' and 'Veiled', the work was later shown at the exhibition *Fashion Revolution* at London's Somerset House in 2009. This new way of displaying and viewing the shoot, filmed in the round, also revealed the model's engagement with the project.

Brown's algorithmic work has taken interaction design into uncharted realms, altering how we interpret and engage with digital imagery. His philosophical approach to the projects he chooses to work with provides audiences with new contexts for fashion and other online experiences. We have succumbed to the instinct to click and drag and are rewarded with spectacles of motion, form, image and colour that are unexpected, emotional and visually rich.

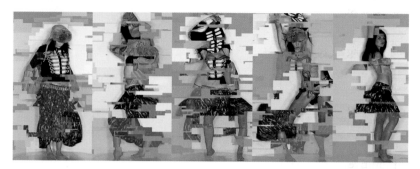

A generative flower work,
from the ongoing series
Play-Create,
2001–present

Each image frame (below)
illustrates a mutation of the
infinite generative design as
it evolves with an additional
softening spatial effect. The
series also explored a rare
CG aesthetic: greyscale.

Daniel Brown
for SHOWstudio,
V_A, 2002

Brown chose items from
the Spring/Summer 2002
collections of four designers
to create interactive brand
experiences (opposite, top
to bottom). A collage of Marc
Jacobs floral prints flow
across the image like fabric;
Missoni's signature colour
and texture is highlighted
in shafts that emanate from
the cursor as it moves across
an otherwise dark space;
Prada's brocaded look is
defined by a richly textured
kaleidoscopic effect,
generated by the cursor;
and Nicolas Ghesquière's
collections for Balenciaga
are described in a Möbius
strip, which oscillates
in the direction of the
cursor against a sparkling
background.

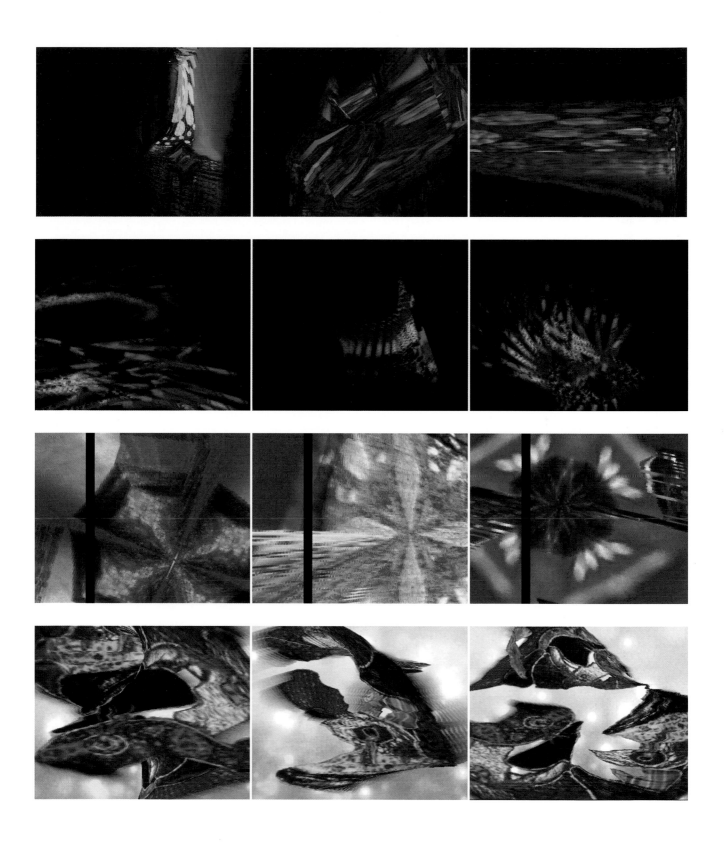

casey reas

While artists and designers use software to manipulate all kinds of visual material, construct 3D forms and explore moving images, it remains unusual for them to write their own. Casey Reas, however, together with Ben Fry, created Processing, an evolving open-source programming language and integrated development environment, while still graduate students at MIT's Media Lab in 2001. This acclaimed platform, described by its creators as an 'electronic sketchbook', is free to download, and allows the fundamentals of computer programming to be learned and adopted.

A theme in Reas's work is the study of dynamic reactive digital systems, which receive and process programmed input as a means of generating and altering visual compositions. He designs digitally constructed kinetic systems, which are realized as 2D prints, software art, animation, large installations and interactive sculpture. Reas's works are continually in flux, as the associations and interaction between the characteristic elements never cease. Perpetually in motion, whether by generative design or by human interaction, intricate

Process 6,
2005

A still image (above) from an infinite series derived from the generative-design software, Process 6. This entire body of work, along with *Process 6 (Puff 1–12)* (ill. p. 155), conveys a particularly haptic, almost textile, quality.

Tissue, 2007
With Cait Reas

In collaboration with
fashion designer Cait Reas,
Reas created the *Tissue*
collection (left and opposite,
below) in conjunction
with 1 of 1, an independent
design studio. This Los
Angeles-based collective
initiates opportunities for
the synthesis of fashion
and art, to devise one-of-a-
kind apparel, which is then
available to order.

flowing lines or complex forms of colour and structure evolve. These works convey a tactile quality, enhanced through touchscreen technology, thus creating an intimate dialogue with the viewer. It is interesting to consider what the 'touch' or haptic quality of his work could physically be, and if this aspect might be included in a future 'Process'.

Reas's *Tissue* series from 2002 (ill. opposite, below and p. 154) was digitally printed onto cloth and translated into a fashion collection in collaboration with designer Cait Reas in 2007. As complementary digital technology evolves, the context for his designs is expanding into fashion, architecture and 3D design. With digital fabrication becoming more sensitive to fine construction procedures, such technology lends itself to artists and designers to convey the otherwise impossible. The status quo of rapid and evolutionary hardware, operating systems and software developments is frequently rendered obsolete due to commercial demands. This has an enormous effect on those who write and develop their own software. Palettes of unique tooling may become impossible to use, and a whole language can be lost in the space of a few years, or even months. Reas, like many artists

and designers, is attempting to resist this by pursuing alternative working methods that exist outside current conventional frameworks.

Increased hardware capability enables advancement of software, and perhaps the prospect of achieving the otherwise impossible. For Reas, each language that emerges through programming has its own attributes, informs us of new behaviour and characteristics, and is even to some extent like a different physical material. In Anthony Burke and Therese Tierney's essay 'Beyond Code', published in *Network Practice: New Strategies in Architecture and Design* (2007), Reas offers an insight into the programming process: '*Process 4* emerged from a simple idea, to give software elements the behaviour of maintaining their own "personal" space. No two elements overlap because they turn away as soon as they touch another.'

For many artists and designers, programming may be, understandably, a barrier between an idea and its execution, and therefore too constraining. But for those persistent enough to pursue the medium, the potential for new types of mark and structure is infinite, and, in many ways, unlike any other process.

Process 18,
2008

Process 14,
2008

An image derived from the
generative system, *Process
18* (opposite), a greyscale
design that is the precursor
of the subtly coloured
designs, *Process 18 (Image
B 1-10)* and *(Image A 1–10)*,
both documented on Reas's
extensive web archive.

A still image from the
generative-design series
Process 14 (above), which
introduces a particularly
painterly quality in terms
of mark-making and
colouration.

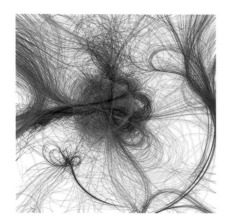
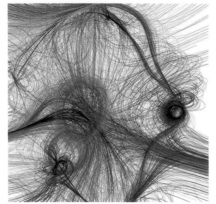

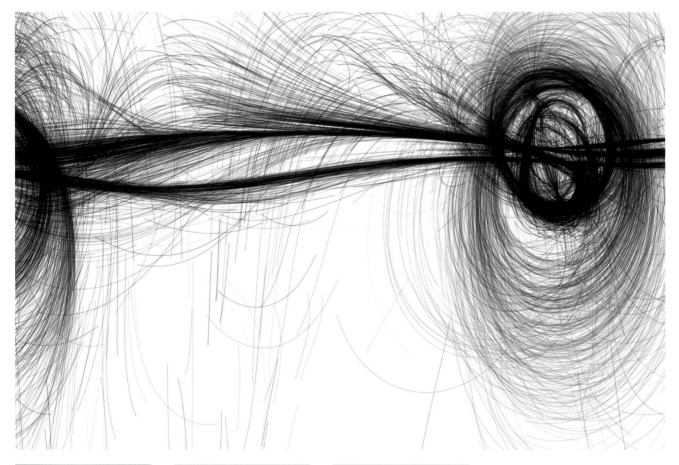

Path Prints 02, 05, 06, 2001	*Tissue Type A-00,* 2002	*TI,* 2004
This early series (top), according to the artist, 'documents the movement of synthetic neural systems. Each line reveals the history of one system's movement as it navigates its environment.'	The *Tissue* series (above) also exposes the movements of synthetic neural systems. Exhibition of the work on touchscreen technology achieves a particularly intimate dialogue with the viewer.	This installation (opposite) conveys *Process 6 (Puff 1–12)* as a series of circular light boxes of varying scales, and transitional phases of the evolving design.

jakob schlaepfer

Jakob Schlaepfer is a textile company based in St Gallen, Switzerland – a town already well known for its textile heritage – and has completely revolutionized the field of embroidery. Founded in 1904 by Rudolf Vogel as an embroidery firm (and trading under its current name since 1934), the company continually invests in the newest technology, allowing them to keep abreast of the constant developments in textile manufacture. High-tech processes are often combined with intricate, handcrafted work to create ink-jet digital prints for both fashion and interiors, which are extremely sophisticated in terms of colour, texture and pattern.

Jakob Schlaepfer was one of the first companies to use laser-cutting in creating perforated and cut textiles for layered and relief effects. The firm designs two haute-couture and two ready-to-wear collections each year, and have provided fabrics for fashion designers including Jean Paul Gaultier and Vivienne Westwood. Their designs, produced on luxurious textiles such as chiffon, are often inspired by nature, the fine or applied arts, or by other cultures. The visionary designer Martin Leuthold is the company's head of creative design; one of his designs for a scarf (1996), which incorporates silk and silvered-metal wire in a satin weave, belongs to the Art Institute of Chicago.

One way of using digital print is to create the look of a technique that would otherwise be too labour-intensive to produce commercially, for example the *ikat*, or 'warp-painted' technique, in which the warp threads in a cloth are dyed or painted. When the weft is inserted, the dyed/painted design becomes diffused or striated, resulting in a characteristically 'smudgy' look. This method is very time-consuming when done manually, but the digital printer speeds up

the process and allows each subtle nuance to be translated to the cloth. Because repeat pattern is no longer necessary, it is possible to reproduce the look of a 'one-off' design in both digital print and laser-cutting. Asymmetric and symmetric looks can be created and key features placed strategically on the human form (a trail of laser-cut flowers and leaves falling over a shoulder and swirling onto the floor, for example). Digital print allows for colours to merge seamlessly, as well as creating the simulation of depth, producing a striking visual effect when related to the body.

Use of the computer-controlled laser enables the creation of both simple or

lavishly intricate forms. Laser-cutting has become a signature for the company, and they have experimented with three-dimensional 'fold' effects and the addition of crystals to further animate a laser-cut surface. All types of materials are treated, from luxurious naturals to sophisticated techno textiles – even fake fur has been laser-cut to create a deep-pile fabric with draped panels.

For their interior textiles, the firm has explored the use of heavier weights of cloth, including metallics and brocades. The design *Orchid* was printed on *Glinka*, a fabric bonded with holographic foil that achieves a very rich visual effect, ideal for wrapped panels or as wallpaper. Another signature is a metallic textile range, in which the addition of metal allows for a malleable, sculptural quality and a strong tactile appeal as the fabric (including *Olya*, a double-layer metal fabric) can be scrunched up into all kinds of three-dimensional forms. Previously digital printing on such 'difficult' fabrics had not been possible, but Jakob Schlaepfer has been able to ink-jet print onto metallic substrates. *Igor*, a Jacquard-woven textile incorporating a holographic yarn, was used in the company's 2008 interiors collection as the surface for digital prints (ill. pp. 158, 159).

Ink-jet printing on the warp of a cloth allows the look of a traditional *ikat*, which, as well as being used for fashion, is also ideal for all kinds of household linen and drapes. The company often experiments with different layers of cloth to result in mesmerizing moiré or trompe-l'oeil effects that appear different, depending on the angle the viewer. Three layers of semi-transparent tulle chosen for one design, *Serge*, were simultaneously digitally printed. The result is dimensional and 'alive' in its character, as the shifting planes of cloth ebb and flow together. A more defined look is achieved when the same design is printed onto a blackout cloth intended for hotels or domestic rooms.

**Jakob Schlaepfer
for Georges Chakra,
Spring/Summer 2009**

Laser-cutting was used to
embellish this ensemble
with relief-effect florals
(opposite). Puffed sleeves,
face-framing lapels and
patch pockets are layered
over a simple strapless dress.

**Jakob Schlaepfer
for Chanel,
Autumn/Winter 1999–2000**

For this design for Chanel
(right), the substrate was
laser-cut in a diamond-
pattern to create a feminine,
fluid effect. Layers of fabric
move against the body,
draping and hugging
simultaneously.

jonathan saunders

After designing a 'bird-of-paradise' print for Alexander McQueen's 'Transitions' collection (Spring/Summer 2003; ill. right) to great acclaim, Jonathan Saunders made his own catwalk debut at London Fashion Week, where he showed his graphic, engineered prints on dresses with capes, layered tunics and pencil skirts. Now well known for his use of bold, geometric colour and dynamic pattern to create modern, form-hugging silhouettes, Saunders has been instrumental in fashion's print revival (after a long period of a minimalist, pared-down aesthetic), by offering an entirely different look with his psychedelic, kaleidoscopic and utterly mesmerizing prints.

Attention to both printed imagery and the body shape is realized by clever 'placement' printing, in which the prints are carefully worked out in conjunction with flat pattern pieces before being screenprinted in his London studio. Saunders's form of 'bespoke' printing allows a feature design to be accurately placed; on a central panel or at the hemline of a garment, for example, or as a particular area of interest on the hip of an otherwise plain shift dress. Scale, proportion and the positioning of imagery are all considered for each pattern piece: centre front, centre back and side panels. By so doing, Saunders enables two-dimensional pattern to become three-dimensional and wearable, in a beautiful and compelling manner. This is a very different process to creating a printed design, available in various colourways, which is then used for several garment designs.

Saunders combines the latest digital technologies with traditional hand-silkscreen printing, in which one design can necessitate up to twenty screens for colour-separation prints. Hand-drawing and computer-generated imagery are brought together and manipulated before the final design to be printed is decided upon. An image is enlarged by projecting it onto a surface, and then drawn by hand with charcoal or pencil before reducing it in size. It might then be further worked on the computer to achieve the final design for each garment shape. By working large and reducing the resulting imagery down, a great amount of detail is made possible. Mirrored effects, in which a pattern is seen in symmetry (like a Rorschach inkblot test, or a child's folded-paper 'butterfly'), have been used to create a perfectly balanced secondary motif; ombré effects, where printed colour is graduated from light to dark, also feature in several of Saunders's collections. He has an innate understanding of the female form; a central coloured feature

Jonathan Saunders for Alexander McQueen, 'Transitions', Spring/Summer 2003

This bold, colourful print, designed by Saunders for McQueen's 'Transitions' collection, with its blending of colours and textures, would be very difficult to achieve without digital means. The resulting floaty dresses were feminine and elegant as they fluttered down the catwalk.

panel flanked by two black side panels can create the impression of an elongated, slim silhouette, for example, while colour-blocking can also create flattering effects (thus ensuring the popularity of his designs). Saunders takes an architectural approach to design with clean, streamlined shapes, which range from body-conscious tube dresses to strictly tailored forms.

The digital has allowed a very different look to emerge in printed textile designs, with digital printers being able to print one motif across the entire width, dispensing with the need for repeat. This gives the designer great freedom, which Saunders takes advantage of to create oversized imagery, in which a single, large motif is the focus. Sources of inspiration are often taken from the world of fine art, particularly

Modernism and Postmodernism. Past collections have made reference to the architecture of Le Corbusier, the essential forms of Constantin Brancusi's sculpture and the colourful designs of Ettore Sottsass's work for the Memphis design group. Patterns shown in his collections can have the look of marbled paper, with their swirling mass of coloured, merging lines, or an optical or moiré appearance through the use of striped prints. Saunders approaches the making of fashion almost as an artist would, treating the female body as a blank canvas, dividing it into sections, and organizing it into sections of colour-blocking and pattern. He is an example of a designer who works across the fields of textile and fashion, combining hand and computer processes, to realize his print designs: a successful mix of craft and the digital.

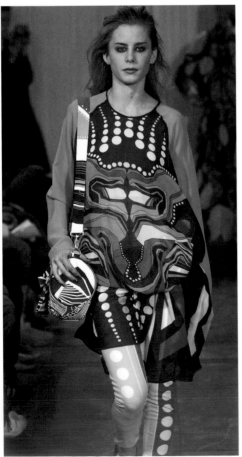

Jonathan Saunders,
Autumn/Winter 2003–4;
Autumn/Winter 2004–5;
Spring/Summer 2004

Jonathan Saunders,
Autumn/Winter 2006–7

The designer's first solo collection for Autumn/ Winter 2003–4 (opposite, bottom left) was inspired by *Transformers* cartoons, Aboriginal art and the photographs of Richard Avedon, as well as the bold patterns and large-scale prints of the 1960s. The Spring/Summer 2004 collection (opposite, right) included strong graphics and mirror imagery, and was inspired by the prints of M. C. Escher and the rave culture of the 1990s, and sealed Saunders's reputation for 'techno-graphic' printing. For Autumn/Winter 2004–5 (opposite, top left), Saunders utilized geometric shapes and blocks/panels of rich, autumnal colour.

The art collection of Peggy Guggenheim was the inspiration behind this collection for Autumn/ Winter 2006–7. It shows strong, geometric prints in black, white and grey, and many of the designs create the illusion of depth. A gradated print gives the impression of feathers on a voluminous skirt (below), while converging vertical stripes create a dramatic form for a full-length dress (right).

sonja weber

Artist Sonja Weber combines various technologies – using photography, painting, computer technology and Jacquard weaving, and drawing inspiration from each – to create compelling and complex woven artworks, which possess a strongly photorealistic quality and demonstrate a deep concern with light and movement. Weber is fascinated by the effect of light falling across a surface (from water and clouds formations to mountain ranges, and even hair), the depth of shadows and the suspension of a particular moment in time, seemingly caught at random. Capturing this ephemeral, often fleeting subject matter in photographs, she then digitally converts the images into woven structures, either as large-scale canvases or panels of smaller 'moments'.

Weber tends to work in series, exploring different ways of looking at a single theme, often looking at a fragment of a whole with an intent focus and close inspection. Abstracted monochromatic images that deal with subtle nuances of shade and light, such as *Blue Mountains* (ill. right), have become her signature. Inspiration comes from a variety of sources, from the grand and monumental, to the more intimate. Seas with calm, smooth surfaces or turbulent waters, the open expanse of skies peppered with cloud formations, and extreme close-ups of human hair, which almost function as portraits of individuals (ill. p. 168), are all part of her repertoire.

Her images of moving water, with their suggested depth, offer the viewer a contemplative arena that inspires reflection. Such is Weber's material skill that in *Speedwater* (ill. p. 169), the interweaving yarns create a life-like image of swirling, turbulent water that threatens to spill over the picture frame. The *Sky Moment* series (ill. opposite)

evokes a similar emotional response; viewers will perhaps be reminded of trying to find faces and animal shapes in the clouds when they were young. Free associations come to the fore constantly when viewing Weber's work, suggestive of a reflective, even spiritual sphere. The representations of clouds suggest a physicality of lightness and softness, and also possess a transcendent quality: they are formed, they merge, morph, and then dissipate.

Interpreted in shades of light and dark, the images take on a different aspect in their reincarnation as woven fabric, acquiring depth, a more significant resonance and a direct physicality that offers different 'faces' to the viewer as light plays across the surface, catching it at different angles. In order to give emphasis to texture, mainly black and white yarns are used to denote substance and space. From a distance, the works appear

Blue Mountains,
2005

In her work, Weber addresses universal themes that have attracted artists for centuries, from the intimate to a feeling of grandeur, imbuing them with a new meaning and bringing them up to date through her use of digital technologies.

almost like large-scale photographs; on closer inspection, the individual pixels of the original digital image are revealed as the interlacing of warp and weft.

Weber's work is reminiscent of the many artists who have created images of skies, clouds and various atmospheric effects – from Turner and Constable in the nineteenth century to the American contemporary photographer William Eggleston, who took photographs from a speeding car by pointing his camera up at the sky. Claude Monet's paintings of skies, with their wonderful brush strokes, and the *Equivalent* series of photographs of clouds (1925–31) by Alfred Stieglitz also come to mind. Photographer Henri Cartier-Bresson addressed the issue of the ephemeral in photography in his book *Images à la sauvette*, published in 1952, by noting that there is 'nothing in this world that does not have a decisive moment'. An image can only exist at one particular moment in time, with that particular light, falling on that subject. A cloud formation can change in the blink of an eye, as it is buffeted by the wind; a head of hair appears one way for a moment, but a casual brush of the hand, a toss of the head or a gust of wind creates a completely different look.

In her representations of vast spaces and more private situations, both of which illustrate constant shifts of motion, Weber records fractions of seconds that mark specific moments frozen in time, taken from life, from our real, perceivable world and its state of constant flux.

Sky Moment, 2007

A computer-operated Jacquard loom enabled the beautiful, ephemeral quality of the movement of clouds to be captured, and every nuance of the shades of blue to be conveyed. The sense of depth and constantly shifting layers achieve a photographic realism.

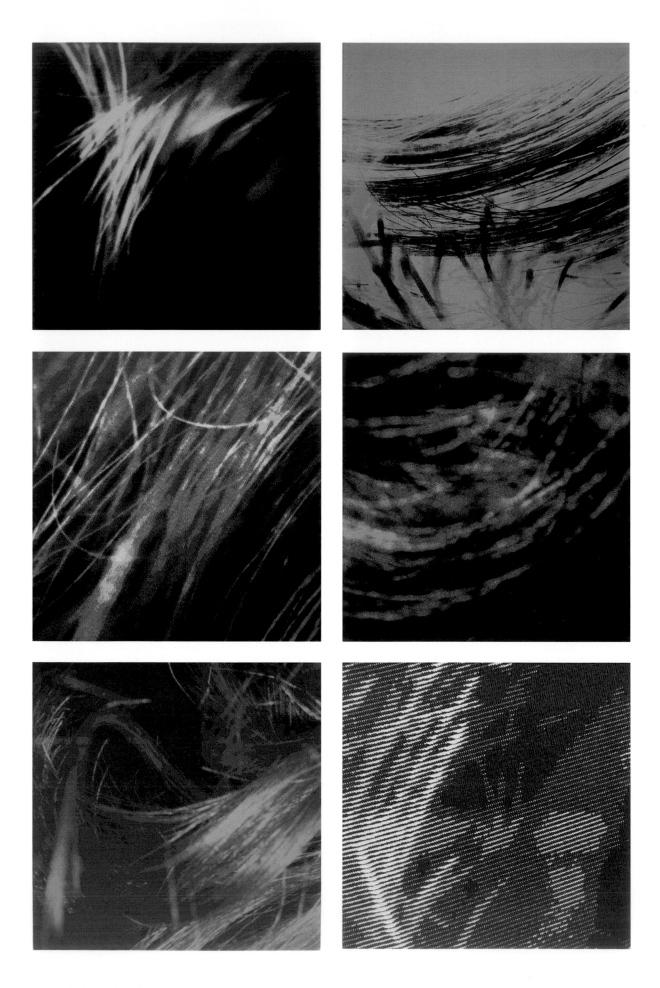

Andrea, 2005; *Verena,* 2004;
Lydia, 2005; *Thomas,* 2003;
Bryan, 2004

Bryan (detail),
2004

Speedwater,
2008

While these computer-controlled Jacquard artworks (opposite) have a print-like quality when viewed from afar, up close they reveal a sense of depth and space. In these depictions of hair, lines stretch and streak across the canvas, or curl and entangle, while layers are exposed as the strands of hair move over and under one another. Top row, left to right: *Andrea*; *Verena*; middle row, left to right: *Lydia*; *Thomas*; bottom row, left: *Bryan*.

By working with a very fine warp and weft, Weber is able to create a hyper-realistic effect that faithfully captures her original imagery (opposite, bottom right). Light and shade are conveyed by bringing white or black threads to the foreground; the mingling of the two contrasts reveals varying shades of grey.

In this particular image (above), which was inspired by Venice's waterways, the combination of black and white threads creates an almost iridescent surface, which catches the light and suggests the fast ebbing and flowing of water. It is easy to imagine that the water could extend and spill out beyond the confines of the frame.

michiko koshino

Japanese fashion designer Michiko Koshino is known for her use of hyper-realistic photographic imagery in digital print. She works with both all-over repeat and non-repeat designs, and creates subversive, streetwise fashion (London's rich cultural mix and youth scene are constant sources of inspiration). This edgy, urban aesthetic incorporates technology that exploits her use of imagery and choice of materials, as well as new ways of cutting and manipulating fabric, fostering an eclectic, unpredictable and challenging vision that she applies to her fashion designs.

The use of the computer has changed the aesthetic of printed textiles for fashion. No longer trapped by the limitations of small-scale repeat, computer-aided designs can be more effective in the form of large, one-off prints that are placed asymmetrically upon the body. Because the printed textile can be closely engineered in conjunction with the cut of the clothing, the placement of the design can likewise be meticulously calculated. A wonderful example of Koshino's enterprising spirit can be seen in her Spring/Summer 2004 collection (ill. pp. 171–75), for which she manipulated photographs of the exotic flowers, plants and vegetation of Hawaii in Adobe Photoshop to create digital prints that were both sophisticated and humorous. Scanning the original photographs into the software allowed for the creation of many different effects: imagery could be layered; scale drastically altered; repeat patterns orchestrated and imagery strategically placed, dictated by the silhouette and detailing of the garment.

Koshino creates two very distinct designs, in which scale and composition are both carefully considered. Firstly, there are the all-over repeat patterns, which are smaller in scale and can be cut and sewn in different directions. Such designs are closer in style to traditional textile designs for fashion, and can be printed on a variety of substrates to expand their potential application to both fashion and accessories, including scarves and footwear, even helmets. Then there are the more 'pictorial' designs, which have a definite orientation and depict recognizable imagery, from people sitting in deckchairs to a sunset over an ocean. The juxtaposition of these two types of design makes for a particularly rich collection, with the large, one-off 'pictures' digitally printed on short dresses or skirts, while the smaller-scale designs work as dramatic foils.

Digital print allows detail to be conveyed in a hyper-realistic manner, and Koshino's designs are further manipulated and layered to create depth. She uses the abundance of nature – grasses, palm trees, water lilies and reflections on water – as a starting point, reinterpreting it into highly representational imagery, which works in a variety of scales, and, when printed, would enliven any grey city environment and transport the wearer to more exotic climes. Koshino's designs also convey a sense of humour (showing the backs of people sitting and looking out to sea, for example); the pieces are both striking 'conversation' pieces and fun to wear.

Working with the digital allows for highly sophisticated imagery that is intricate and complex. By designing digitally, it is possible to layer imagery to create plays of transparency and opacity, an aspect that Koshino readily employed for her Spring/Summer 2004 collection. It is clearly apparent that the imagery has its source in the real world. With this collection, Koshino manipulated it to create a fantasy world, quite apart from the everyday.

Digital artwork, Spring/Summer 2004

Koshino captures the exotic look of hibiscus flowers, grown in warmer climates for their delicate and shockingly bright colours. These 'all-over' designs were scanned into Photoshop and manipulated to create a repeat pattern that was digitally printed and used for various items of clothing.

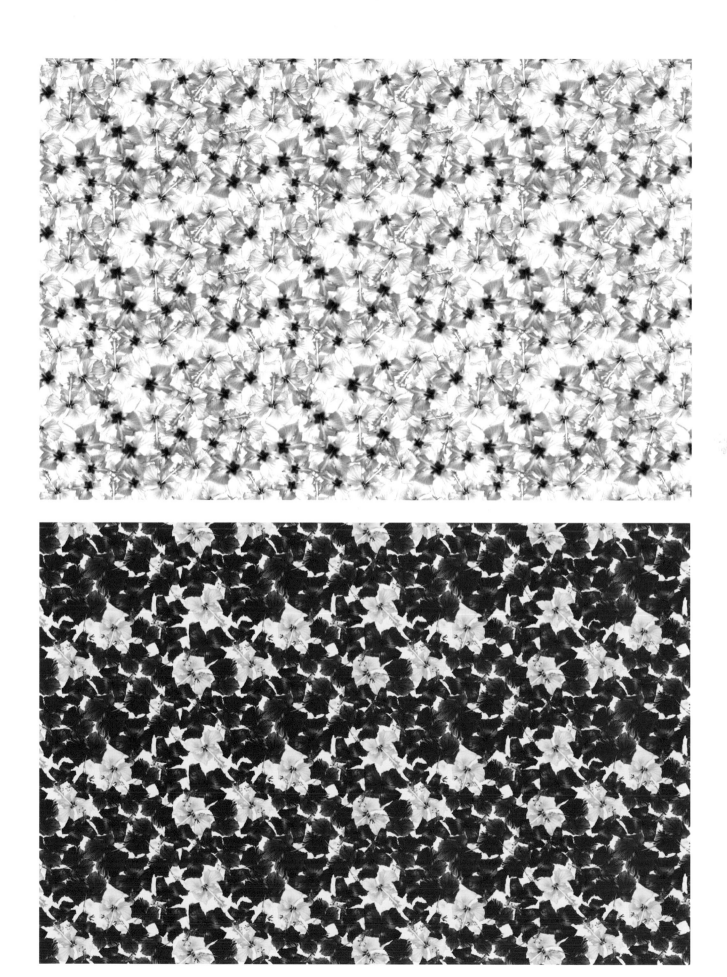

Photographs of palm trees were digitally manipulated to create a repeat pattern that could be turned and placed according to the cut of the garment and position on the body. For this vest-shaped top and mini-skirt (below, right), the imagery (below) was used in a large scale and rotated to create a bold design.

**Digital artwork,
Spring/Summer 2004**

Photoshop manipulation
allowed for the bright
colours in this image of
water lilies to be altered
and enhanced (above, left).
A dress accessorized by
a printed scarf with the
same design (above, right)
softens and breaks up the
descriptive imagery.

The scale and placement of the digitally printed design (below, left) were carefully considered, and different substrates were chosen for printing to create a fully coordinating outfit. The design was printed on a garment and a scooter helmet (below, right).

basso & brooke

Brazilian-born Bruno Basso and Nottingham native Christopher Brooke established their fashion partnership in 2002, and a mere two years later were the winners of the inaugural Fashion Fringe award, an event that now accompanies London's Fashion Week. The duo produce flamboyant, digitally printed textile designs, exploiting the full gamut of colour and pattern possible to achieve sumptuous fabric surfaces. Their accomplished use of imaging software led Tim Banks, fashion commentator for *Vogue* Online, to describe their label as 'the Pixar of clothes'.

Basso & Brooke evolved at a time when digital-print technology was just emerging and still quite costly, and yet the potential of these tools, specifically for printed textiles for fashion, was apparent. The first designers to implement the use of digital print throughout an entire catwalk collection, Basso & Brooke unleashed a new, technically ambitious surface vocabulary for fashion. Collections became more refined as their command of the technology, both imaging and production, developed. The scale of the imagery, combined with intricate patterning and colour ranges, is always demanding. Each collection set a challenge for the next, as the visual sophistication of their designs increased. The duo tend not to follow obvious fashion trends, preferring instead to design instinctively, creating forms to connect with the imagery that they conjure, an unusual and challenging approach. Complex, bold designs are specifically positioned to look part of the garment shape, rather than merely a decorative addition.

Attracted to the emerging possibilities of digital fabric-printing machines and imaging media from very early on, Basso & Brooke managed to shirk the trappings of imaging filters and software gimmickry in their

'The Succubus and Other Tales', Spring/Summer 2005

Basso & Brooke's debut collection, shown at London's Fashion Week, signalled the pair's innovative approach to combining historical and futuristic aesthetics to achieve richly unique fashion narratives that are only achievable through digital-print innovation.

designs. Early users of Photoshop distorted imagery in stylized, often immediately recognizable ways, with a range of filters; use of these special effects was rarely seen as considered or discerning. If the odd filter entered Basso & Brooke's creative process, it was certainly not evident in their detailed visuals. Taking inspiration from artists such as Fiona Rae, Peter Halley and, for their 'Neo Pop' collection (Spring/Summer 2010; ill. p. 181), Jeff Koons and photographer Herb Ritts, the duo combine these interests with a technology twist, referencing the Big Bang, H. G. Wells and Jules Verne. The subtle use of fine, indecipherable ASCII (American Standard Code for Information Interchange) text on the billowing dresses that featured in their 'Turning' collection (Autumn/Winter 2007–8; ill. pp. 178, 179) appeared to form folds of delicate shading around the body.

This was accompanied by pieces inspired by imagery from Tetris, a video game from the 1980s, programmed by Alexey Pajitnov.

In 2006, Basso & Brooke presented their 'Exotique' collection (Spring/Summer 2007) at Shepherd's Bush Empire, in London. A combination of spectacular lighting, grand atmosphere and couture-like garments, the designers took the audience through the world of the exotic with images of endangered species, luxury graphic fur and skins. For Autumn/Winter 2007–8, they returned to the main venue at the BFC Tent with the 'Turning' collection. Introducing fluidity and lightness, characteristics that are unusual in their designs, the duo presented abstract and pixellated prints that appeared on cloud-like, billowing clothing.

As their work has evolved, Basso & Brooke have worked in partnership with Massimo Ferretti and the Italian fashion and luxury goods brand Aeffe. Regular collaborators include Swarovski and in particular milliner Stephen Jones, who devises experimental headpieces that add a complementary twist to the designers' collections – including a range of geometric headpieces inspired by the Italian designer and computer enthusiast Ettore Sottsass for Spring/Summer 2008 (ill. right). Having perfected an accomplished use of digital media over the years, their work can appear wonderfully off-piste, quite unlike anything else emerging from the catwalk. Recent collections, however, show a maturity and sophistication in both the textile and garment form, ensuring their future design success.

Technology and the Far East combined in the 'High-Tech Romance' collection (Spring/Summer 2009; ill. p. 181), which was packed with a balanced collage of brilliantly coloured prints. Recognizable references to Japanese printmaking (Hokusai's wave, for example) and other motifs including flowers, calligraphy and *sumi-e* strokes work amid coded geometrical patterns. The imagery was enhanced with beading, embroidery

or Swarovski crystals. Laser-cutting techniques were also employed to further enrich the fabric surfaces. This collection was complemented by a twist on traditional Japanese accessories associated with geisha, such as origami-like obi belts, highly sculpted platform shoes, traditionally known as *okobo*, by Raouda Assaf, and oversized hair adornments by Jones.

Beyond the catwalk, the pair's graphic imagery has begun to permeate the interiors sector with innovative surface design. Wall coverings and furnishing materials look set to become as inspired as their catwalk collections.

'Brave New World', Spring/Summer 2008

For this collection, the pair drew inspiration from Aldous Huxley's novel, artist Fiona Rae's abstract paintings, and the designs of Ettore Sottsass, which inspired the use of a range of Formica laminates and surfacing as a material for millinery, translated into a series of abstract geometric forms by Stephen Jones.

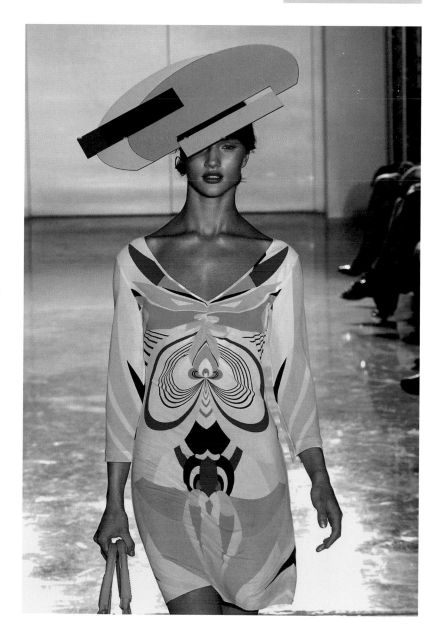

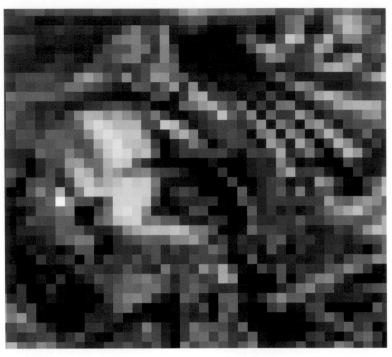

'Turning',
Autumn/Winter 2007–8

This print (top) was inspired
by references to emerging
popular computing, such
as Tetris, a video game from
the 1980s, programmed by
Alexey Pajitnov.

'Vanity Fair',
Spring/Summer 2006

This collection (above)
offered a theatrical mix of
1950s- and '80s-inspired
silhouettes with an edgy
undertone.

'Turning',
Autumn/Winter 2007–8

A complex print (opposite)
merges ASCII code with
the depiction of a stone
statue and draped garment,
creating an illusion of drape
evident in the print.

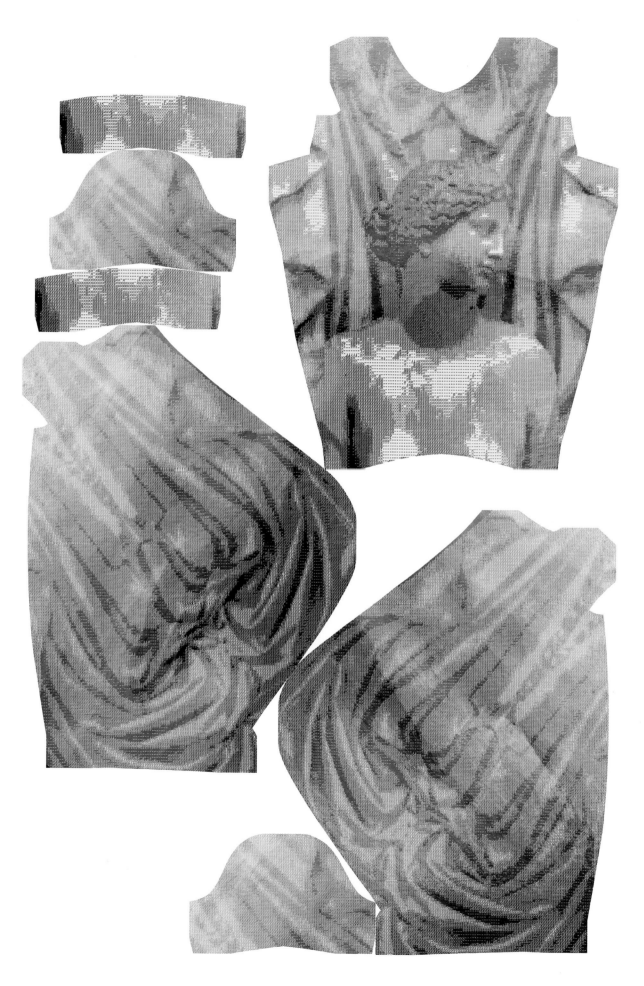

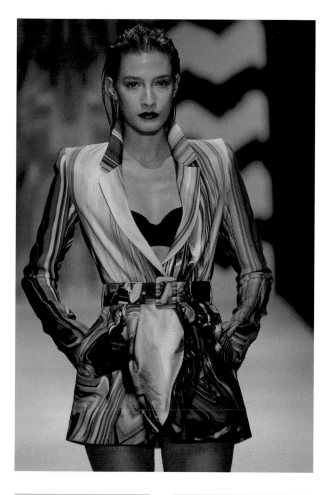

Big Bang,
from 'Science and Fiction',
Autumn/Winter 2006–7;
'Neo Pop',
Spring/Summer 2010

'High-Tech Romance',
Spring/Summer 2009;
'Le Roi Soleil',
Autumn/Winter 2009–10

The series of prints, including *Big Bang* (opposite) developed for Autumn/ Winter 2006–7 conveyed a particularly rich fusion of Victorian and science-fiction influences. The imagery and tone are mysteriously dark yet highly detailed, both pixellated and painterly in style, emulating delicate drape in a wide range of light and heavy materials. For Spring/Summer 2010, the painterly, high-octane 'Neo Pop' collection (above) was influenced by Herb Ritts and Jeff Koons. Dynamic patterning was enhanced with shimmering surfaces to add a particular energy.

For Spring/Summer 2009 (above, right), technology and the Far East were combined to create a kaleidoscope of brilliantly coloured prints, fashioned into simple, fitted garments with kimono and origami structural twists. An exquisite tonal Rococo collection for Autumn/ Winter 2009–10 (right) included decorative trompe-l'oeil additions, such as furs, lace and pearls. Powdered faces and two-dimensional wig-like headpieces by Stephen Jones evoked a 'period' event.

joshua davis

Having originally trained as a painter and illustrator, New York-based web designer Joshua Davis is one of an influential generation of practitioners that were among the first to raid the earliest commercial software and hardware for ideas, and to recognize the potential of the Internet. Somewhat unconventionally, Davis took the technician out of code, and in so doing legitimized the designer–programmer. His early work invigorated otherwise static web pages for a number of key commercial clients, at a time when moving image on the web was relatively new, and companies were only just beginning to take the possibility of a web presence seriously. During this new dot. com era, Davis became a major contributor to web design. To make his own practice more accessible, Davis developed a series of sites, including Once-upon-a-forest.com and Praystation.com, for which he created an open-source Flash lab and community.

Davis references Jackson Pollock as an artist with whom he identifies conceptually, in that he relates to the idea of being detached from conventional tools. Working mainly with 2D graphics packages, such as Flash and Adobe Illustrator, Davis has pushed the limits of these media by developing his own programming techniques, and pioneered a generative computational process that he describes as 'dynamic abstraction'. Parameters of code are defined to operate in conjunction with the visual information that he inputs: hand-drawings, forms from nature, distorted patterns, even a colour palette from a digital photograph to produce a mutating collage. The design engine is, essentially, 'sent off' to generate extraordinarily complex and random compositions.

At this stage, the process is effectively outside of the designer's control. The results are infinite and unpredictable, and an enormous number of possible final images

Tropism, 2007
Espeis Gallery, New York

This installation work formed part of *Tropism*, the last in a series of three exhibitions at New York's Espeis Gallery organized by online gallery Maxalot. The exhibition featured floor-to-ceiling digital prints of frozen visual representations of Davis's 'dynamic abstraction'.

are produced. One image may be composed of several thousand image layers, impossible to originate or recreate by hand, but which perhaps take minutes to create digitally. With this immense quantity of output, however, some discerning decision-making processes must be implemented, as many images simply fail or their aesthetic composition doesn't work.

Together with programmer Branden Hall, Davis designed Genetic Aesthetic, a software that attempts to develop a system within a system, which would effectively analyse designs, assessing the aesthetic of compositions in any one algorithmic exercise. The system is fed with information on all kinds of characteristics that are considered 'beautiful', with the aim that the system will eventually learn to make constructive decisions. Some element of risk or deviation is incorporated into the program to accommodate the all-important, in Davis's words, 'beautiful accident'. These 'accidents' in Davis's imagery are reminiscent of Pollock's canvases, in that each visual seems to contain a vast energy in action-based patterns and structures, which are composed of organic geometries. The designs are beguilingly complex, linear and dense in form, and employ subtle colour palettes of intricate and rich hues.

Inspired, too, by Japan and Japanese culture, Davis has perhaps unconsciously created his own *ukiyo-e*, or 'pictures of the floating world', an art form that encompasses woodblock prints and paintings. Artists associated with this tradition created works of incredible energy and detail in their depiction of nature in flat 2D form; Katsushika Hokusai's famous *Great Wave off Kanagawa* (c. 1829–32) and the landscapes of Utagawa Hiroshige (1797–1858) are but two examples. Davis's digital apparitions similarly depict unworldly atmospheres, composed of synthetic cloud and dust systems in flux. As if in mid-process, each image looks set to unfold unfathomable possibilities. Davis's own digital *ukiyo-e* works have evolved into large and small-scale surfaces, in the form of a range of products, wallpapers and textile pieces for home-furnishings company Umbra, and to building projections. Each of his unique artworks can be purchased as a download for printing.

Working with vector-based drawing tools means that the execution of Davis's work can be vast, without any image distortion, making the potential range of clients seemingly limitless. Davis seamlessly operates between creating artworks for exhibition (such as online gallery Maxalot's *Tropism* exhibition in 2007; ill. opposite) and designs for commercial clients such as Nike, Barney's New York, Nokia, Diesel, Motorola and BMW, together with the rock band, the Red Hot Chili Peppers. His generative process is intriguing to companies, who, once they buy into a design, become interested in negotiating rights to evolving imagery from an algorithm (originally conceived for the advertising campaign of a specific brand, for example).

Davis has also deployed methods of creating truly interactive, multi-user image works that attract huge crowds of participants. Random Assistant has now appeared at a number of festivals, including the 2008 OFFF Festival, held in Lisbon, where 2,500 attendees worked on four black-and-white prints, 1m × 3m each. The audience becomes engaged as part of one of Davis's random generative systems, as they select and determine the colour palettes for these pieces. Davis worked on a panel alongside this human software, for eight to ten hours over three days.

In continuing to test the limits of software capability, Joshua Davis has defined an extremely exciting and inclusive modus operandi for digital-image design, which, refreshingly, has no boundaries of practice.

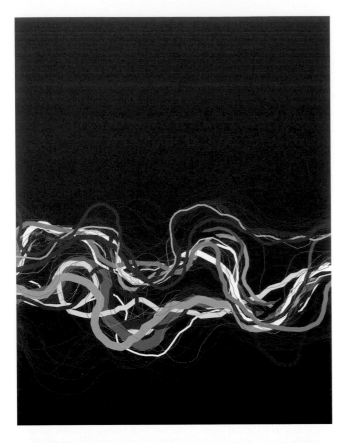

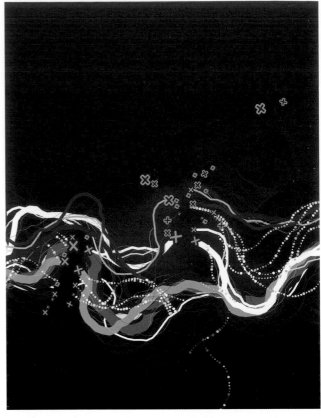

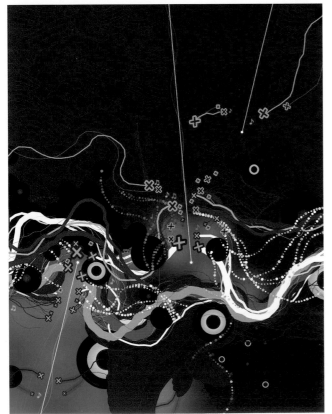

**Joshua Davis
for Motorola,
Soundwires,
2007**

The graphic-image
production process appears
as infinite and variable as
generative design itself, and
has become familiar through
numerous commercial
clients. This image sequence
(above and left) was
commissioned by Motorola
to promote the company's
S9 wireless headphones.

**Joshua Davis
for Omega Code,
Omega Code Bézier Tests,
2008**

These two images (opposite,
left) were part of a series
commissioned by the
Brazilian band, Omega Code.
The experimental series of
prints was the first, says
Davis, to use the Bézier curve
– used in computer graphics
to model smooth curves – to
map random architectural
shapes.

TA, 2007
Todays Art Festival,
The Hague

OFFF Lightboxes, 2007
Online Flash Film Festival,
Barcelona

For an annual art festival,
artwork was precision-
beamed onto the surface
of a building (above, right).
Davis's images possess such
clarity that they are capable
of withstanding large-scale
projection.

The *OFFF Lightbox* series as
interior installation (right)
shows how light adds a
vibrancy to otherwise flat 2D
graphics, the details of which
are accentuated, almost as
animation, when presented
in this format.

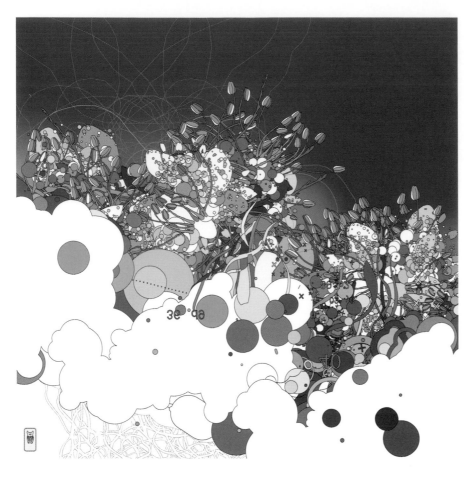

Moss Pyrus, 2007;
Snow Medusa, 2007

Moss Pyrus (left) and *Snow Medusa* (below, left) are limited-edition works from the *Tropism* series, available via online digital-print gallery Maxalot, which makes accessible high-resolution digital artworks.

Once-upon-a-forest 016, 2005

One of a series of artworks (opposite) that formed part of the Once-upon-a-forest compositions. It was created for Maxalot, which has represented digital artists since 2003.

louise goldin

In Louise Goldin's revolutionary designs for knitwear, cloth and garment are constructed simultaneously on computer-controlled machinery to achieve distinctive cut-out, body-conscious shapes with a science-fiction appeal, resulting in clothes that are far removed from knitwear's more homespun image. Her collections are driven by an innate understanding of both technology and craft. She digitally develops structure and form that surpass those created by conventional methodologies, and combines her use of the computer as a primary tool with a knowledge of craft skills and an appreciation of the inherent properties of knit (stretch, flexibility and drape).

Rather than creating knitted separates, Goldin is interested in the 'look' of an entire outfit. Her ready-to-wear womenswear designs are presented on the catwalk as succinct collections, with long, linear lines that elongate and emphasize body curves, following the contours and smoothing as they go to achieve a flattering silhouette. Often the garments are cleverly engineered to 'fit and flare', fully exploiting the ability of knit to both hold a shape and to be fluid. Goldin's trademark is graphically strong, heavily patterned, computer-generated knitwear, a particular aesthetic achieved by creating designs that challenge the whole concept of the medium. The comfort, homeliness, bulkiness and warmth often associated with knitwear have long gone.

Over the last two decades, ever-inventive structures have been produced, thanks to seamless three-dimensional knitting. Japanese company Shima Seiki, a producer of computerized flat-knitting machines, reinvented the idea of whole-garment knitwear, as opposed to parts that are then assembled. The seamless garment is knitted in three dimensions, from yarn to end product, on the knitting machine, with no post-production (cutting, piecing and sewing) needed. Goldin's first collection in Spring/Summer 2007 (ill. opposite, top) was dynamic and strong, and featured panels that accentuated the torso and all-in-one jumpsuits that gave a lean appearance. Sweater dresses worn over leggings presented a contemporary and very wearable look – one that is simultaneously athletic and sexy. Her sense of colour is sophisticated and acute: vibrant colours such as electric blue, deep terracotta and acid green shine out. The collections also offer strong, monochromatic looks with dense blacks, or graphic contrasts of black, grey and white.

Goldin experiments with different computer programs to mix traditional knitwear patterns with the type of digital pixellation viewed on a computer screen. Such pixellated imagery can be translated into knit with incredible detail, the digital allowing fantasy to become a reality. Not only

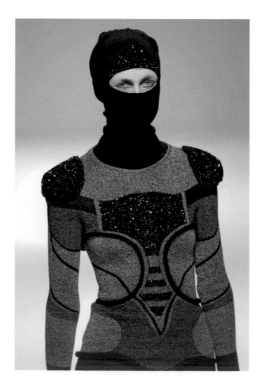

Louise Goldin, Autumn/Winter 2007–8

A sombre grey and black palette with marled textures uses dramatic patterning made possible through the use of CAD/CAM tools. Traditional aspects of tailoring are subverted where exterior shoulder pads are bejewelled with Swarovski crystals to turn what normally remains hidden into a feature.

is the imagery considered, but also the very construction of the knit. Working digitally allows for complex interlacing, the equivalent to computer-assisted Jacquard weaves where individual threads can be controlled. By using digital technology, knit is literally taken into a whole new arena. Goldin's designs are wide in their reference, from Inuit culture to science-fiction space suits with their protective padding.

Her Spring/Summer 2008 collection (ill. p. 191) was based on the work of Russian painter Wassily Kandinsky, and featured colliding patterns and clashing blocks of colour. Goldin's particular look owes a debt to performance wear for extreme sports, which streamlines the body (as if for speed) with vertical panelling. Likewise her collection for Autumn/Winter 2008–9 showed vivid abstraction with strong linear and zig-zag patterning (ill. right, below). Superwoman and intergalactic warriors came to mind as the models strode forth in jersey garments that clung to their bodies, hugging and controlling in a modern way. Fitted panels flared from the hip and encircled the body, or were ruched and secured with cords to create 'puffed-up' shapes.

Knitwear in fashion is distinct from working with woven fabrics, as the designer is involved throughout the process, from the choice of yarn to the presentation of the finished product. The construction of the textile and the garment are one, and Goldin enjoys both the level of control this offers, and the transformation from two dimensions to three. Meticulous in her research into new techniques and the integration of old ones (including macramé techniques developed in Brazil), Goldin has, in a relatively short space of time, delivered innovative, luxurious knitwear, and looks set to continue to bring knit into the foreground of fashion. By using her understanding of low-tech methodologies together with her knowledge of code and computing, Louise Goldin is a true visionary.

Louise Goldin, Spring/Summer 2007

Goldin's first collection of super-lightweight, fine-gauge, body-conscious knitwear was dramatic in its appeal and yet very wearable. The symmetrical design, achieved by resurrecting the interlacing technique of macramé (used predominantly in the 1970s), divided the body and suggested stylish bondage, or a modern form of lace.

Louise Goldin, Autumn/Winter 2008–9

This futuristic outfit features a subtly padded top with graphic linear outlining, highlighted with Swarovski crystals, and teamed with a mini-skirt with zig-zag 'flame' patterning. Goldin's designs often begin on the computer, and here the pixel is evidenced as blocks of black, grey and white for a gradated effect.

A space-age aesthetic is
offered with this cosmos-
inspired collection,
featuring an all-in-one sheer
bodysuit, with strategically
placed Swarovski crystals,
and trompe-l'oeil belt.
Other designs reference
geographical studies of the
earth's surface. This type of
imagery is made possible by
using a computer-controlled
knitting machine.

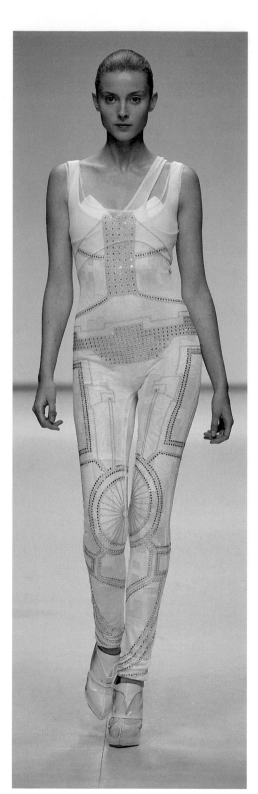

**Louise Goldin,
Spring/Summer 2008**

**Louise Goldin,
Spring/Summer 2008**

For this body-conscious mini-dress (above), up to three layers of semi-sheer, ultra-fine-gauge knits were used to create vest shapes overlaid with shoestring-strapped slips. The cutaway swimwear styling is balanced with a flirty skirt. Continuing the sportswear theme, latex skullcaps and headbands with chin straps feature as streamlined accessories for the collection.

In another sporty design (above, right), Goldin displayed her expertise with colour. Sea-turquoise and coral-red were used together with clashing pinks and oranges for a distinctive summertime look. The patterning on the lower part of the dress appears like thermal imaging, and contrasts well with the nautical stripes.

tom gallant

London-based artist Tom Gallant trained in traditional fine art, printmaking and material processes. Drawing inspiration from Japanese paper techniques, his delicate works are produced by hand, using only a cutting board and scalpel. Recent digital methods have enabled an attempt to reverse-engineer his image-construction process, and to repurpose it in a very different context. A proposal to translate his paper constructions into 3D wearable form has led to an ongoing partnership with fashion designer Marios Schwab – one that illustrates Gallant's significant craft skill.

Laser-cutting technology has enabled increasing potential for intricacy of pattern and material design. For Schwab's Autumn/ Winter 2008–9 collection (ill. pp. 192–94), composed of simple garment silhouettes, Gallant created a series of fine fabrics, in part referencing William Morris's floral designs. Computer drawing and laser-cutting and layering enabled a complex and exacting transition from his paper works to fabric form. The delicate line, achieved by the laser-cut surfaces, operated as a type of visual camouflage for the imagery beneath, which was originally sourced from archived pornographic magazines. Each garment required a precise construction plan, informed by laser-cutting tests that took into account the distinct differences between working with paper and with cloth. The resulting garments were composed of a variety of surface effects that subtly alluded to the female form underneath – a material invention that displayed a skilled balance of craft and digital methods, while subverting the conventional process of fashion design.

The collaboration between Gallant and Schwab continued in the latter's 'Placement Patterns' collection for Spring/Summer 2009

(ill. p. 195), with the development of digitally generated, trompe-l'oeil imagery for printed textile finishes. Gallant's image sources included paper workings from a series he created in 2008, which revisited Gustave Doré's elegant black-and-white illustrations for the Bible and Dante's *Divine Comedy*, dating from 1866 and 1867, respectively. Inspired by Doré's 2D illusionary depiction of cloth and drape, Gallant recreated this line, describing the cloth form by using a hand-cut paper technique, layered against pornographic imagery, emulating a fine veil effect. On the catwalk, the garment interplayed between the physical body of the model and the imagery hidden in the 2D print. The overall effect was simpler and less dramatic than the laser-cut series, but the image development and placement on both garment form and body was exacting and specifically crafted, so that the combination of drape imagery on 3D draped constructions worked in accord.

The aim for Schwab's collection for Autumn/Winter 2009–10 (ill. pp. 196, 197) was to create a digital print series, composed of abstract stereoscopic prints, to be fully realized using 3D glasses to view on the catwalk. Swarovski crystals were photographed from two angles, close to

each other, and the images converted into cyan and red, and then overlaid and collaged, resulting in a 3D optical effect. To fully achieve this illusion, the 2D image development process entailed a complex design procedure requiring the use of 3D glasses while working on the computer. The resulting sharp angular imagery in blue, red and green gradating tones set against stark black and white background and highlights were reproduced using digital printing. The stereoscopic effect was enhanced by combining layers of transparent and mat materials, with additional printing on top of a translucent sequinned layer. Schwab's garments achieved dramatic technical tailoring that incorporated cracks and fissures through the layered fabrics to complement Gallant's crystalline abstractions.

The dialogue between Gallant and Marios Schwab illustrates how digital media can enable artists and designers to extend practices and reposition themselves in new 'spaces'. Collaborations of this nature are rare, however, and Gallant's skill was paramount in enabling such a precise response to the task, without compromise to either his or Schwab's creative endeavour.

Tom Gallant
for Marios Schwab,
Autumn/Winter 2008–9

Gallant collaborated with Schwab to realize the translation of his paper works into twenty catwalk garments, each unique in their surface construction, achieved with engineered laser-cutting methods to create intricate body-conscious forms.

Tom Gallant
for Marios Schwab,
Autumn/Winter 2008–9

Backstage at the Autumn/
Winter 2008–9 catwalk show
(left). The delicate, lace-like
forms worn by the models
are seen to great effect in
this close-up photograph.

Tom Gallant
for Marios Schwab,
Autumn/Winter 2008–9

The dress and detail shown
here (below, left and right)
illustrate the translation of
Gallant's hand-cut works
into digitally printed and
laser-cut forms for fashion.

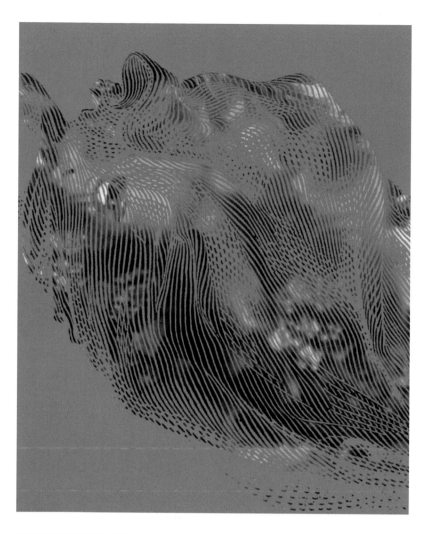

**Tom Gallant
for Marios Schwab,
Spring/Summer 2009**

Gallant's digitally generated
trompe-l'oeil effect leads
the eye to partially hidden
pornographic imagery, cut
from archived magazines.
This informed the drape and
form of Schwab's 'Placement
Patterns' collection.

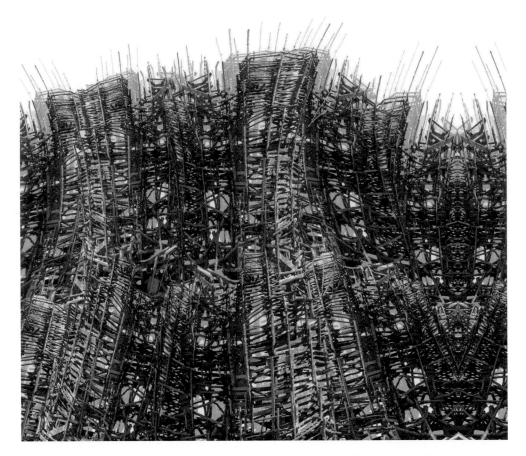

Tom Gallant
for Marios Schwab,
Autumn/Winter 2009–10

To achieve an optical 3D
effect for the catwalk,
Gallant created a series of
stereoscopic digital prints,
the illusionary qualities
of which were enhanced
through the use a variety
of sheer fabric layers.

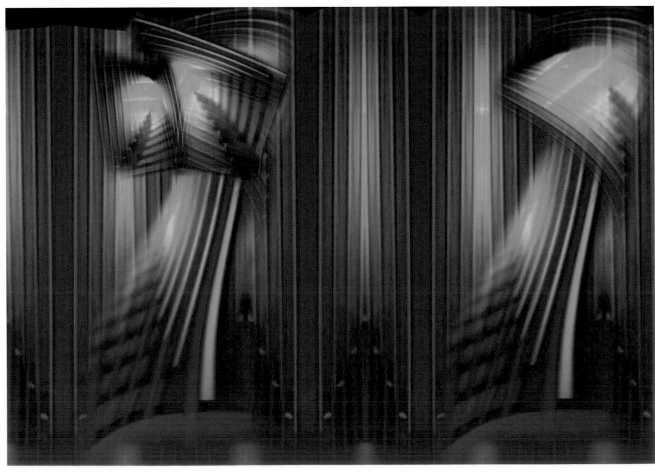

iris van herpen

Despite having been born into an already digitally native generation, as a child designer Iris van Herpen preferred the physicality of making, doing and being occupied outdoors to the screen environments of television or games consoles. Apart from her admittedly invaluable computer, she still prefers to have limited distraction from what she is most passionate about: exploring a hybrid approach to fashion that sits between avant-garde artefact and body architecture. Van Herpen has established a style for combining industrial and fine-crafted fabrication processes to express a range of limited-edition, show-stopping body concepts, and her practice has recently turned to 3D printing and rapid-prototyping tools, driving this technology into new terrain and challenging aesthetic perception of the media.

Having graduated from the ArtEZ Institute of the Arts in the Netherlands in 2006, van Herpen struggled with mastering the mechanics of computing and its relevance to her aims. Even the emerging possibility of 3D printing was not initially appealing, owing to the limited aesthetic of the available materials, and in particular their crude, synthetic finish – a far cry from the qualities achieved by experimenting with more established media and processes. After internships with Alexander McQueen and Dutch designer Claudy Jongstra, van Herpen launched her own label in 2007.

Early collections such as 'Mummification' (Autumn/Winter 2009–10), 'Radiation Invasion' (Spring/Summer 2010) and 'Synesthesia' (Autumn/Winter 2010–11; all ill. p. 200) employed meticulous use of a range of complex and challenging materials, such as leather, metal, rubber and plastic, tempered with fine cutting, construction and manipulation techniques that teased and

belied their material origin. Both industrial-machine techniques and hand-construction and finishing skills were employed to fashion the intricate garment forms to a very high level. Van Herpen's collections are small but rich in their elaborate content, drama and illusion, while also being delicate and wearable. She has attracted commissions from the singer Björk and choreographer Nanine Linning, as well as collaborations with shoemakers United Nude.

The unpredictability of water inspired 'Crystallization' (Spring/Summer 2011; ill. below and p. 202), a capsule collection launched at Amsterdam Fashion Week, in which laser-cutting and 3D printing were

**'Crystallization',
Spring/Summer 2011**
With MGX by Materialise and Daniel Widrig

This stunning, fully articulated 'cape' was 3D printed in one piece that perfectly clipped onto the shoulders of the model's body. Advancing the capability of digital fabrication, this unique wearable garment accessory formed part of a bespoke group of pieces.

introduced to the designer's palette of processes. The centrepiece of the collection – a structured and moulded leather dress, framed by a clear, highly finished armature – emulated a fully animated splash of water, as if the model has just jumped into a pool. To achieve this experimental CAD work, van Herpen collaborated with conceptual architectural designer Daniel Widrig, who has also worked for Zaha Hadid. Widrig translated van Herpen's designs, starting primarily from a series of powerful hand-drawings that sculpted the form of her fashion around the body.

Van Herpen and Widrig's partnership evolved into a now-established creative dialogue in the digital manufacture of futuristic couture, as seen in a series of 3D printed garments for the 'Escapism' collection (Spring/Summer 2011; ill. pp. 201, 203), shown at Paris Fashion Week. The intricate, intriguing body-hugging silhouettes demonstrated a significant development in van Herpen's approach to 3D printing technology. The wearability of computer-manufactured creations, as opposed to being merely decorative, was central to the collection, which evidenced a fusion of innate material capability and a developing use of digital tools.

It is testament to the combined analogue and digital craft of van Herpen and Widrig that the resulting garments were virtually fashioned without the use of body-scanning equipment or an avatar, and that, once printed, they connected to the body form as if tailored. While quite solid and rigid-looking, the pieces were in fact composed of feather-light articulated components, produced in one complete unit to be malleable. MGX by Materialise computer-manufactured the pieces, using a laser-printing process that fused fine layers of polyamide to make otherwise impossible forms. The painstakingly crafted finish resulted in many mistaking the 3D printed works for entirely hand-crafted pieces.

While 3D rapid-prototyping tools have been used over the last two decades for high-tech manufacture in the automotive and aviation industries, they have only recently become technically and financially accessible to designers. As innovations abound, novelty and gimmickry prevail, particularly in fashion and product contexts, where structural design is often not limited enough and untreated printed materials are aesthetically undesirable. The applications of these media are reliant on material developments to refine the printing processes, so that the output becomes ever-more sophisticated for designers or consumers.

Science and engineering sectors will begin to consider high-performance, low-cost, recycled, organic and more malleable materials specific to fashion and textiles as the resolution, scale and speed of 3D digital printing continues to improve. Despite its aesthetic failings, the perceived capability of 3D printing is being elevated by makers who are challenging its use. Van Herpen illustrates the importance of material skill in this design–science engagement, and the potential of collaborative cross-disciplinary approaches to developing new technology. Unfazed by the current limitations of 3D printing, she embraces the chance to employ emerging materials that offer more adaptable properties. Printed food, for example, may provide previously unimaginable solutions to conceptual design thinking.

In the meantime, the realm of fashion provides a lucrative vehicle for van Herpen's challenging yet exquisite works, which offer new modes of self-expression for those who inhabit the futuristic couture she creates. In the future, her ambition could even lie in the design of more challenging structures, including furniture, buildings and environments, in both physical and virtual forms. The future of 3D printing technology looks set to enable this designer to achieve the currently inconceivable.

'Radiation Invasion',
Spring/Summer 2010;
'Synesthesia',
Autumn/Winter 2010–11;
'Mummification',
Autumn/Winter, 2009–10

Van Herpen's collections – 'Radiation Invasion' (below), 'Synesthesia' (right) and 'Mummification' (below, right) – demonstrate the inventive use of industrial media, such as leather, rubber and plastics, and the designer's extensive material skill in crafting such striking, intricately constructed and innovation-driven garment forms.

The collaboration between van Herpen and Widrig became more assured with this collection (opposite), which advances the use of digital fabrication in creating these surprisingly feather-light garment forms. Again, van Herpen combines both digital and analogue media in this collection to stunning effect.

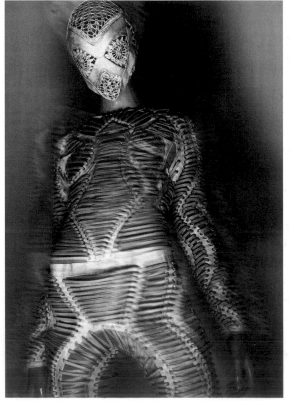

**'Crystallization',
Spring/Summer 2011**
With Joost Vandebrug

Experimentation with
a range of digital practices
emerges in van Herpen's
'Crystallization' collection,
including 3D printing
to capture a 'splash' of
clear water, laser-cutting
on synthetic media and
moving-image composition,
developed for the catwalk
in conjunction with
photographer and film-
maker Joost Vandebrug.

Shown at Paris Fashion
Week, this collection
challenged the conventions
of couture. The headpieces
were designed by Stephen
Jones and the shoes by
architect Rem Koolhaas's
company, United Nude,
in collaboration with
van Herpen.

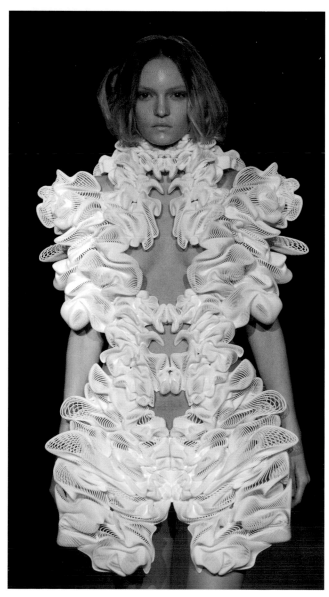

3 the future of digital pasts

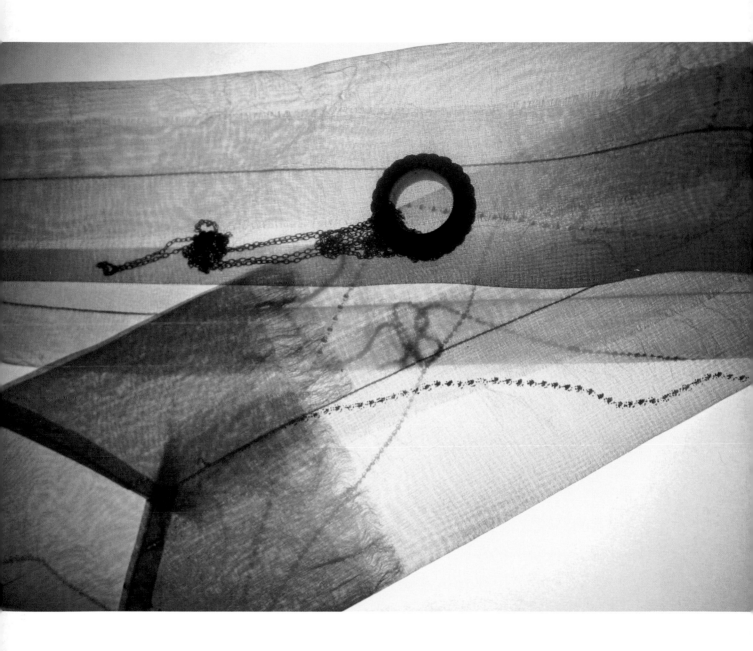

Tomoko Hayashi,
Intimacy, 2003

This series of artefacts was
designed for people in
long-distance relationships,
and linked conceptually to
memory and the notion of
digital communication. The
fabric of a delicate accessory
– a tie or undergarment – is 3D
embossed on its surface by the
pattern of a partner's jewelry.

'If a fabric can be wiped and rewritten with a fresh image, like a computer screen, what would be the need for textile designers? And, more importantly, what would be the need for more than one garment in that shape? ... Seasonal print collections could become obsolete. Instead, consumers might ... download new collections of surface design into their "digital" garments as and when they chose.'

Suzanne Lee, *Fashioning the Future: Tomorrow's Wardrobe* (2005)

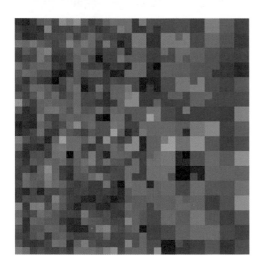

Tomoko Hayashi,
***Mutsugoto*, 2007**

Created with Stefan Agamanolis and Matthew Karau at Media Lab Europe, *Mutsugoto* is an interface for intimate communication over distance. A stroke of the body is digitally traced, appearing beside a partner in another space.

Michael Hansmeyer,
Subdivided Quad,
2006

This 2D study, based on
the subdivision of a quad
for ten iterations, was
generated and visualized
using the open-source
software, Processing.

In an incredibly short space of time, computing technology has become both extremely sophisticated and almost invisible, normalized by daily use and influenced by the imagineering narrative of film. In *The Matrix* (1999), our world is envisaged as a computer simulation, a vortex of embedded layers, composed of thousands of three-dimensional synthesized images that effectively 'delete' the real. In reality, life's pace has accelerated to the point that we are no longer aware of the effect of computing on our everyday existence. Microchips and processors are to be found in everything from cars to clothing, and computers have evolved from mainframes that were big enough to fill a room to smart phones that fit in the palm of one's hand. Once-fictionalized concepts such as implanted memories and eye-scanning, as seen in the retro-futuristic film *Blade Runner* (1982), in which irises are digitally scanned to differentiate between the eye of a human and that of a genetically manufactured albeit deceptively similar 'replicant', have already been realized.

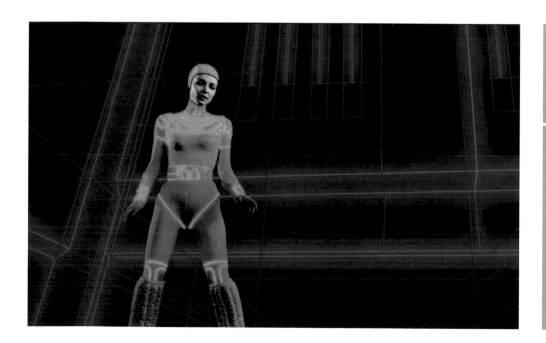

Steve Lisberger
(director),
Tron, 1982

This landmark film, which portrayed the concept of being inside a computer mainframe, was one of the first to use early computer-graphic imaging techniques. The film's aesthetic has influenced many creative genres, including fashion and product design.

Early computing entailed a geographical separation of material and digital practice; now these practices have been superseded by an array of portable and micro methods, partnered by the Internet, which support an ever-shifting range of communication environments. Having already radically altered and hybridized many working processes, what does the digital future offer the fashion and textile sectors? The next generation of computing technology promises to be enticing, ambitious and unimaginably powerful.

Coded material

The industrial-design technique of rapid-prototyping, or digital fabrication, was originally developed towards the end of the twentieth century to aid engineers by removing both the hand-making and manufacturing processes from the product-design equation. The technology has inevitably filtered into fashion design, and 3D products can now be machine-produced directly from a data file via computer numerical control (CNC) milling or three-dimensional printing processes. CNC milling is a reductive process, digitally carving from

a block of material, such as wood or metal, while 3D printing processes include stereo-lithography, which combines laser and liquid photopolymer to print 3D forms (similar to ink-jet printing) and selective laser-sintering (SLS), in which 3D models are built up using coloured synthetic powder (available in an array of colours), printed in the desired form and fused by an adhesive solution.

Product designers Janne Kyttänen and Jiri Evenhuis of Freedom of Creation pioneered the use of these processes, investigating, for example, the 3D printing of textile forms using SLS. Such research has produced chain mail-like material, configured into clothing and accessories such as their *V_bag* (ill. below). Collaborating with Kyttänen, Philip Delamore at the London College of Fashion progressed this idea by working on the digital manufacture of finer mesh-like links in order to achieve more complex 3D wearable structures, such as gloves.

Currently, rapid-prototyping material outputs appear aesthetically quite plastic and solid; it is likely that the next stage of development will refine the printing media so that they are more robust and capable of finer, more fluid constructions. This

Freedom of Creation,
V_bag, 2005

Kyttänen and Evenhuis fabricated a malleable, cloth-like material consisting of 3D printed links, assembled like chain mail. This results in a lucrative substrate for smaller artefacts, a precursor to future 3D fabrication media, which is likely to become more fluid, textile-like and sustainable.

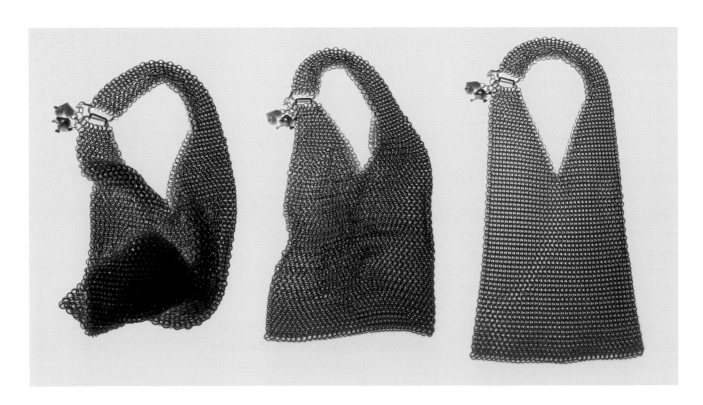

may in time even offer a manufacturing advance from the Shima Seiki computerized flat-knitting machine, which produces complete garment forms in one piece, or the digital construction tooling employed by Issey Miyake (see pp. 94–99) for A-POC. The invention of such flexible, sustainable materials is dramatically altering design, construction and printing processes, with the traditional methods of working with textiles becoming obsolete. Buying cloth by the metre to be tailored into bespoke garments, necessitating hours of fittings, is being replaced by fully dimensional clothing and accessories that can be quickly made to order, with integrated fastening systems or even their own packaging, at the push of a button.

The advantages to the small-scale designer, who cannot compete with the low costs of overseas production, and to the planet in terms of waste reduction

and sustainability, are clear. This type of production also offers more control to the consumer, who can engage collaboratively in the design process – an idea explored by Hamish Morrow, whose CoutureLab website offers 3D CAD-modelled jewelry with three different purchasing options, and by product designer Lionel Theodore Dean, whose own FutureFactories website shows pre-modelled CAD forms that can be morphed on screen via bespoke generative software, thus creating a number of different versions of an original design. While observing a form in transition, the consumer can pause to select the changing artefact at any point and have it digitally printed. With alteration options for shape, scale, surface and colour, this concept may be applied to the rapid 'making' of anything, forever altering the relationship between designer, consumer and product.

J. Morgan Puett and Mark Dion, *RN: The Past, Present and Future of the Nurse's Uniform*, 2003–4

A computer-generated diagram, created in collaboration with Iain Kerr, for one of four proposed nurse's uniforms, the 'Diagnostic Nurse' (c. 2027). The uniform features a range of bio-sensing functions, including touch-driven, biometric and acupoint sensors, enabling the nurse and patient to respond and adapt to ever-changing situations and circumstances. This work was created for the Fabric Workshop and Museum, Philadelphia.

Code and generative-system design offer limitless tools for design solutions. Given parameters, code can have in-built strategies that can digitally populate surface and space with pattern and form. Because it can be challenging to work with, programmers have developed software such as Automake, by Justin Marshall and Ertu Unver, which uses randomly generated 3D matrices to allow maker and consumer to co-design without any experience of code. Software that is developed in a public, collaborative manner is known as 'open-source', which itself has become a metaphor for ethical access to code innovation. This kind of access allows the user to develop it, change it, use it and share it, unencumbered by interfaces that mechanize the creative process. The capability of programming languages is infinite, and the freedom to utilize the full potential of a language, outside of commercial

constraints, is vital to those who are passionate about the potential of code.

The British band Radiohead decided to open-source the music video for their single, 'House of Cards' (ill. above and opposite), and the data was released, in collaboration with Google, using a Creative Commons license (an evolving digital-rights management system), which meant that anyone could fashion their own version. In the video, a moving cloud of digitized points of light, seemingly moulded to singer Thom Yorke's otherwise invisible head, follows his facial movements and suggests a fluid and responsive surface. The phosphorescent-like data, gathered without the use of conventional cameras or lighting rigs, seems vibrant and alive. Data-gathering technology is, in fact, already in common use, from smartphones to digital cameras. Using GPS technology, people can 'draw' their journeys,

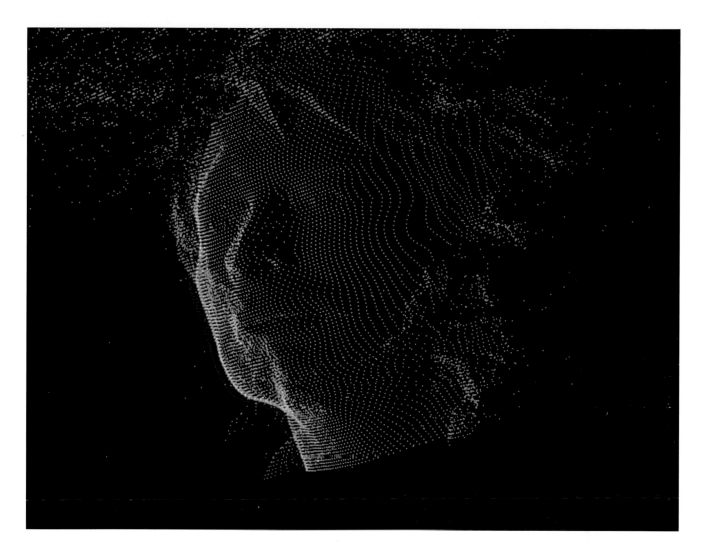

feeding the meta-tagging data back to their
computers, while miniature cameras produce
images that can be similarly meta-tagged
with location, time and date information.
The technology itself becomes a creative
source for the design of the future.

Meta skins
It would seem that fabric itself is becoming
digitally composed and data driven. *RN: The
Past, Present and Future of the Nurse's Uniform* (ill.
p. 211), an installation by J. Morgan Puett and
Mark Dion, in collaboration with the Fabric
Workshop and Museum in Philadelphia,
featured four proposed uniforms that
anticipated a world in which bio-sensing,
touch-driven sensors are the norm, and fibre
and fabric technology is ultra-sensitive and
can constantly access updated information.
In Austria, the data-visualization project
News Knitter (ill. p. 214) by Ebru Kurbak and

Mahir M. Yavuz of the Interface Culture Lab,
University of Art and Design Linz, consisted
of ten sweaters, produced on a Shima Seiki
flat-knitting machine, on which were printed
patterns that originated from live data
streams of news. Two software processes were
used: one to receive the online data, and the
second to convert it into visual patterns.

Wearable computers are now a reality,
whereas not long ago they were thought of
as the kind of science fiction portrayed in 2001:
A Space Odyssey (1968), which showed garments
with embedded wireless communication
devices. The potential of wearable computing
was initially explored by the military and
academia, but soon mere possibility became
reality, and technology developed to allow for
flexible boards and miniaturized components,
with items such as wireless laptops and
digital personal organizers incorporated into
garments and accessories. The commercial

Radiohead,
'House of Cards'
music video, 2008
Directed by James Frost

Geometric Informatics
technology was used to
capture the singer's head in
motion, while a Velodyne
Lidar scanner data-captured
the landscape of West Palm
Beach, Florida. Once collated,
the data was made available
to the public, so individuals
could create their own
version of the beguiling 360°
visual. The web, open-source
programming and the
Creative Commons culture
is generating a new kind of
dialogue between designer
and audience.

Ebru Kurbak
and Mahir M. Yavuz,
News Knitter, 2007

News Knitter (below)
demonstrates how live
data becomes physically
manifest in fabric form.
The project employed jersey
knit as an alternative screen
on which to host live data
from news on the Internet.

CuteCircuit,
Hug Shirt, 2002

The *Hug Shirt* (above)
effects the sensation
of being hugged over
a distance. Through sensors
embedded in the fabric, the
recipient feels the sensation
of touch from the sender,
who may also be wearing
a shirt or sending a 'hug'
via a mobile phone.

success of computer couture has largely been illusory, owing initially to cumbersome hardware and cost, but small companies like CuteCircuit, headed by Francesca Rosella and Ryan Genz, are proving that with innovation, good design and tenacity, wearable computing has a future. Their garments, including the award-winning *Hug Shirt* (ill. opposite, right), operate as dynamic interfaces around the body, connecting people and places. As hardware becomes ever-more invisible, designers can prioritize functionality, comfort and beauty.

Contemporary e-textiles are becoming increasingly intuitive and interactive, as responsive elements are embedded into fabric and triggered by sensors. Photonic fibres, made up into textile forms and linked to microcomputers, will enable changes in colour and pattern, depending on conditions such as light, temperature and stress impacts. As textiles metamorphose into screens, they become even more versatile as a surface for 3D forms. Scientist and inventor Susumu Tachi is among those who have been experimenting in the development of this kind of technology. For *Optical Camouflage* (ill. right, above and below), Tachi designed a jacket made from retro-reflective material. A camera takes images of what is immediately behind the wearer, and sends the photographs via computer to be projected onto the front of the garment, thus rendering the person almost invisible. As computing power increases and the data generated by individuals becomes harnessed, carried on almost invisible hardware components to the point of being practically fluid, it is becoming possible to embed micro-gadgetry in our clothing, and potentially into our very being – a concept that was once kept firmly to the realms of science fiction.

Alongside the computational potential of the skin of our bodies, the skin of our habitat is also being redefined. Architecture has been the most forward-thinking design sector when it comes to the adoption of computer processes for drawing, modelling and visualization, and CAD/CAM tools can now facilitate the creation of 'futurescapes', in which it is possible for digital fabrication to achieve new kinds of physical form without any structural inhibition. Computational architecture has given rise to a new fluid aesthetic (as seen in the buildings of Zaha Hadid and Frank Gehry), in which concrete and steel can take on the appearance of cut and draped cloth. Interactivity and in-built sensory controls are becoming part of the modern architect's vocabulary, as futuristic membranes are developed that are smart, responsive, shape-changing and functional.

One such intuitive membrane is *HypoSurface* (ill. p. 216), a smart display system

Susumu Tachi,
Optical Camouflage,
2003

To make the wearer seem almost invisible, imagery of the view immediately behind is captured on video, relayed through a computer, and projected onto the front of the coat. The garment is made from a retro-reflective material that bounces the imagery straight back to its source, allowing the image to be readable even in daylight conditions.

that behaves like a digitally controlled liquid,
moving in waves, patterns, logos, even text.
In its current form, its component parts are
delicate but visible platelets; the aim is to
incorporate biotechnology principles into
this mechanically articulated screen surface,
creating a responsive skin that could clad
an entire building. Parametric modelling
methods are used to create highly conceptual,
seemingly improbable surfaces and forms.
Additional scripting and programming,
combined with data on environmental and
structural characteristics, will influence
how an algorithm will run; as the algorithm
evolves to become the design tool, the
conventional role of the designer alters.

For practitioners like architect and
programmer Michael Hansmeyer, open-
source software (such as Processing) provides
a coherent and accessible language for
the realization of innovative architectural
environments. Through his explorations
into self-generating forms, Hansmeyer
implements relatively simple procedures

to create intricate and diverse structures,
composed of complex subdivisions
(ill. opposite and p. 208). Their multiple
surfaces define an aesthetic that is both
unique and potentially flexible. What now
seems almost impossible to build, at least in
the traditional sense, may yet become viable
as computer-simulation programs improve
our ability to test complex forms, and in the
longer term advance digital fabrication or
3D printing techniques. When combined with
emerging material science, these processes
will realize otherwise intangible concepts.

Mette Ramsgard Thomsen, director of
the Centre for Information Technology and
Architecture, Copenhagen, explores the
dynamic intersections between architecture
and digital technology, as well as tactile,
material and malleable approaches to
the design and construction of habitats.
Using a camera interface, *Sea Unsea* (2006),
an interactive dance/architecture piece
conceived by Thomsen and choreographer
Carol Brown, has both performers and public

drawing out movement patterns informed by nature (swarming insects, shifting seas and blossoming flowers). A room-size installation, *Slow Furl* (ill. p. 218), examines the use of pliable material technology as a reactive shape, or 'assemblage', in architecture. Formed of a pliable, tactile skin, this intelligent membrane shape-shifts slowly, over long periods of time, forming a subtle dialogue with those that inhabit the associated space.

Data touch

Textiles, with their variable characteristics of weight, solidity and softness, present a particular challenge to interactive haptic technology. Touchability is central to fabric's physical appeal, but the digital creation of touch and texture is complex, reliant on individual interpretation and sensory experience. The development of haptic tools to facilitate 3D computer-graphic modelling is evolving towards convincing sensory devices that emulate the 'touch' of a range of materials. If fully achievable, such technology would prove invaluable for shopping and gaming online, and enhancing the museum experience. Digital textile simulation, for example, could enable the virtual handling of a historic garment that is hidden away from the deteriorating effects of physical touch (see Jane Harris; pp. 126–31).

Commercially available software such as FreeForm from Sensable provides a 3D-modelling and hand-held tool system that enables the recognition of a virtual object and its surface as if it were a physically present form. A digitized feeling of touch is fed directly to the hand as it works the digital tool, a sophisticated pen-like mouse, while it engages with the computer-generated form. The sensation is as yet a little robotic and strange, but nonetheless effective. The Tacitus Project, based at the Edinburgh College of Art, explored the role of haptics in the CG modelling experience. Researchers developed new methods of analysis, incorporating, for example, the sound of making associated with human–object interaction, and how sound informs the decision-making processes of a maker. Developing a means of believably digitizing this information will serve to improve the haptic experience.

Just as the believable 3D modelling of fabric has proved particularly complex, simulating the feel and very materiality of textiles has posed further challenges. HapTex (2004–7), a project from the MIRAlab group at the University of Geneva, successfully integrated a tactile interface with visual representations of virtual textiles, enabling the user to 'feel' the virtual garment form. The visual simulation and the haptic rendering were based on the physical properties of the simulated textile, taken from measurements of real textiles using the Kawabata Evaluation System, making it

Michael Hansmeyer, *Subdivided Pavilions*, 2006

Hansmeyer's initial subdivision studies used a cubic frame as an input. The subdivision process then determines the shape of each of the 150,000 faces, their colour and transparency. The computer program was written in Processing, and rendered in Autodesk Maya 3D computer-graphics software.

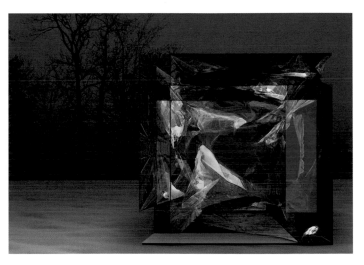

possible for the user to identify, by 'touch', different computer-generated fabrics.

Click2Touch was another interface concept that aimed to create the 'feel' of a range of textiles through visualization and touch reflection. Using the mouse or touchscreen technology to handle the fabric, the user would choose between different texture options: smoothness, stretch, creasing, hairiness, softness, fullness, prickliness, drape, thickness, elasticity and rigidity. Thickness, for example, may be visually denoted by the lifting and dropping of cloth to convey its weight, and the effect of hairiness achieved by stroking the digitized material and seeing fibres move. The realization of haptic interaction with real-time animated textiles remains complex, and the technical advancements that would facilitate it fully remain, for now, in the future. A system that is capable of conveying a full range of fabrics, with all their subtleties, would provide a radical shift in the way fabric is modelled and constructed in a 3D environment, and achieve an effective remote design system between maker and manufacturer.

Physical interaction with digital media will be a key driver in determining our future design experiences. The mouse has maintained pole position as the primary interaction tool for almost forty years without much competition, but most laptops now operate without a mouse,

and touchscreen technology is changing even further the conventional use of desktop computers. Hand-held devices such as Apple's pioneering iPhone and iPad very quickly illustrated the commercial potential for touchscreen technology, as did Nintendo's Wii, operated using gaming technology via movement sensors and controlled by the body's motion in space.

San Francisco-based artist and designer Rachel Beth Egenhoefer conceptually works with code, digital hardware and analogue material processes to explore our physical engagement with computers, and the space or interface between body and machine (see *Space Between*; ill. opposite). Collaborating with scientist Kyle E. Jennings, Egenhoefer coded her own version of a Wii game, *KNiiTTiiNG*, in which the controls take on the role of knitting needles, with the result of both teaching the user how to knit and allowing gaming technology to become the interface to link with traditional craft skills.

Multi-touch technology has been around as a concept since the mid-1980s, and most famously appeared as the beguiling interface of the future in the film *Minority Report* (2002). Set in 2054, in Washington, DC, the film shows 'pre-crime' officer John Anderton operating a vast, curved glass screen; wearing data gloves, his hands travel across it at great speed, without actually touching the surface. The screen is responsive, as imagery, film and data reports appear at his fingertips.

Mette Ramsgard Thomsen, *Slow Furl*, 2008; *Reef Pattern*, 2008

As visitors approach and move alongside *Slow Furl* (below, left), the material membrane moves imperceptibly, creating new cavities and spaces. The wall is formed by its very slow action, reacting to human presence and interaction. *Reef Pattern* (below, right), created in the same year, investigates the forming of sheet material in architecture, using hybridized 3D modelling and pattern-cutting techniques.

Text and images zoom in and out, discarding and collating evidence, visually compiling the past, present and future. This concept is quickly emerging as a design tool, enabling fast thinking and collaborative design processes, in one space and across distance.

The intuitive Microsoft Surface computing platform similarly recognizes hand gestures, touch and physical objects, and enables multi-interface computer use. Wireless phones and cameras connect to the 'surface' without any plugging-in, so that images can be linked together or transferred seamlessly from one device to another, simply via their placement on the table top-like screen. Fingers become drawing and painting tools as they sweep across the screen, advancing the digital experience of drawing and painting from previously rigid, pen-like tools to something more sensitive and fluid. Using concepts such as remote desktop access (now more usually employed by computer companies to repair or reinstall software), collaborative design practices are evolving as processing power facilitates more live or real-time image-based communication.

Digital consumer
As early as 1996, multimedia artist and designer Pia Myrvold understood the commercial and environmental potential of digital printing for fashion. Having launched Clothes as Publishing, a project for which artists, writers, musicians and architects were invited to print text and images onto clothing, in 2000 she set up Cybercouture, an interactive website that allowed the customization of a digitally printed dress. The website introduced sound, images, film and text to the digital presentation of finished collections, along with the instruction that consumers undergo 3D body scans and email their measurements – an early form of bespoke cyber couture. Another fashion innovator was Thierry Mugler, who in 1998 first experimented with the idea of a virtual fashion show, using Vicon motion-capture systems in combination with very early 3D cloth-animation software (supplied by REM Infografica ClothReyes) to achieve the motion-data of a moving model. Mugler oversaw the CG construction of a simple signature dress form; colour and pattern variations were also built into the design. That same year, Helmut Lang also shunned the traditional catwalk for a live Internet broadcast, via his newly launched website, for his Autumn/Winter 1998–99 collection.

In even earlier experiments with computer couture, MIRAlab has been researching the possibilities of digitally dressing an avatar, virtual actor or model since 1989. Founded by Nadia Magnenat-Thalmann, the Swiss group initiated the development of virtual catwalk systems and e-commerce for fashion and textiles. The design and manufacture of clothing is attracting investment in digital

Rachel Beth Egenhoefer, *Space Between*, 2008

Created in collaboration with Jon Buck of the University of Brighton, *Space Between* comprised a 3D resin cast that depicted the space between the body and the computer. The transparency of the resin material enables a view of an otherwise intangible relationship in the round.

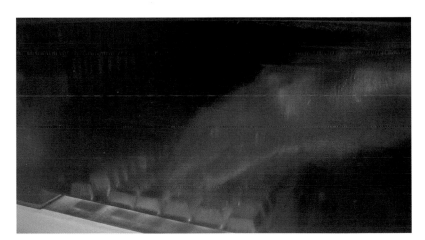

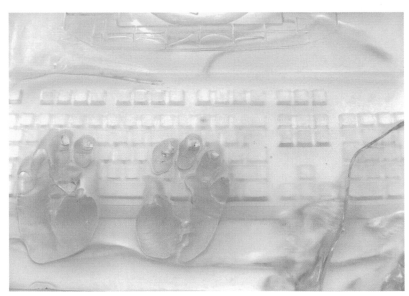

technology in order to become faster and more flexible in delivering knowledge-driven production, with re-engineering and data-driven intelligent automation informing future customization processes of the final garment.

The realistic rendering of moving fabric has challenged the capabilities of most software development and, until recently, processing power. The believable digital portrayal of the subtle differentiations between a tight or loose fit, or of a silhouette embellished with pockets, linings, buttons and zips remains complex. Various types and gauges of knit, different weave structures, and printed, stitched, manipulated, coated, lacquered, chemical or heat-treated finishes all need to be convincingly conveyed. The digital visualization of the transformation of fabric to garment involves 2D cloth manipulation, 3D modelling, and the communication of the garment cut and underlying body shape – even the effect of air and gravity in digital space contribute to the final form. Textures can be 2D-scanned or digitally constructed, and then virtually projected and positioned onto the 3D object.

The mechanics of motion and the articulation of the body greatly enhance the overall visual, and are best achieved using motion capture of real human-movement data to implant into the digital garment form. Computing has had much to achieve in order for it to appear truly viable, but there is now enormous scope. Smaller fashion design houses are taking their shows away from the catwalk, and we can distinctly see the evolution of CG animation and the Internet as valuable tools for the fashion designer. A digital technician on the design team could provide new methods of exploring cloth and 3D form in a live presentation context.

In *Minority Report*, data emitting from John Anderton's body as he walks through a large shopping mall seems to trigger responses from billboards that are programmed to know the names, interests and habits of passers-by. As real-time and network computing connect personalized information from bank accounts to shopping preferences, this kind of public interaction will become less confined to the realms of fiction. Online shopping is now accompanied by a hyper-realistic, digital impression of the virtual high street, with film and gaming technology employed to make the experience credible and pleasurable. Established sites include the customizable Virtual Mall, in which shoppers can organize the layout of their 'malls' according to personal taste, and Near London, which brings over six hundred traders from the chaos of the West End high street to the comfort of one's living room. But the Internet is more than a digital retail tool – designers, stylists and writers also view it as a visual forum, in which to consider new ideas and engage creatively with unrestricted audiences.

In 2004, fashion designer Martin Margiela provided a new experience in co-designing with a live event hosted by SHOWstudio. Margiela posted a pattern for a simple but incomplete shift dress, inviting anyone to contribute to the design; the results were then exhibited on the SHOWstudio website. Alexander McQueen, Hussein Chalayan, Ann-Sofie Back and London-based brand Swash were also among the designers invited to participate. In the website's virtual space, fashion becomes an interactive communication tool, providing connectivity and a unique kind of fashion democracy in a rapidly changing arena. This type of two-way communication is instilling co-design principles, and small studio-based groups can engage in intriguing dialogues with an unlimited audience through movies, live competitions, blogs, virtual worlds and, of course, mobile communication. The landscape of fashion engagement is rapidly shifting.

Buying clothes remains for most people, however, a direct and sensory experience that involves a number of decisions, from

As the breathtaking finale to McQueen's Paris Fashion Week show, model Kate Moss appeared to float above the catwalk at a time when she (for legal reasons) was unable to leave the UK. In reality, Moss's 'appearance' was due to a 3D holographic effect, created by Dick Straker of the visual effects company Mesmer.

looking at the cut, handling and gauging the weight of the fabric, trying the garment on, and viewing the entire effect. The realistic CG imaging of soft, flexible materials is incredibly complicated, and in this respect the fashion world faces certain challenges – including the 'virtualization' of the self – that do not exist to the same extent in other design sectors. While it is currently possible to create a 3D computer-graphic model of ourselves, there are anomalies within us that ensure we are not akin to our digital double: a 'perfect' image of our imperfect selves is somewhat disconcerting. This is where the avatar comes into its own – while the generally accurate form and proportions of oneself may be viewed while 'trying on' clothes during an online shopping experience, some distance can be achieved by the selection of, for example, a different face or hair. As the digital rendering of human simulation becomes more believable, this solution may be a possible compromise.

Three-dimensional models of the virtual self also enable consumers to visualize the design of a garment in digital form, pre-production. Smart cards are used to order made-to-measure clothing online, and to ensure data security. One such system is Bodymetrics, which uses body-scanning booths to provide accurate measurements. Initially offering made-to-measure jeans from fashion designer Tristan Webber's 'Digital Couture' line (2005), the concept provides a unique retail experience that works particularly well for fitted garments, such as suits and jeans. Expensive in comparison to the average high-street purchase (one pair of customized jeans costs several hundred pounds, with a four-week turnaround), the argument for the cost-effectiveness of this kind of technology is levied at bespoke tailoring, and the idea that the average woman buys many pairs of jeans in the quest for the perfect fit. This process provides not only the elusive fit, but also less waste for the sustainability conscious.

The ultimate goal is to achieve advanced infrastructures for virtual retailing services that provide custom-made clothing. The precise 3D measurements afforded by body scanning means that, after receiving the information, perhaps by email, the designer or manufacturer can then make up the selected garment without the need for fittings. E-manufacturing initiatives for design and retail are appearing, and, unlike early software models, companies are monitoring the progress of these developments. C-Design and OptiTex currently provide the most accessible industry-standard fashion software, with the latter offering a 3D computer-graphic construction and visualization system that allows designs to be viewed on an avatar.

Visually, this is still a very different experience to shopping on the high street. Now that consumers have Internet access via smartphones, they can bypass the high street altogether and buy entire wardrobes online. Bespoke this is not, but the practice of e-commerce, particularly in relation to fashion, is embedded in this technology-driven culture. With 3D body-scanning measurements to hand and ready access to the web, it is not difficult to imagine how the customization of mass-market fashion will evolve, especially in countries such as China and India, where the technology uptake is accelerating.

Future worlds

Augmented reality, a visualization and communication tool, blends real-world and digitally generated imagery into live footage, in real time. Eventually, motion-tracking techniques, marker recognition and the construction of controlled environments may offer new approaches to co-creation processes. For his 'Widows of Culloden' collection (Autumn/Winter 2006–7; ill. p. 221), Alexander McQueen presented a low-tech augmented-reality effect based on the illusionary principles of the nineteenth-century technique, 'Pepper's Ghost'. At the finale of the catwalk show, a life-sized 3D hologram of model Kate Moss was projected, appearing through a billowing trail of rippling chiffon. Moss then appeared to metamorphose into an indistinguishable form, and vanish into the ether before an enraptured audience.

Italian fashion company Diesel also used this relatively low technology for their Spring/Summer 2008 collection (ill. below), to portray a CG-animated virtual journey through time, a future 3D realm of interplanetary forms, luminescent giant pods and aquatic beasts, which interacted with the action on the catwalk throughout the show. Augmented reality enables fashion collections to be presented simultaneously in 3D form in different venues across the globe. True 3D imaging in space is evolving, and requires an intricate combination of camera and laser technology. In time, the 'on-screen' experience is likely to be fully three-dimensional, 360° in real space, without the need for a monitor.

Brain–computer interfacing is an accelerating science, and offers control mechanisms that merge the relationship between humans and machines. Currently, the technology enables the opening of doors, switching lights on and off, operating phones and controlling specially designed robots. Interfaces that are driven by the power of thought promise new experiences for users, and to enhance those of people with disabilities. This kind of interface will link gaming technology with augmented reality, and will be more broadly linked to a range of entertainment, theatre and cinema. In years to come it might even be possible to capture creative thought as it evolves, to be disseminated in some physical form on the computer screen.

The concept of being physically inside computer space was an inspirational one for William Gibson, the prophetic author of *Neuromancer* (1984), who coined the word 'cyberspace'. In an interview with Tim Adams of *The Observer* in 2007, Gibson recalled the video arcades of the early 1980s, and being 'struck by the idea that the kids pushing the buttons wanted, more than anything, to be on the other side of the screen'. Two years before the publication of *Neuromancer*, Disney

had released one of its riskiest feature-film ventures, *Tron* (ill. p. 209). Inspired by director Steve Lisberger's experience of video games, *Tron* explored digital media as tools with which to convey one of the earliest imaginings of what it might be like to be inside the otherwise invisible workings of a computer. The storyline explored associated digital experiential ideas and visual effects, including immersive worlds, real-time gaming and virtual space.

The film was groundbreaking on many levels, not least because it was a huge departure from Disney's established style. It also included some of the earliest computer effects, the cost of which contributed to the $20,000,000 budget – enormous by 1980s standards – and resulted in only fifteen to twenty minutes of actual digital footage. The product of a collaboration with the four leading computer-graphics firms of the day, *Tron* was celebrated as a milestone by the computer-animation industry. Traditional film techniques were augmented by numerous new processes employed to create the 'computer aesthetic', which generated greater workloads than conventional cell animation, and consequently were never used again. Ironically *Tron*, the first commercial film to use digital media, was refused a nomination for special effects, because at the time using a computer was seen as cheating. But the film's influence has been lasting and wide-ranging; nearly thirty years later, Disney released *Tron: Legacy* (2010), effectively illustrating the longevity of computing in film.

New worlds, whether on land or in outer space, have had an enduring fascination. The desire to believably portray the physical world in a virtual space, in real time, continues to challenge the technical and aesthetic capabilities of digital media. As processing power increases, and we become more accustomed to engaging with computer-graphic gaming technology, it is perhaps easier to envisage creative potential in live digital space as an extension of our physical experiences. Hardware capabilities, cost and the high expectations of computing, particularly in the early 1990s, have to some extent limited how virtual space has evolved. The gaming, entertainment, medicine and military sectors have dominated real-time developments, with attention levied upon technical innovation. Surprisingly little aesthetic advance has been made regarding real-time spatial development since 2000, perhaps due to the dot.com crash and shifting research and development trends. The potential for the design of virtual spaces remains wide open, and judging by the success of the real-time gaming market alone, there is much yet to exploit.

Real-time technology has taken a while to evolve into an accessible form. In the early 1990s, software developer Softimage was one of the few companies that made graphics tools for artists. At a time when technical developments were considered key to commercial success, Softimage sought a level of creative engagement in the development of code that would parallel aesthetic objectives. Char Davies, the company's director of visual research and an artist herself, created 'immersive virtual reality environments', which operated in real time. *Osmose* (ill. opposite), in particular, was considered revolutionary, and illustrated the untapped potential between artist and computer. Immersive experiences are commonly accompanied by joysticks, data gloves and cumbersome headwear, but with *Osmose*, the experience of immersion is determined by sensory devices on the body that, unusually, monitor breathing. A feeling akin to diving underwater is achieved, offering similar manoeuvres, such as the facility to accelerate and slow down. This experience alone has had a profound emotional effect on those emerging from *Osmose*'s virtual space back into the physical world.

Previously, the aim of those making virtual reality worlds had been to make

Char Davies,
Subterranean Earth and
Tree Pond, digital stills
from *Osmose*, 1995

Richard Brown,
Mimesia, 2004

Osmose (opposite) is an immersive real-time virtual environment with a highly considered aesthetic, developed using 3D modelling and animation by Softimage, on a Silicon Graphics Onyx, the most powerful supercomputer at the time.

Brown applied a painterly aesthetic to *Mimesia* (above), a real-time virtual world. Using head gestures, the viewer navigates the space via an IntelligentCamera interface, which is rendered using Games Engine Technology.

digital realms look 'real'; early results were often slightly crude. *Osmose* deliberately crossed realism with abstraction to achieve something that was believable, although not 'real'. Nature was portrayed as delicately constructed layers of transparency, translucency, light, particles and water; the 'immersant' navigated through a series of spaces that included a clearing, a forest, a pond, an abyss and fog. Appropriately, the final space was composed of code. *Osmose*'s feat was to challenge what could be experientially and visually accomplished, using real-time computing as a medium. Davies's work remains a benchmark for virtual-reality environments today.

Mimesia (ill. p. 225) by Richard Brown is a 'dream-like, hyper-real artificial world', built using gaming technology. Brown applied a distinctive painterly quality to his work, which, he says, is not a film (there is no story), or a game (there is no quest). Instead, *Mimesia* is an interactive painting that unfolds in a story-less narrative. Brown borrowed from painting, film and gaming to produce a work that incorporates aspects of all three, and yet is completely different. This new approach to graphic-based, real-time spaces coincided with the rising popularity and commercial success of interactive virtual worlds, of which *Second Life*, developed by Linden Lab, and *Entropia Universe*, by MindArk, both launched in 2003, are the most accessible and established.

The explosion of simpler and accessible real-time graphic spaces would appear to have eclipsed the rich and considered cultural realms of *Osmose* and *Mimesia*. *Second Life*, for example, has evolved into and currently remains an environment most used for commercial, social and educational purposes. In these virtual worlds, the principles of gaming, costume and fashion come together to define new online markets. Designers exploring these alternative modes of operation have found that the concept of developing forms for digital spaces,

Vexed Generation
for *Entropia Universe*,
2006

Adam Thorpe and Joe Hunter unusually relocated their design operation in the real world to a virtual one. Virtual clothing for dressing avatars is proving to be a commercially lucrative sector in real-time spaces such as *Second Life* and *Entropia Universe*.

which will only ever exist virtually, can be challenging. Almost everything within these environments is created with the internal building and scripting tools provided. 'Residents', or users, have the option to consume 'off the shelf', create and customize their own environment, objects, clothing and identity. The 'freeholders' of these virtual online spaces allow their subscribers to retain the intellectual property rights to all that they construct, so that practitioners can fully exploit the commercial potential of whatever they choose to make.

Among the designers who have recognized the potential of this form of commercial practice are Adam Thorpe and Joe Hunter of Vexed Generation. In 2006, they repositioned their already internationally recognized operation from the real world to a virtual one (*Entropia Universe*). While no longer trading from physical premises, the pair have found that their designs are highly coveted in the digital environment. *Entropia Universe* has become a successful commercial arena in which designers can sell their wares; in 2004 and 2008, it achieved world records for producing the most expensive virtual-world objects ever sold. Digital garments (ill. opposite) are purchased via users' avatars or online personas, with social 'spaces' (for clubbing, for example) providing the incentive to create new guises and different identities, and thus purchase digital couture.

Design colleges around the world are exploring virtual worlds and real-time spaces for the development of new design and communication methods, particularly in the architecture and built-environment sectors. The scripting tools that facilitate the building of basic virtual forms have a tendency to lend themselves to solid-object modelling. The subject areas of fashion and textiles are more challenging to portray. *Second Life Island* (ill. right) hosted an installation that featured the work of the Textile Futures Research Centre, a collaborative whose members are drawn from Central Saint Martins, Chelsea College of Art and Design and the London College of Fashion, as part of an investigation into the use of *Second Life* as a space for the communication and exhibition of fashion. These types of digital real-time spaces are, for many, simply a mirror reflecting how we already engage with the physical world. For some, they provide a space in which to exist in a completely different and freeing guise. The avatar-making process provides the chance to assume a new identity in any form the user purchases or designs for him or herself: animal, 'human' or hybrid. This can, in equal measure, be considered both intriguing and circumspect. The gap between the physical and digital worlds is narrowing, with sensory technology providing a means to merge the two, and designers are exploring what the distinct spaces have to offer in terms of human interaction, and how digital and analogue may work together to provide new modes of communication.

Artist and designer Tomoko Hayashi uses textile language as an interface for

Textile Futures Research Centre, *Second Life Island,* 2008

Curated and 3D constructed by Jane Harris, Caryn Simonson and Andrew Sides, this real-time installation was created from image components of members' individual works in the physical world. The resulting digitized pieces take on a new form in virtual space, transforming pattern, object or figurative images. Illustrated is the work of designers Rachel Wingfield, Garth Lewis, Becky Earley, Emma Neuberg, Philip Delamore and Melanie Bowles.

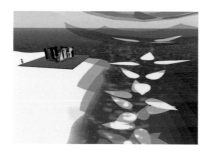

developing conceptual, technology-driven applications. Her work seeks to improve the connection and communication between two people who live at a distance from each other. One project, *Intimacy* (ill. p. 205) features undergarments with mementoes embedded in them, which three-dimensionally emboss the fine, transparent material. The intention is that before parting, one half of the couple removes a small object to keep, while the other partner holds the memory of the object in its embossed form. *Intimacy* is a concept piece that, while informed by digital communication, aims to counteract the pervasiveness of communication tools using more considered and desirable forms. Another work, *Mutsugoto* (ill. below and p. 207), offers an intimate interface for communication, bypassing email and text. A computer vision and projection tool enables a user, who is lying down, to draw the outline of his or her body. A remote

partner receives this seductive light drawing by digital transmission, and experiences the 'feeling' of the distant companion. The linear image can take many forms as the body changes position. Hayashi's sensitivity towards material languages, using tacit hand-making skills, contributes to new approaches in technology innovation.

As digital media become accessible, a number of key projects have evolved to illustrate how digital technology alters and enhances our everyday space, particularly in the home environment. *House_n* is an MIT project that has been running for over ten years, exploring new design strategies in this context, while *Curious Home*, part of the design project *Equator* from the Interaction Research Studio at Goldsmiths, University of London, considers what an emerging digital world has to offer beyond the computer. Bringing together artists, designers, social and computing scientists, *Curious Home*

Tomoko Hayashi, *Mutsugoto*, 2007

This project evolved into choreographic and performance concepts, which envisage invisible hardware and technology interfaces. Digital interaction is embedded, instinctive and intuitive, regardless of geography and time, with the human supplementing the computer.

reconsiders design methods, resulting in the creation of unique objects for the everyday. Philips Design regularly present research concepts on how the digital and physical worlds combined can be exploited to improve everyday engagements. Carole Collet and Tobi Schneidler's project *Remote Home, One Home, Two Cities* (2003) demanded that digital media and material processes were considered in unison. The project comprises two separate spaces, in two cities, which communicate through object and surface design, responding to human presence. Designed to overcome the difficulties of two people living remotely, the traditional boundaries of home are eroded by technology and craft interventions. Furnishings change shape or colour as these visual and tactile indicators imply the remote presence of a partner in a corresponding space. Textiles are a fundamental component to this work. It is unusual to see knitting, for example, alongside sensory devices, but this kind of analogue and digital partnership is an attempt to consider human emotion, and to counterbalance the isolationism of digital media.

With computing becoming ever more invisible and our progression into cyberspace showing no sign of abating, manual processes and emotional considerations become increasingly important and appealing. Knowledge of materials is still relevant in an emerging technology, helping to drive discerning decision-making processes. Traditional and advanced media are converging, and future computer-generated aesthetics are likely to be composed of both analogue and digital techniques. In *The Laws of Simplicity* (2006), John Maeda extols the virtues of simplicity in our complex, over-designed physical and digital worlds. As a pioneering designer of digital 'stuff', he had engaged in a highly productive relationship with computing technology, but his current mission is to rethink these earlier efforts. Maeda's

thoughts on simplicity are timely, as he explores coping strategies for the difficulties of a society that is driven by technology – one to which he has been a vital contributor.

The computer seems to simultaneously enlarge and narrow our environments. On the one hand, we are functioning in larger global contexts, but on the other we are working from home and in smaller work or creative communities. The hybrid 'office space' or 'studio', real or virtual, reaches into new arenas; collaboration is expanded through exchange and real-time online communication, with certain technology practices requiring collaboration to make them viable. While this state initially arose due to the complexities of computing, what has evolved is a cross-fertilization of science, engineering and design disciplines. The lone practitioner has given ground to many different types of creative partnership. Engineers working with designers have contributed to the development of programming and software languages over and above a creative objective that perhaps set the path. Ideas can be pooled and problems solved by communicating online, areas of research can be set up and creative solutions found. Artists and designers have taken more control of creative digital practice, and have become part of a global collaborative team.

In this era of invisible computing, the designer, maker and artist have quickly adopted new vocabularies, visual languages and codes to enable expansive commentary on our emerging lifestyles, desires or dreams. Digital media have provided revolutionary forms of creative expression through a myriad of methods, from the screen-based, with its abstractions and hyper-real macro and micro-scenarios, time-based, self-generating, fast-evolving imagery and media that have evoked consideration of new kinds of space and infinite zones, the potential future for which, in creative terms, is shifting, flexible, complex and unbounded.

biographies & histories

Mitsuko Akutsu
Textile artist

Akutsu studied industrial design at Tokyo National University of Fine Arts and Music, graduating in 1977. In 1999 she undertook a workshop at the Montreal Centre for Contemporary Textiles, working with Louise Lemieux Bérubé. She has exhibited her work extensively, with solo exhibitions at MCCT and Tokyo's Senbikiya Gallery and group shows in Canada and New York. Akutsu is a Professor at Aoyama Gakuin Women's Junior College in Tokyo.

Savithri Bartlett
Researcher and textile designer

Bartlett received her BA from Edinburgh College of Art (1992), an M.Phil from the Royal College of Art, London (1997) and a PhD from Loughborough University (2006). The results of her research at the RCA were applied to the creation of moulded hats for Chanel's Autumn/Winter 1997–98 collection. Bartlett has established a fruitful collaboration with avant-garde fashion label Boudicca, working on many of their collections, including 'Leave' (Spring/Summer 1998), 'Immortality' (Spring/Summer 1999), 'We Sell Disguises' (Autumn/Winter 2003–4), 'Performance' (Spring/Summer 2004) and 'Hunter Gatherer' (Autumn/Winter 2004–5). Bartlett is Senior Lecturer in fashion design at the University of Winchester.

Basso & Brooke
Fashion design label, established UK, 2002

Co-founders Christopher Brooke graduated from Kingston University, in Surrey, in 1995, receiving an MA from Central Saint Martins in 1997, and Bruno Basso studied journalism at Universidade Católica de Santos, Brazil, and advertising at the Universidade Santa Cecília, graduating in 2001. The pair won the prestigious London Fashion Fringe award in 2004. Soon after, they presented their first collection for London Fashion Week, 'The Succubus and Other Tales'.
www.bassoandbrooke.com

Markus Benesch
Industrial and interior designer

Benesch established his studio Marcus Benesch Creates in Münich in 1989, adding an office in Milan in 2001. He uses the digital at both the design and manufacture stages to transform bland spaces, such as offices and hotel corridors, and create imaginary settings for trade-fair stands. His 'Colourflage' collection makes use of the digital to blend furniture into the background by using similar colours and patterns; wallpaper, fabric and furniture are camouflaged, or 'colourflaged', by colour. Benesch and his team develop materials, products and interiors that engage the aesthetic and the sensorial with the functional. Clients include Abet Laminati, Benetton, Paul Smith and Memphis Milano. Benesch is a Visiting Professor at various design schools in Münich and Milan.
www.markusbeneschcreates.com

Hardy Blechman
Fashion designer

Blechman founded UK fashion label Maharishi in 1995, and is now the company's Creative Director and Head Designer. His previous experience was in international military and industrial clothing. Maharishi has its roots in workwear and military surplus, often incorporating digital camouflage patterning. Blechman is considered a worldwide expert on camouflage, its history and contemporary appropriation, and is the author of *DPM: Disruptive Pattern Material* (2004).
www.emaharishi.com

Blommers/Schumm
Photography studio, established Netherlands, 1996

After meeting while students at the Gerrit Rietveld Academie in Amsterdam, Anuschka Blommers and Niels Schumm have worked as a team on fashion, portrait and still-life photography. Their breakthrough came in 1997, when fashion designers Viktor & Rolf commissioned a photo shoot for *Purple* magazine. In 2006 they published *Anita and 124 Other Portraits*, which spanned ten years of collaboration. Their work has been included in numerous books and catalogues, as well as in leading fashion magazines.
www.blommers-schumm.com

Bodymetrics
Body-scanning company, established UK

Co-founder Suran Goonatilake received his BA in computing and artificial intelligence from the University of Sussex in 1989, followed by a PhD from University College London. Bodymetrics is a bespoke clothing system that uses 3D body-scanning technology to achieve the perfect fit, particularly for garments such as jeans, shirts and suits. In collaboration with PrimeSense, Bodymetrics is newly evolving as a virtual try-on system for clothing retail. The system is capable of creating a precise 3D model of the body, which 'wears' a selected item of clothing that has been mapped onto it and mimics body movement as an onscreen avatar.

Boredom Research
Digital design collaborative, established UK, 1996

Vicky Isley and Paul Smith both graduated in multimedia from Southampton Institute. In 2003 they completed 'Hello World', a year-long residency at ArtSway. Isley and Smith have produced interactive sound applications and computational soundscapes in the form of online projects, prints and generative objects, which have been exhibited internationally and showcased at such events as Ars Electronica, Data:Base and Electrohype, and within online exhibitions, including Soundtoys.net, E-2.org and Mobilegaze.com. Isley and Smith are currently Research Lecturers at the National Centre for Computer Animation, Bournemouth University.
www.boredomresearch.net

Philippa Brock
Textile designer

Brock graduated from Goldsmiths, University of London, in 1991, and the Royal College of Art in 1993. She was Senior Research Fellow at Winchester School of Art (1994–96), and served as consultant designer for the Taiwan Textile Federation, designing and producing twice-yearly fabric collections. Her work for the *Nobel Textiles* project, initiated by Carole Collet and the Medical Research Council, was exhibited in London (2008) and Haslach, Austria (2009), and as part of the Crafts Council's *Labcraft* exhibition (2010). Brock is currently Woven Textiles Specialist Subject Leader at Central Saint Martins.

Daniel Brown
Designer and artist

Brown specializes in the creative application of digital technology and interactive design. Through his company Play-Create, his client base is extensive and varied, and includes Nick Knight, Saatchi & Saatchi, *Dazed & Confused* magazine, Lady Gaga and the BBC. Acknowledged as a pioneer in the new media field and chosen as London Design Museum's Designer of the Year in 2004, he has since been named as one of the *Observer*'s '80 people who will define the next 10 years' and *Design Week*'s 'hottest 50 designers'. His original and experimental works are in the collections of the San Francisco Museum of Modern Art and the Victoria & Albert Museum, London.
www.danielbrowns.com, www.play-create.com

Richard Brown
Artist

Brown graduated with a BSc in computers and cybernetics and MA in fine art, and was a Research Fellow in computer-related design at the Royal College of Art (1995–2001). He received a two-year fellowship grant from the National Endowment of Science Technology and the Arts (2002), and was Honorary Senior Research Fellow at Victorian College of the Arts, Melbourne University (2002–3), and artist-in-residence at the Natural History Unit at the ABC and School of Informatics, University of Edinburgh (2005–8). Brown is the author of *Biotica: Art, Emergence and Artificial Life* (2001).
www.mimetics.com

James Bullen
Textile designer

Bullen graduated from the Royal College of Art in 1999, winning acclaim for his trompe-l'oeil printed textile collection, with designs that simulated pierced, slashed, buttoned and folded fabrics. His prints were subsequently applied to a wide range of accessories for fashion and interiors, a laminate range for Formica, and major projects such as the Merrill Lynch building in London. Bullen is a recipient of the Peugeot Design Award for Textiles, and continues to develop his digitally designed, 3D graphic illusionary prints.
www.jamesbullendesigns.co.uk

Hussein Chalayan
Fashion designer

After graduating from Central Saint Martins in 1993, Chalayan launched his own label in 1994. He was named British Fashion Designer of the Year in 1999 and 2000.

In 2001 his work was featured in the exhibitions *Century City* (Tate Modern) and *Radical Fashion* (Victoria & Albert Museum), and in 2009 his work was the subject of a major retrospective at the Design Museum, London. Acknowledged as one of fashion's most influential innovators, Chalayan was awarded an MBE in 2006, and in 2011 was named an Honorary Fellow of the London College of Fashion. He is the author of *Hussein Chalayan* (2011). www.husseinchalayan.com

Simon A. Clarke
Artist

Clarke graduated from Middlesex University in 1986, later receiving his MA (1987) and PhD (2005) from Birmingham City University. His work has been featured in international exhibitions, including *Artists at Work: New Technology in Textile and Fibre Art*, Prato Textile Museum, Italy (2003), and he has lectured at a number of institutions, including Kenyatta University, Kenya; Savannah College of Art and Design, Georgia; and Goldsmiths, University of London. An authority on African textiles, Clarke was Textile Fellow at the University of Plymouth at Exeter (1989–90) and is the author of *Textile Design* (2011). He is Senior Lecturer in printed textiles at University College Falmouth.

Malcolm Cocks
Textile designer

Cocks studied at Manchester Regional College of Art and the Central School of Art, London (later Central Saint Martins), receiving an MA in early computer imaging for printed textile design from the Royal College of Art in 1991. Cocks established the first computer studio in the school of fashion and textiles at Central Saint Martins, and coordinated the pioneering T_3Ph_2 research project (1993–97), which led to an exhibition at the Fashion Institute of Technology, New York, in 1999. A project with Warner & Sons and Eddie Squires resulted in six of the first entirely digitally designed and printed textiles, now in the collection of the Cooper-Hewitt National Design Museum in New York. Cocks is currently researching *Drawing with the Keyboard*, a project that involves fine-art printmaking from programming environments and landscape. www.csm.u-net.com/ph2_12.htm

Harold Cohen
Artist

Cohen studied and later taught painting at the Slade School of Fine Art, London (1961-65). He represented Great Britain in the Venice Biennale, and Documenta 3, and designed textiles for London department store Heal's, which are now in the collection of the Victoria & Albert Museum. In 1968 he visited the visual arts department at the University of California, San Diego, where he became a professor in 1971, director of the Center for Research in Computing and the Arts in 1992 and Emeritus Professor in 1994. A guest scholarship at Stanford University's Artificial Intelligence Lab (1973–75) led to the creation of the generative computer program AARON, the first artificial intelligence 'artist' (subsequent artworks have been attributed to AARON). Cohen's work is in numerous private and public collections,

including Tate Modern, the Arts Council of Great Britain and the British Council. www.aaronshome.com

Carole Collet
Textile designer

Collet established the MA Textile Futures course at Central Saint Martins in 2001, and has since implemented future thinking for resilient design in the textile-design sector. She has contributed to numerous international conferences and events on the subject of future textiles, technology and sustainable design practice. Collet has collaborated with Tobi Schneidler (notably on the project *Remote Home*), a designer who works between the physical and mediated worlds and is the co-founder of the Smart Studio, Interactive Institute, in Sweden. Collet's work has been exhibited at the Institute of Contemporary Art, Victoria & Albert Museum and the Science Museum, London. She is a Reader in textile futures and is Deputy Director of the Textile Futures Research Centre at Central Saint Martins. www.carolecollet.com

Rory Crichton
Illustrator and textile designer

Crichton received his BA from Glasgow School of Art in 1992. Now established as a freelance textile designer, his first clients included Prada, Missoni and Katherine Hamnett, and he has acted as consultant to such leading international brands, as Bottega Veneta, Gucci, Givenchy, Louis Vuitton **and, more recently,** Marc Jacobs and Giles Deacon. Crichton also created the illustration for Pulp's *We Love Life* album cover, and collaborated with Peter Saville Associates on publicity material for footwear brand Audley.

CuteCircuit
Fashion and design company, established UK, 2004

Based in London, CuteCircuit is a wearable technologies and interaction design firm, founded by fashion designer Francesca Rosella and artist and anthropologist Ryan Genz It was the first company to successfully merge wearable and telecommunication technologies into viable commercial products for the fashion, sport and communication industries. The duo's designs were featured at Wired NextFest in New York (2006) and Los Angeles (2007), and their *Hug Shirt* was nominated as one of *Time* magazine's 'best inventions of the year' in 2006. www.cutecircuit.com

Char Davies
Digital media artist

Davies received her PhD in new media philosophy from the Centre for Advanced Inquiry in the Interactive Arts, University of Plymouth, in 2005. Originally a painter, Davies transitioned to digital media in the late 1980s, and became a founding director of the 3D software company Softimage. Her virtual environment *Osmose* (1995) is considered a landmark in the history of new media art. She has also published numerous essays on virtual space. Davies is based in Quebec and San Francisco. www.immersence.com

Joshua Davis
Digital designer, artist and author

Having experimented with programming languages while a student at Brooklyn's Pratt Institute, Davis was an early pioneer in the use of Macromedia Flash. He has written a book about the program (*Flash to the Core*, 2002), and builds his own Flash-based programs to create generative imagery for online, commercial and public artworks. Davis was behind three influential websites (Once-upon-a-forest.com, Praystation.com and Dreamless.org), and counts Sony, Nokia and Motorola among his clients. His work has been exhibited at the Cooper-Hewitt National Design Museum, Tate Modern and the Centre Georges Pompidou. He is a Professor at the School of Visual Arts, New York. www.joshuadavis.com

Philip Delamore
Textile designer

Delamore graduated in 1990 from Cheltenham School of Art with a BA in fashion and printed textiles, followed by a diploma in computing for fine art in 1996. He has digitally created imagery, fabrics and artefacts for clients including Tristan Webber, Hamish Morrow, Gillian Wearing and Nutters Saville Row, and more recently MOU and Gareth Pugh. Current research looks at the impact of new and emerging technologies on the fashion industry. Delamore has given presentations at the Victoria & Albert Museum, the Institute of Contemporary Art, Stanford University and the Royal Institute, among others, and sits on advisory panels for university textile and fashion courses, as well as acting as a design innovation consultant for industry. Delamore is Senior Research Fellow and director of the Fashion Digital Studio, London College of Fashion.

Deuce Design
Design company, established Australia, 2000

Founded by Bruce Slorach, now its Creative Director, and Sophie Tatlow, Deuce Design is a multidisciplinary graphic design studio, which produces products that are both contemporary and culturally significant, from graphics for the public domain and environmental designs to branding, print, web, fashion and lighting. Slorach received his BA in fine art from the Victorian College of the Arts, University of Melbourne, and established fashion label Abyss Studio in the early 1980s. He has also worked as Creative Director at Mambo Graphics. An accomplished designer and visual artist, Slorach has had his works exhibited at the Victoria & Albert Museum, the National Gallery of Australia and the Powerhouse Museum in Sydney. www.deucedesign.com.au

Diesel
Fashion label, established Italy, 1979

Founded by Renzo Rosso, Diesel soon became known for its functional, edgy clothing in quality materials. Its first flagship store opened in New York in 1996. DieselStyleLab, a more experimental line for both men and women, was launched in 1998. Making use of the latest developments in technical textiles and finishing treatments, Diesel then adopts these techniques to create fashion collections

that have achieved a cult following. The company works closely with specialist textile mills, mixing traditional natural materials with the latest synthetics and combining inventive choices of materials with expert cutting and styling. Diesel has many stores worldwide, with the largest in Milan.
www.diesel.com

Hil Driessen
Textile designer
Driessen graduated from the Academy of Visual Arts, Maastricht, in 1990, and founded her design studio *De Textielkamer* in 1998. She has employed both digital print and computer-controlled Jacquard weave. In 2002 she was artist-in-residence at the European Ceramic Work Centre, in 's-Hertogenbosch, Netherlands. Driessen often collaborates with spatial designer Toon van Deijne, and they have worked together ever since their first exhibition at Galerie Ra, Amsterdam, in 2002, under the name Driessen + van Deijne. Their work has been featured in exhibitions at the Museum at the Fashion Institute of Technology, New York (2005), and the Rhode Island School of Design (2008).
www.hildriessen.com

Emily DuBois
Textile artist
DuBois graduated with a BFA from Rochester Institute of Technology, New York, in 1970, followed by an MFA from the California College of Arts and Crafts in 1980 and postgraduate studies at the Indian Institute of Handloom Technology, Varanasi. Her work has been exhibited at TNCA Gallery, Taiwan (2004); Renwick Gallery, Washington, DC (2005); the De Young Museum, San Francisco (2005); SOFA Chicago (2000, 2005 and 2011); Honolulu Academy of Arts, Hawaii (2011) and the Textile Museum, Washington, DC (2011); and in group shows at the Museum of Contemporary Art, Montreal (2000-3) and the Irish Craft Council (2005). Her most recent work has been a departure away from 2D pieces to encompass three dimensions, using sophisticated, digitally woven structures to enable one-off shaped textile works. DuBois has been based in Hawaii since 2002.
www.emilydubois.com

Warren du Preez
Designer
Du Preez and creative partner Nick Thornton Jones began their collaboration in 1998 through a shared fascination of the image-making process and the possibilities of combining analogue and emerging digital domains. Their distinctive approach in visual communication and experimentation has resulted in striking and highly original artworks and imagery, with clients that span the realms music, fashion and beauty. They have created editorials for *Numéro*, *i-D*, *Big* and *Dazed & Confused* magazines, and worked for numerous clients, including Lancôme, Shu Uemura, Issey Miyake, Cartier, Thierry Mugler, Pierre Cardin, Nike, Björk and Massive Attack. Their work has been exhibited at the Fondation Cartier, Paris and the National Portrait Gallery and Institute of Contemporary Arts, London.
www.wnstudio.tv

eBoy
Pixel art group, established Germany, 1997
Founded by Steffen Sauerteig and Svend Smital, both born in East Germany, and Kai Vermehr from Venezuela, the group is best known for its *eCity* project. Imagery from the series has been used for posters, T-shirts, jigsaw puzzles, and even on the back of a Dublin bus. As well as their own products, eBoy creates work for magazines, advertisements, websites, toys and games. The group has collaborated with fashion designer Paul Smith, Kidrobot, Adidas, Diesel, DKNY, Levi's, Nike, British Telecom, and many others.
www.hello.eboy.com/eboy

Rachel Beth Egenhoefer
Textile artist
Egenhoefer received her BFA from the Maryland Institute College of Art in 2002, and MFA from the University of California, San Diego, in 2004, where she was a graduate researcher at the Center for Research in Computing and the Arts. Her work has been exhibited at the Corcoran Gallery of Art, Washington, DC, the Banff Centre, Alberta, Canada, the Institute for Contemporary Art, London, and the Lighthouse in Brighton. Egenhoefer is currently Assistant Professor of Design, University of San Francisco.
www.rachelbeth.net

Eley Kishimoto
Fashion and textile label, established UK, 1996
Mark Eley studied weaving at Brighton Polytechnic, and Wakako Kishimoto received her BA and MA in fashion and print from Central Saint Martins. The London-based duo began working together in 1992, and their designs have graced the world's catwalks, via collaborations with Louis Vuitton, Marc Jacobs, Alexander McQueen, Alber Elbaz and Jil Sander. Their print designs have also been found on wallpaper, furniture, mobile phones and computers, and even architecture. In 2003, the Victoria & Albert Museum staged a retrospective exhibition of their work as part of the *Fashion in Motion* series to celebrate Eley Kishimoto's ten years in the fashion and textile industries. The pair were creative directors for Paris-based fashion label Cacharel (2008–9), and since 2010 have been artistic directors for Laura Ashley London, a new line for the Japanese market.
www.eleykishimoto.com

Freedom of Creation
Design company, established Finland, 2000
Founder Janne Kyttänen studied at ELISAVA (Barcelona School of Design and Engineering), before graduating from the Gerrit Rietveld Academy, Amsterdam in 2000. The company relocated to the Netherlands in 2006, where Kyttänen teamed up with Jiri Evenhuis. Freedom of Creation produces its designs with 3D printing technologies, which then either become part of the FOC collection or are commercialized by other design labels. The company's products have been published and exhibited internationally, and feature in the permanent collections of numerous museums.
www.freedomofcreation.com

James Frost
Digital-imaging director
Frost began directing with Alex Smith at Ridley Scott Associates in 1997. Since 2002 he has worked with musical artists including Norah Jones, the White Stripes, Elvis Costello, Phish, Robyn and Interpol, entailing the use of data visualization in collaboration with Aaron Koblin. His video for Radiohead's single 'House of Cards', for which he was technically assisted by Koblin, was nominated for the Best Short Form Music Video at the 51st Grammy Awards in 2009. The video premiered on Google, and was showcased by Saatchi & Saatchi in Cannes. Frost's video for the band OK Go in 2010 achieved the AICP award and is in the collection of Museum of Modern Art, New York.

Dai Fujiwara
Textile designer
Fujiwara graduated from Tama Art University, Tokyo, in 1994 with a degree in textile design before joining the Miyake Design Studio. As a member of the Issey Miyake Collection design team, he launched A-POC with Miyake in 1998. Fujiwara has the mind of an engineer, and spent five years researching industrial knitting machines and the accompanying software needed to program A-POC, winning the Good Design Award in 2000 and the Mainichi Design Award in 2003. Fujiwara was appointed creative director of Issey Miyake in 2006.
www.isseymiyake.com

Jonathan Fuller
Textile designer
Fuller received his BA from Glasgow School of Art in 1992 and MA in printed textile design from the Royal College of Art in 1996. With fellow designer Elvira van Vredenburgh, Fuller set up the London-based print studio Vredenburgh Fuller. He uses Adobe Photoshop and Adobe Illustrator software to generate and manipulate imagery, allowing for a multitude of visual effects, layers of transparencies and opacities, the mimicry of brush marks and other hand processes, and the distortion of regular patterns. Fuller lives and works in Cornwall as a freelance textile designer, with agents in Los Angeles and Tokyo.
www.jonathanfuller.co.uk

Tom Gallant
Artist
Gallant received his BA in graphic design from Southampton Institute of Higher Education in 1997, followed by an MA in fine art print from Camberwell College of Arts in 2000. He completed a fellowship in fine art print at the Royal Academy Schools (2000–1), and was an artist-in-residence at Foundation B.A.D., an artists' initiative in Rotterdam (2003–4). His work has been included in numerous exhibitions, including *Media in Transition II*, Hamish Morrison Galerie, Berlin (2010), *Change Happens*, Mimmo Scognamiglio, Milan (2011) and *The Yellow Wallpaper*, Danson House, London (2012).
www.tom-gallant.com

Louise Goldin

Fashion designer

Goldin received both her BA (2001) and MA (2005) in fashion from Central Saint Martins. Her graduate collection was bought and produced exclusively by London department store Selfridges; soon after, she launched her own label. After being spotted by Lulu Kennedy, Goldin was invited to show her Autumn/Winter 2007–8 collection at Fashion East, London Fashion Week's alternative offshoot, and made her London Fashion Week debut with her Autumn/ Winter 2008–9 collection. Goldin was the recipient of New Generation sponsorship from the British Fashion Council, and has won the Deutsche Bank Pyramid Award, the Chloé Award and the Swarovski Emerging Talent Award at the British Fashion Awards 2008, as well as the British Fashion Council's Fashion Forward prize in 2010.

www.louisegoldin.com

Kate Goldsworthy

Textile designer

Goldsworthy received her MA from the University of the Arts London, and is currently completing a PhD as part of the Arts and Humanities Research Council -funded project *Ever & Again: Rethinking Recycled Textiles* with the Textiles Environment Design research cluster at Chelsea College of Art and Design. Goldsworthy is currently Course Director of MA Textile Futures at Central Saint Martins, and is a core member of the Textile Futures Research Centre.

www.kategoldsworthy.co.uk

Mark Goulthorpe

Architect

Goulthorpe founded the dECOi atelier, based in Boston and Paris, in 1991 to create impressionable design, including *HypoSurface*. The collective has received awards from the Royal Academy, the French Ministry of Culture and the Architectural League of New York. Goulthorpe has given and written numerous lectures and publications, including *The Possibility of (an) Architecture: Collected Essays* (2008), and receives frequent guest-professorships, from a design unit at the Architectural Association, London, to the École Spéciale d'Architecture in Paris. Goulthorpe is currently Associate Professor of Architecture at MIT.

www.hyposurface.org

Naoki Hamaguchi

Artist

Hamaguchi received his BA in textiles from Goldsmiths, University of London in 2004, and MA in fine art from Central Saint Martins in 2006. He was the recipient of the Christine Risley Prize in 2006. Exhibitions include *Free Range*, Atlantis, London (2004); *Kimono, Canvas of my Japanese Spirit*, Constance Howard Resource and Research Centre, Deptford (2006); and *Quick and Dirty*, The Bargehouse, London (2006). Hamaguchi is currently practicing in the UK.

www.naokihamaguchi.com

Michael Hansmeyer

Architect

Hansmeyer graduated with an MBA from Insead Fontainebleau, France, and an MA from Columbia University, New York. He has worked for McKinsey & Co and Herzog & de Meuron architects. Recent projects have included *Subdivided Pavilions* (2006), *Voxel-Based Geometries* (2009) and *Subdivided Columns: A New Order* (2010). Hansmeyer is currently based in the CAAD group at ETH Zürich's architecture department.

www.michael-hansmeyer.com

Jane Harris

Designer and artist

Harris studied textile design at Glasgow School of Art, followed by PhD research at the Royal College of Art (1995–2000). She has pioneered a practice in digital-imaging design and creative computing disciplines, and has won recognition from numerous institutions, including the Arts Foundation, the Arts Humanities Research Board and the National Endowment for Science, Technology and the Arts. Her work has been widely exhibited at museums such as the Victoria & Albert Museum and Institute of Contemporary Art in London, the Fine Arts Museums of San Francisco and the Tokyo Design Centre, and is in the collection of the Whitworth Art Gallery, Manchester. Harris co-founded the Textile Futures Research Centre at University of the Arts, London, in 2007, and she is currently Professor of Design at Kingston University, Surrey.

www.janeharris.org

Tomoko Hayashi

Artist and textile designer

Hayashi received her BFA from Kyoto Seika University in 2002, and MA from Central Saint Martins in 2004. She was invited to develop an intimate communication device in collaboration with Stefan Agamanolis and Matthew Karau of the Media Lab Europe, in Dublin. The piece was first installed in the *Touch Me* exhibition at the Victoria & Albert Museum in 2005; a new version, developed with the same team at the Distance Lab in Inverness, Scotland, was exhibited at *Skin of/in Contemporary Art* at the National Museum of Art, Osaka, in 2007. Hayashi currently works at the Ishikawa Oku Laboratory, University of Tokyo.

www.tomokohayashi.com,
www.tokyotomoco.blogspot.com

Daniel Herman

Fashion designer

Herman received his BA from Central Saint Martins in 1998. He won the Swiss Federal Award in 1999 and 2002, and the Swiss Textiles Award in 2000. Herman has worked for Jakob Schlaepfer and the luxury clothing firm Akris, and developed textiles for Gessner, a manufacturer of finishing machinery (2002–6). A consultant and freelance designer for the lingerie company Triumph since 2003, Herman's main focus has been technological innovation, and he established the Triumph Inspiration Award, an international lingerie competition for fashion design students. Along with his own label, based in Zürich,

Herman has also collaborated on a research project with the Geneva University of Art and Design since 2010.

www.danielherman.com

Marie Hill

Textile designer

Hill received her BA in fashion print from Central Saint Martins in 2009. Having served internships at Alexander McQueen and Stine Goya, where she designed prints for the Spring/Summer 2008 collection, her graduate collection, which featured fluorescent cocktail dresses with spider-back detailing, won the L'Oréal Professionnel Young Designer Award. After graduation, Hill designed a capsule collection for Browns Focus and prints and embroideries for Givenchy's womenswear, prêt-à-porter and haute couture collections. She is currently Print and Embroidery Designer for the fashion house Balmain in Paris.

www.balmain.com

Ainsley Hillard

Textile artist

Hillard received her BA from Middlesex University in 2000, and MA from Curtin University, Australia, in 2003. Her works are often site-specific, informed by places and memories, and her interdisciplinary approach embraces both textile and non-materials and processing, combining the direct physicality of materials with the detachment of digital technologies to create multi-sensory installations. Hillard's work has been included in many international exhibitions, and her first solo show in the UK was held at the Mission Gallery, Swansea, in 2008. In 2012, she received an award from the Arts Council of Wales. Hillard is a lecturer in surface pattern design at Swansea Metropolitan University.

www.ainsleyhillard.com

Eunsuk Hur

Textile designer

Hur studied at KonKuk University, Seoul, before receiving an MA in design for textile futures from Central Saint Martins in 2009. Her work has been featured in exhibitions, including *Future Form*, Trafalgar Hotel, London (2010) and the Gwangju Design Biennale 2009, South Korea, the trade show Tent London (2009), and in such publications as *Vogue Nippon* and *Elle Decoration*, both in 2009. Hur is currently a student at the School of Design, University of Leeds.

www.eunsukhur.com

Jakob Schlaepfer

Textile company, established Switzerland, 1934

Jakob Schlaepfer began life in 1904 as an embroidery firm founded by Rudolf Vogel. After being bought in 1934 by employee Jakob Schlaepfer, who had joined the company in 1908, the rebranded company was taken over in 1957 by Schlaepfer's son, who managed it until 1995. In 1964 the company, based in St Gallen, Switzerland, showed its first haute couture collection. The firm has pioneered the use of textile technology, introducing computers in 1968, and has won many awards, including the Red Dot Design Award, the Preis Schweiz and the Imagination Prize at Première Vision.

www.jakob-schlaepfer.ch

Janis Jefferies

Artist, writer and curator

Jefferies studied woven construction in the late 1970s under the tutelage of Magdalena Abakanowicz at the Academy of Fine Arts, in Poznán, Poland. With numerous solo exhibitions, together with a prolific written and curatorial practice, Jefferies is recognized as a leading practitioner and theorist of her generation. She has collaborated with computer scientist Tim Blackwell, a Senior Lecturer in computing at Goldsmiths, University of London, whose research spans computational swarm intelligence, art and music computing. Jefferies is Professor of Visual Arts and Research at Goldsmiths, University of London, Artistic Director of Goldsmiths Digital Studios and co-director of the college's Centre for Social and Creative Technologies.

Mary Katrantzou

Fashion designer

Katrantzou studied architecture at Rhode Island School of Design, before transferring to Central Saint Martins to complete a BA in textile design and an MA in fashion. Katrantzou opened the Central Saint Martins 2008 graduate show with a collection that featured trompe-l'oeil digital prints of oversized jewelry on bonded jersey dresses. She worked for Sophia Kokosalaki and sold samples to Bill Blass, and is now an independent fashion designer based in London. After receiving New Generation sponsorship, Katrantzou made her debut at London Fashion Week with her Autumn/Winter 2009–10 collection.
www.marykatrantzou.com

Patricia Kinsella

Textile designer and curator

Originally from the USA, Kinsella is now based in Italy, where she is curator at the Prato Textile Museum. She was chosen to take part in Müller Zell's Art and Industry project in 1991, in which strong links between the digital and textile were forged. Kinsella lectures at many institutions, including SACI (Studio Art Centers International), Polimoda and Art Studio Fuji, in Florence, and Syracuse University and the Fashion Institute of Technology, in New York.

Nick Knight

Fashion photographer

Knight studied at Bournemouth and Poole College of Art and Design. Having published his first book of photographs, *Skinheads*, in 1982, Knight went on to challenge conventional notions of image and beauty. He is a director and founder of the pioneering fashion website SHOWstudio, launched in 2000. His prolific practice includes editorial work for *Vogue*, *Dazed & Confused*, *W*, *i-D* and *Visionaire* magazines, and fashion advertising for clients including Christian Dior, Alexander McQueen, Calvin Klein, Levi Strauss, Yohji Yamamoto and Yves Saint Laurent. Knight's work has been exhibited at the Victoria & Albert Museum, Saatchi Gallery, Photographers' Gallery, Hayward Gallery and Tate Modern.
www.nickknight.com, www.showstudio.com

KnoWear

Design studio, established USA, 2000

New York-based Peter Allen and Carla Ross Allen met in 1998 while graduate students at Cranbrook Academy of Art, Michigan. Prior to this, Peter Allen received his BA in sculpture from the University of Hartford, Connecticut, and studied 18th- and 19th-century furniture reproduction at the North Bennett Street School, Boston. Carla Ross Allen received her BFA in industrial design from the California College of the Arts. Their work has been exhibited at the Cooper-Hewitt National Design Museum and the Eyebeam Gallery, New York, the National Museums of Scotland, and Zeche Zollverein, Germany, and included in numerous publications.
www.knowear.net

Michiko Koshino

Fashion designer

Koshino, the daughter of Hiroko Koshino, one of Japan's most famous designers, moved to London in 1973. Her labels include Motorking, launched in 1987 in collaboration with Adachi, a producer of motorcycle racing wear; and Yen, a jeans brand launched in 1995 that uses Japanese denim woven onto original American 1940s fabric. Koshino's collections have been shown at London Fashion Week since its inception in 1984, and three of her outfits were included in the exhibition *Street Styles (1950–1994)*, held at the Victoria & Albert Museum in 1994. In 2007, Koshino represented her native Japan at the World Fashion Awards in Los Angeles. She lives and works in London.
www.michikokoshino.co.uk

Ebru Kurbak

Designer

Kurbak received her BArch and MSc degrees in architecture from Istanbul Technical University. She is currently a PhD candidate at Kunstuniversität Linz, where she also lectures. Recent projects have explored the instrumental, aesthetic and semiotic potentials of body-worn interfaces. Her work has been published internationally, and exhibited at the Ars Electronica, Siggraph and FILE festivals.
www.ebrukurbak.net

Barbara Layne

Textile artist and researcher

Layne received her BFA from the University of Colorado in 1979, and MFA in textile design from the University of Kansas in 1982. She co-founded the Hexagram Institute for Research/Creation in Media Arts and Technologies in 2001, and collaboratively explores textiles and new technologies to communicate visual information. Her work has been included in the International Symposia of Electronic Arts, Istanbul (2011), Kaunas Biennial (2011) and the touring exhibition *Futurotextiles* (2011–12). Layne is Professor of Studio Arts and director of Studio subTela at Concordia University, Montreal.
www.subtela.hexagram.ca

Kyu Jin Lee

Textile designer

Lee graduated with a BA in fashion (2001) and MA in textile futures (2005) from Central Saint Martins. During her MA studies, she developed a poetic fusion of analogue and digital drawing processes and imaging-making, which she applies to fashion textiles. Her work has been exhibited at Texprint, Paris, the Seoul Museum of Art, and the Daeduk Science & Culture and Arts Centre, South Korea. Lee is a freelance designer and artist, and lecturer in fibre and fashion at Mokwon University, South Korea.

Loop.pH

Design studio, established UK, 2003

Loop.pH is a London-based art and design studio founded by Mathias Gmachl and Rachel Wingfield. Their practice mediates between digital and biological media, facilitating participatory design and urban crafts. The studio specializes in the design and fabrication of ephemeral textile architecture and living environments, devising urban interventions informed by ecologically based parametric design and principles of community engagement, and has received support from the Leverhulme Trust, Audi Design Foundation and the Technology Strategy Board. Their installation work is in the collections of the Museum of Modern Art, New York, and the Victoria & Albert, London.
www.loop.ph

Lost in Space

Digital special-effects studio, established 1990

Founded by Christian Hogue, Lost in Space is a pioneering studio that specializes in cutting-edge moving-image work across all sectors, including visual effects for music videos, advertising, television and films such as *Terminator 2*, *Judge Dredd* and the James Bond series. The studio has also created visionary imagery for *Big*, *Dazed & Confused* and *Wired* magazines, as well as the iconic cover artwork for Coldplay's *A Rush of Blood to the Head* album. Other clients include Roger Sanchez, Björk, Smirnoff, Sony, Nike, Adidas, Orange, MTV, Disney, the BBC and Channel 4, and music groups the Rolling Stones, Simply Red and Metallica.
www.lostinspace.com

Roland Maas

Artist and designer

Maas graduated from art college in 1990, and since 2002 has been developing the toon model Babelle (or 'Baboes', as she is known in the Benelux countries), in collaboration with editor Maurits Brands. Babelle has become well known in the Netherlands through trend reports in the fashion trade magazine *Link*, and is regularly 'booked' by editors, manufacturers and designers to model their collections.
www.rolandmaas.nl, www.babelle.nl

John Maeda

Digital media artist

Maeda arrived at MIT in 1984 with a first-generation Macintosh computer. After completing his BS and MS degrees in computer science, he received a PhD in design from the University of Tsukuba, School of Art and Design

in Japan. Having pioneered a fusion of the art, design and technology fields, Maeda has subsequently influenced many digital creatives, including his student Casey Reas. Among his notable publications are *Maeda @ Media* (2000) and *The Laws of Simplicity* (2006), and his work has been widely exhibited, including at the Museum of Modern Art, New York, and the Fondation Cartier, Paris. He was appointed President of the Rhode Island School of Design in 2008.
www.maedastudio.com

Florence Manlik
Artist and designer
Manlik's signature fluid and delicate designs, achieved by utilizing very fine 0.20 pens, are highly saturated with a maze of lines, and she uses the computer as a tool with which to further manipulate and 'clean up' her handmade designs with Adobe Photoshop software. In addition to her personal work, she has supplied designs to Hermès for its *Carré* scarves and patterns, Lin, Inc., in Tokyo, for interior design; and Selfridges in London for its 'Wonder Room' advertising campaign. She has also collaborated with fashion designer Robert Normand on his women's prêt-à-porter collections (2006–9). Manlik lives and works in Paris.
www.florencemanlik.com

Ben Maron
Computer scientist and designer
Maron graduated from MIT in computer science in 2004, and received a BA in fashion from Central Saint Martins in 2008. He was a lead architect on the Cyclops (Blue Gene/C) supercomputer team at MIT, and worked with the wearables unit at MIT Media Lab. Straddling the fields of computer science and fashion, he has worked for such companies as IBM, as well as fashion designers including Donna Karan and Jonathan Saunders. Maron's interests lie in the fusion of complex circuitry, generative design and the interaction of fabric with the human body, and he aims to fuse the two fields by creating new methods of garment design.
www.benjaminmaron.com

Christy Matson
Artist
Matson graduated from the University of Washington in 2001, and received her MFA from the California College of the Arts in 2005. She has been artist-in-residence at the Experimental Sound Studio, Chicago, the Harvestworks Digital Media Arts Center, New York, and the Museum of Contemporary Craft, Portland, Oregon. Matson has taught at the Haystack Mountain School of Crafts, Maine, and has been Assistant Professor at the School of the Art Institute of Chicago. Her work has been featured in many exhibitions, including the Kaunas Biennial (2007 and 2011) and *40 under 40: Craft Futures* (2012–13), at the Renwick Gallery, Washington, DC.
www.cmatson.com

Bruce Mau
Designer
After studying at Ontario College of Art & Design, Mau worked for design group Fifty Fingers, followed by Pentagram in London, before returning to Toronto to found Public Good Design and Communication. Mau was Creative Director of *I.D.* magazine (1991–93), and Design Director of Zone Books until 2004. He has been awarded the Chrysler Award for Design Innovation (1998), the Toronto Arts Award for Architecture and Design (1999) and the AIGA Gold Medal (2007). In 2003 Mau founded Institute without Boundaries, a studio-based postgraduate programme for designers of the future, in collaboration with George Brown College, Toronto. In 2004, Mau and his students created the groundbreaking exhibition *Massive Change*. He is the co-founder of the Massive Change Network, and his design work involves collaboration for positive change. Mau is the founder and Chairman Emeritus of Bruce Mau Design, with studios in Toronto and New York.
www.brucemaudesign.com

Alexander McQueen
Fashion designer
McQueen received his MA from Central Saint Martins in 1991, and served apprenticeships at Savile Row tailors Anderson & Sheppard and Gieves & Hawkes before launching his own label in 1992. He was head designer at Givenchy (1996–2001), and was named British Designer of the Year in 1996, 1997, 2001 and 2003. McQueen was awarded a CBE in 2000. One of the most influential fashion designers of his generation, McQueen consistently challenged catwalk conventions, resulting in innovative performances and installations. After his death in 2010, a memorial exhibition, *Alexander McQueen: Savage Beauty* (2011), was held at the Metropolitan Museum of Art; it proved to be one of the most popular exhibitions in the museum's history.
www.alexandermcqueen.com

Me Company
Digital-imaging company, established UK, 1985
Founded by Paul White, Me Company became prolific, specializing in high-impact imagery, photography, CGI illustration and brand development for such clients as the singer Björk (including the sleeve artwork for the Sugarcubes' first UK single), fashion designers Hussein Chalayan, Kenzo and Lanvin, and *Numéro* and *Big* magazines.
www.mecompany.com

MIRAlab
Interdisciplinary research lab, established Switzerland, 1989
Founded by Nadia Magnenat-Thalmann at the University of Geneva, Switzerland, MIRAlab is a pioneering interdisciplinary computer-science research lab working in the domains of mixed reality, personality and emotional models, social robotics, 3D medical simulation, cultural heritage, virtual humans, 3D multimedia application and the simulation of hair and clothing. Since 1992, MIRAlab has participated in more than forty-eight European funded projects.
www.miralab.ch

Issey Miyake
Fashion designer
Miyake studied at Tama Art University, Tokyo, and the Chambre Syndicale de la Couture in Paris. After graduation, Miyake worked for fashion houses Guy Laroche and Givenchy in Paris, and Geoffrey Beene in New York. On returning to Tokyo in 1970, he set up Miyake Design Studio with Makiko Minagawa. In 1993 Miyake launched Pleats Please, followed in 1998 by A-POC with Dai Fujiwara and a team of young designers. That same year a retrospective, *Issey Miyake: Making Things*, was held at the Fondation Cartier in Paris. In 2000, A-POC won Grand Prize at the Good Design Awards. Miyake established the Miyake Issey Foundation in 2004, and is co-director (with Taku Satoh and Naoto Fukasawa) of 21_21 Design Sight, an exhibition venue in Tokyo, which opened in 2007.
www.isseymiyake.com

Hamish Morrow
Fashion designer
Morrow moved to London from South Africa in 1989 to study at Central Saint Martins, and graduated with an MA in menswear fashion design from the Royal College of Art in 1996. Morrow has worked in ateliers in New York, Paris and Milan, and collaborated with Louis Feraud, Fendi, Kangol and Krizia, and launched his own label in 2000. His second collection, 'The Life Cycle of an Idea' (Autumn/Winter 2001–2), caught the attention of the fashion press. His own-label collections have integrated high-tech concepts with traditional methods of making clothes, and more recently he has produced capsule collections that combine luxury and technology.

Pia Myrvold
Multimedia artist and designer
Born in Norway, Myrvold began her career as a painter. Now based in Paris, she is a 'polymath', exploring painting, sculpture, music, video, installation and fashion. Myrvold is inspired by the links between electronic music, digital video and CAD/CAM, and she has created fashion via her website Cybercouture, using digital means, manufacture and presentation. She has exhibited her work at New York Fashion Week and in galleries worldwide.
www.pia-myrvold.com, www.cybercouture.com

Nicola Naismith
Designer and artist
Naismith received her MA from Norwich School of Art and Design in 2003. Her practice explores the relationships between historical production methods and contemporary innovations in design and manufacturing. She has been awarded numerous residencies, including *Digital Making* at the Hethel Engineering Centre, Norwich, in 2010, and *Spatial Divisions* at the former Bally factory in 2007. Commissioned works include a site-specific exhibition for London's Foundling Museum in 2007.
www.nicolanaismith.co.uk

Rupert Newman

Textile designer and light artist

Newman received his BA from University College Falmouth (2006) and MA from the Royal College of Art (2009). In 2006, he was selected for Texprint, and showed his designs at Indigo in Paris. After graduating from University College Falmouth, Newman spent a year in Berlin, where he set up a studio to paint and continue with his textile designs, and to develop a new concept that merged textiles with light projections and sound. He works with Adobe Photoshop and After Effects software, experimenting with static and moving imagery. Newman also designs sophisticated repeat patterns for fashion prints, and from these he creates moving light projections for events.

www.rupertnewman.com

Nuno

Textile design company, established Japan, 1984

Founded by Jun'ichi Arai and Reiko Sudo, Nuno produces textiles for fashion and interiors that combine the inherent properties of natural with synthetic textiles, and traditional techniques with the latest technological advances. The main retail shop and textile studio are in Tokyo's Roppongi district, with smaller boutiques throughout Japan. In 2002, Nuno Works was launched, producing prints created through a combination of ancient techniques and new materials. Nuno's fabrics are sold by Sain AG, Switzerland and MOKUM, Australia, and are imported and distributed throughout the USA by Material Things. The company was the subject of a touring exhibition, 21:21: *The Textile Vision of Reiko Sudo and Nuno* (2005–7), and has produced several publications devoted to its innovative textiles.

www.nuno.com

Hanna Palmgren

Artist

Palmgren received her BA in textiles from Goldsmiths, University of London in 2004. Together with fellow graduate Anna Hughes, she explores the urban context of cities through videos and installations, focusing on the relationships between exterior spaces and the domestic setting. In 2005, they took part in the Transart05 festival, in Bolzano, Italy.

Nick Phillips

Designer

Phillips initially trained in sculpture at Sheffield Hallam University, and pursued a career as a graphic designer, specializing in computer games. He used his materials knowledge to create the illusion of 3D on the computer screen, and to convey believable representations of such complex forms as hair, skin and clothing. A founder of the Designers Republic, a Sheffield-based graphic design company, Phillips has worked on numerous CGI projects, including *Wip3out* (winner of a BAFTA for Game Graphics in 1999) and *To End All Wars*, a game based on World War 1.

Jo Pierce

Textile designer

After receiving an MA in textile futures from Central Saint Martins in 2003, Pierce established her own company, Re-surface Design, through which she continues to develop her practice. She was a course leader for the BA Textile Design and MA Contemporary Crafts (Textiles) at University College Farnham, and was part of the UCA Crafts Futures research cluster and a founding member of the experimental textile group, Circle. Pierce is currently Senior Lecturer and Print Pathway Leader for textile design at Central Saint Martins, and is a member of the Textile Futures Research Centre.

Prada

Fashion label, established Italy, 1913

Founded by Mario Prada, whose granddaughter Miuccia Prada took over the company in 1978 and turned it into a household name with partner Patrizio Bertelli. Prada Woman was launched in 1988, followed by Miu Miu in 1993, Prada Menswear in 1994, and Miu Miu Men and Prada Sport in 1999. In 2002 Miuccia Prada was voted one of the thirty most powerful women in Europe by the *Wall Street Journal*, and one of *Time* magazine's 100 most influential people in 2005. Interested in the links between fashion and contemporary art, Prada and Bertelli launched Fondazione Prada in 1993, which hosts permanent installations and temporary exhibitions.

www.prada.com

J. Morgan Puett

Artist

Puett received her MFA in sculpture and film-making from the School of the Art Institute of Chicago in 1985. Having operated her own fashion label and storefront projects in New York (1984–2000), she has exhibited her work internationally and is a recipient of the Smithsonian Artist Research Fellowship (2009) and a USA Simon Fellow (2011). Puett co-founded Mildred's Lane in the Upper Delaware River Valley with award-winning artist Mark Dion, whose work has been included in exhibitions at the Tate Gallery, London (1999) and the Museum of Modern Art, New York (2004). Puett teaches and designs at Mildred's Lane and the Mildred Complex(ity), which often hosts collaborative projects with international artists.

www.jmorganpuett.com, www.mildredslane.com

Karim Rashid

Industrial designer

Rashid received his BA from Carleton University, Ottawa, in 1982, and completed his postgraduate studies in Italy. He has over 3,000 designs to his name, including designs for interiors, fashion, furniture, lighting, art, music and installations. Among his award-winning creations are the *Garbo* waste bin and *Oh Chair* for Umbra. He has designed furniture for Artemide and Magis, brand identity for Citibank and Hyundai, and luxury goods for Veuve Clicquot and Swarovski. His work has been featured in numerous publications, including *Time* magazine, the *Financial Times*,

Design Futures (2011) and *Living Modern* (2010).

www.karimrashid.com

Casey Reas

Digital designer and artist

Reas studied at MIT, where together with Ben Fry he created the open-source programming language, Processing. In 2001 he set up the website Processing.org, and co-wrote *Processing: A Programming Handbook for Visual Designers and Artists* in 2007 with Fry and John Maeda. Reas received a Media Arts Fellowship from the Tribeca Film Institute in 2008. His ongoing series *Process* generates software, prints and installations that explore the relationship between naturally evolved and synthetic systems. He has exhibited his work internationally, and has lectured at institutions including the Royal Academy of Art, The Hague, and the NTT InterCommunication Center, Tokyo. Reas is currently Associate Professor and Chair of Design | Media Arts at the University of California, Los Angeles.

www.reas.com

Vibeke Riisberg

Textile designer

Riisberg studied at the School of Arts and Crafts, Copenhagen (1977) and the School of Visual Arts, New York (1987), before completing her PhD thesis in 2006. She was a co-founder of Tastemain & Riisberg design studio, Paris, where she worked from 1982 to 1992. In 1998 she was awarded the Thorvald Bindesbøl medal from the Royal Danish Academy. Riisberg has been a guest lecturer in the UK, Norway, Iceland and Australia, and is currently Associate Professor at Kolding School of Art and Design, Denmark.

www.vibeke-riisberg.dk

Ismini Samanidou

Textile artist

Samanidou received her BA from Central Saint Martins in 2000, followed by an MA from the Royal College of Art in 2003. In 2004, she was a recipient of the Crafts Council's Next Move scheme, and in 2006 won a Crafts Council Development Award. Her work has been included in the exhibitions *Making it Digital* (2008) for the Hidden Art Cornwall design fair, and *Jerwood Contemporary Makers* (2009) at the Jerwood Space, London. Samanidou is an Associate Researcher with the Autonomatic group at University College Falmouth, and a Visiting Lecturer at Central Saint Martins and the University of Brighton.

www.isminisamanidou.com

Jonathan Saunders

Fashion designer

Saunders received his BA from Glasgow School of Art in 1999, and an MA from Central Saint Martins in 2002, specializing in printed textiles. After catching the attention of the world's fashion press with his 'bird-of-paradise' print for Alexander McQueen's 'Transitions' collection (Spring/Summer 2003), his work was featured on the cover of British *Vogue* (January 2004), and he was named Scottish Fashion Designer of the Year (2005). In 2006 he won the

British Fashion Council's Fashion Enterprise Award, and in 2007 was named the *Elle* Style Awards Designer of the Year. Saunders has acted as a consultant for Pucci and Chloé, and was appointed Creative Director for the Italian label Pollini (presenting his first collection in 2008), as well as designing capsule collections for UK high-street giant Topshop and US brand Target.
www.jonathan-saunders.com

Simon Schofield
Artist and computer scientist
Schofield graduated with a PhD in non-photorealistic rendering from Middlesex University, London, in 1994. Following graduation, he was a Research Fellow at Westminster University (1996–98) and a lecturer at the Slade School of Fine Art (1997–2000). Schofield has developed several software systems, including the Piranesi 3D painting tool, used by architects and 3D designers worldwide, and the interactive music system AudioROM, for which he won a BAFTA in 1998. In 2005, he was awarded a NESTA Fellowship. Schofield is currently a Senior Lecturer in computing technology at Nottingham Trent University.
www.simonschofield.net

Romy Smits
Artist and designer
Smits creates bespoke designs for both fashion and interiors. Her designs have been seen in the department store Barneys New York, and exhibited at the Dutch Textile Museum. She has collaborated with Peugeot, Lexus, L'Oréal, Libeco Home and Procter & Gamble. Her work has been featured in many publications, including *100 New Fashion Designers* and *Quick Puff Design*, both published in 2008.
www.romy-smits.com

Eddie Squires
Textile designer
Squires studied at Grimsby School Art (1956–59) and the Central School of Art, London, graduating in 1962. He joined Warner & Sons in 1963, becoming chief designer of printed textiles in 1971, and ultimately director in 1984. Squires was a Fellow of the Chartered Society of Designers, a member of the Design Council's Design Centre Selection Committee (1983–88), and juror for the Royal Society of Arts Student Design Awards (1988–94). In 1969 he designed *Lunar Rocket*, a screenprinted fabric to commemorate the moon landing; the design was chosen as the poster image for Warner's 100th anniversary exhibition at the Victoria & Albert Museum. Credited with preserving Warner's reputation for high-quality, traditional fabrics, Squires was also committed to modern design and encouraged collaboration with new designers and processes, including the digital work of Malcolm Cocks.

Norma Starszakowna
Textile designer and artist
Following graduation from Duncan of Jordanstone College of Art & Design in 1966, Starszakowna set up her own design studio in Dundee, Scotland. She served as Head of Textiles and Fashion (1984–95) and Chair of Design (1995–98) at

DJCAD; Director of Research Development at the University of the Arts London (1999–2005); and Director of Research for the University of Lincoln, Faculty of Art, Architecture and Design (2005–8). Clients have included Miyake Design Studio and Shirin Guild Ltd. A solo exhibition of her work, *Textiles and Innovation*, was held at the Technical University of Lodz, Poland, in 2011. Starszakowna's designs are in the collections of the Whitworth Art Gallery, Manchester, the Victoria & Albert Museum and the Scottish Arts Council.

Rainer Stolle
Artist and designer
Stolle studied at the Fachhochschule, in Krefeld, Germany, and received an MA in textile design futures in 2005 from Central Saint Martins, where he explored the potential of digital textile print in combination with traditional print and dying techniques. Stolle has used digital tools in fashion and textile contexts, as well as advancing a practice in special effects, working with television graphics and visual effects in film for projects including *The Borgias* (2011) and *Avatar* (2009). He created digital environments and matt paintings for such international film productions as the *Lord of the Rings* trilogy (2001–3) and *The Da Vinci Code* (2006). His work has been featured in many exhibitions, including *Cute Circuit: FutureFashionEvent*, Pisa (2006), and *Where Fashion Steps, It Leaves a Print*, Paris (2005). He is currently director of the visual effects company, Timed.ltd.
www.digitanalogue.com

Elisa Strozyk
Designer
Strozyk graduated in textile and surface design from the Kunsthochschule Berlin (2007), and received her MA in future textiles from Central Saint Martins (2009). That same year she exhibited work at the Salone di Mobile, Milan, and the Gwangju Design Biennale, South Korea. She has also completed interiors installations for the Circus Hotel and the Buffalo Shop in Berlin, and her work was featured in the exhibitions *Industrious|Artefacts*, Zuiderzeemuseum, Netherlands (2011–12), and *Power of Making*, Victoria & Albert Museum (2011–12). In 2011 Strozyk was named Textile Designer of the Year by *Elle Decor*.
www.elisastrozyk.de

Peter Struycken
Artist
Struycken graduated from the Royal Academy of Art, The Hague, in 1961. In 1968 he studied electronic musical composition and computer programming at Utrecht University's Institute of Sonology, and in the mid-1970s experimented with computer-operated colour monitors at Delft University of Technology. He was invited to be a Fellow at MIT (1978–79), where he worked with astrophysicist Walter Lewin for the Architecture Machine Group. He was Visiting Professor at Eindhoven University of Technology (1988–89), and a guest lecturer at the Dutch Art Institute in Enschede (1999–2003). In 2007, he was the subject of a monograph devoted to his work.

Sølve Sundsbø
Fashion photographer
Sundsbø studied at the London College of Printing, leaving after four months to become Nick Knight's assistant. He is now an image innovator in his own right, and clients include Cartier, Dolce & Gabbana, Hermès, Armani, Louis Vuitton and Yves Saint Laurent. Sundsbø has also created editorials for Italian *Vogue*, *Love*, *Dazed & Confused*, *Visionaire*, *V*, *Interview* and *i-D* magazines, and directed short films for Chanel, Gucci and SHOWstudio. A video gallery for the *New York Times*, entitled *14 Actors Acting*, won an Emmy in 2011.
www.solvesundsbo.info

Susumu Tachi
Scientist and inventor
Tachi received his PhD from the University of Tokyo in 1973. He was director of the biorobotics division at the Mechanical Engineering Laboratory (1975–89), in Tsukuba Science City, Senior Visiting Scientist at MIT (1979–80) and Professor of Information Physics and Computing at the University of Tokyo (1989–2009). Among his designs are *Telexistence* (1980–present), which enables the highly realistic sensation of existence in a remote place without actual travel, and *Optical Camouflage*, named by *Time* magazine as one of the coolest inventions of 2003. Tachi is Professor Emeritus at the University of Tokyo and Professor at Keio University, where he also heads the Tachi Lab. Ongoing research projects include *TWISTER*, *Repro3D* and *TELESAR V*.
www.tachilab.org

Eros Tang
Digital-image designer
Tang studied at Chelsea College of Art and Design, followed by an M.Phil at the Royal College of Art (1995–97), researching the use of 3D computer-imaging in 2D printed textiles. He has worked as a 3D digital-imaging artist at DC Studios UK, and as a senior artist at both Rocksteady Studios, where he worked on the video game *Urban Chaos: Riot Response*, and Argonaut Games. Tang is currently a 3D digital artist at Rockstar North, the developers of the *Grand Theft Auto* series.
www.3rd-dimension.net

Textile Futures Research Centre
Research centre, established UK, 2007
Based at the University of the Arts London, the group is formed of textile researchers from Chelsea College of Art and Design and Central Saint Martins. Members investigate the future design and implementation of textiles by uniting traditional craft skills and knowledge with cutting-edge technologies in sustainable, digital and science sectors. Current members include Rebecca Earley, Carole Collet, Kay Politowicz, Melanie Bowles, Philippa Brock, Kate Goldsworthy, Anne Marr, Caryn Simonson and Jenny Tillotson.
www.textilefutures.co.uk

Mike Thomas
Artist and photographer
Thomas received his MA in photography from the London

College of Printing. Having started out as an assistant to Nick Knight, Thomas's work has since appeared in numerous international publications, including *Arena*, *Dazed & Confused*, *Details*, *Esquire*, *The Face*, the *Independent*, *Wallpaper*, *L'Optimum* and the *Observer*. He lives and works in London. www.mikethomas-studio.com

Mette Ramsgard Thomsen

Architect

Thomsen's practice focuses on digital crafting as a way of questioning how computation, code and fabrication challenge architectural thinking and material practices. Her work has received funding from the Arts and Humanities Research Council, the Arts Council England, and the Arts Foundation, Copenhagen. She has researched and taught at the Bartlett School of Architecture and University College London, and is currently Professor at the Royal Academy of Fine Arts, School of Architecture, Copenhagen, and heads the Centre for Information Technology and Architecture. www.cita.karch.dk

Nick Thornton Jones

see Warren du Preez

Simon Thorogood

Fashion designer and artist

Thorogood graduated from Central Saint Martins in 1992, and in 1998 launched his design practice with the multimedia installation *White Noise*. He focuses on finding and applying novel ways of creating and communicating fashion design, and his work has been featured in exhibitions including *The Art of Fashion: Installing Allusions*, Museum Boijmans van Beuningen, Rotterdam (2010), and *Block Party: Inspired by the Art of the Tailor*, a Crafts Council touring exhibition in 2011. Ongoing research projects have included *SoundWear* (in collaboration with composer Stephen Wolff), a website and installation concerned with the generation of garment form, colour and surface decoration, and *Clothe-cess*, an investigation into adaptive and interactive fashion-design systems. Thorogood is a Research Fellow at the London College of Fashion. www.simonthorogood.com

Nancy Tilbury

Fashion designer

Tilbury graduated from the Royal College of Art in 1997. She has since worked as a member of Philips Design's Interdisciplinary Design Probes team, and collaborated with Philips Design on a number of conceptual design projects, including *New Nomads*, *Skin Probes* and *Fractal Living Jewelry*. Past commissions included the development of a strategic business model for the *Digital Athlete* project for Nike, and a connected clothing line for Levi's Europe, which featured the first wearable technologies for the fashion industry. Her client list includes EMI Music, ITV television channel (UK), Goose Design and the Black Eyed Peas. Tilbury is currently Course Director, MA Fashion, Kingston University; a Reader at Northumbria University; and director of Studio XO, a fashion and technology brand in London. www.studionancytilbury.com

Timorous Beasties

Textile design company, established UK, 1990

Alistair McAuley and Paul Simmons studied textile design at the Glasgow School of Art, graduating in 1988; Simmons went on to pursue MA studies at the Royal College of Art, London. After designing fabrics and wallpapers for other companies, the pair began to manufacture their own designs. They now have shops in Glasgow and London, and are represented across the globe. The company also undertakes special commissions, including fabrics for milliner Philip Treacy and for the interiors of the Arches Theatre, Glasgow, and London casino 50 Piccadilly. Timorous Beasties was shortlisted for the Designer of the Year prize in 2005. They have collaborated with UK department stores John Lewis and Liberty, Nike and the National Portrait Gallery, Edinburgh. www.timorousbeasties.com

Katherine Townsend

Digital textile designer

Townsend completed her PhD thesis, *Transforming shape: a simultaneous approach to the body, cloth and print for garment and textile design*, in 2004. Her research explored the integration of 2D surface imagery with the contour and 3D form of a garment to create new sculptural approaches to image generation, pertaining to natural body shape. Ongoing research includes enquiry into the design potential of 3D body-scanning. Townsend is Principal Lecturer in textile design for the MA Applied Design Futures pathway, Nottingham Trent University.

Iris van Herpen

Fashion designer

Van Herpen studied fashion design at ArtEZ Institute of the Arts, in Arnhem, Netherlands, graduating in 2006, followed by internships with Alexander McQueen and Claudy Jongstra. She established her eponymous label in 2007, and defined a new direction for couture, combining fine craft techniques with futuristic digital technology. Her work has been featured in many exhibitions, including her first solo show, *The New Craftsmanhip: Iris van Herpen and her Inspiration*, held at the Centraal Museum Utrecht (2011), which juxtaposed her designs with art from the 16th to the 19th centuries. In 2010, the museum was the first in the Netherlands to acquire several of van Herpen's pieces for its permanent collection. www.irisvanherpen.com

Eugène van Veldhoven

Textile designer

Van Veldhoven graduated from the Willem de Kooning Academy, Rotterdam, in 1993. He specializes in print techniques and coatings, and has created textile designs for fashion designers Christian Lacroix and Marithé + François Girbaud, and interiors fabrics for Jack Lenor Larsen and Calvin Klein Home. His designs have been included in the exhibitions *Radical Lace and Subversive Knitting*, Museum of Arts and Design, New York (2007) and *Evolution/Revolution: The Arts and Crafts in Contemporary Fashion and Textiles*, Rhode Island School of Design (2008). His work is in the collection of the Netherlands Textile Museum, Tilburg. www.eugenevanveldhoven.nl

Vexed Generation

Fashion label, established UK, 1994

Founded by Adam Thorpe and Joe Hunter, Vexed Generation was a response to the perceived increasing infringement of civil liberties in the 1990s (Thorpe and Hunter have cited in particular the Criminal Justice Bill of 1994 and the rise of CCTV). Among their designs, collectively known as 'stealth utility', were the one-shouldered rucksack, an iconic product described by *i-D* magazine as 'the bag that ate the world', and *Vexed Parka*, which was made from blast-proof ballistic nylon sourced through the Ministry of Defence. The company also sells 'real-world' items within the virtual environment *Entropia Universe*. Thorpe is a Reader with the Design Against Crime Research Centre at Central Saint Martins, and Hunter is a Senior Lecturer in fashion design at the University of East London.

Moritz Waldemeyer

Designer and engineer

Widely recognized as one of the most innovative designers of his generation, Waldemeyer moved from East Germany to London in 1995, where he trained as an engineer at King's College, completing his MA in 2001. Since then he has collaborated with many of the world's top architects and fashion designers, including Ron Arad, Zaha Hadid and Hussein Chalayan, as well as working for numerous artists such as U2, OK Go, Rihanna and Kylie Minogue. Waldemeyer's work is a fusion of technology, art, fashion and design. www.waldemeyer.com

Kerri Wallace

Textile designer

Wallace graduated from the MA Textile Futures course, Central Saint Martins, in 2007. Her graduate project, *Motion Response Sportswear*, explored the use of thermo-chromic ink and digital-print technology to create responsive body- and motion-sensitive wearable textile 'displays'. Wallace has embarked upon PhD research at Loughborough University, funded by the Arts and Humanities Research Council in conjunction with the Society of Dyers and Colourists. The project explores the design potential of new laser-dye methods of surface patterning for textiles and other product applications.

Junya Watanabe

Fashion designer

Watanabe studied at Bunka College of Fashion in Tokyo. In 1984 he went to work for Rei Kawakubo, first as a pattern cutter, then as a designer for Comme des Garçons' Tricot line, before setting up his own label in 1992. Watanabe made his Paris debut in 1994 under the name Comme des Garçons Junya Watanabe. His collections are described as 'techno couture', as he uses the latest technological developments in materials as new ways of constructing clothing, experimenting with high-performance textiles made possible Japan's advanced textile industry. Watanabe

established his menswear line in collaboration with Levi Strauss in 2001; other collaborations have included Converse, Nike, Carhartt, New Balance and Fred Perry.
www.comme-des-garcons.com

Sonja Weber
Artist
Weber studied at the Textile School, Münchberg, the Academy of Fine Arts, Nuremberg, and the Academy of Fine Arts, Münich, graduating in 2002. The following year she won the Düsseldorf award for young artists, and in 2006 the *Nürnberger Nachrichten* art prize. Weber has exhibited throughout Europe, in shows including *Artists at Work: New Technology in Textile and Fibre Art*, at the Prato Textile Museum, Italy (2003). She has had many solo exhibitions, and in 2010 the German Parliament in Berlin added her work to its collection. Weber has also worked on projects with architects to create art for various public venues.
www.sonja-weber.net

Daniel Widrig
Architect and designer
After graduating from the Architectural Association, London, Widrig established his own studio. He is the recipient of the Far Eastern International Digital Architectural Design Award, the Autodesk Masters Award and the Rome Prize. Widrig was artist-in-residence at the German Academy Villa Massimo in Rome (2009-10), and his work has been exhibited at Art Basel, Paris Fashion Week, the Martin-Gropius-Bau, Berlin, and the Victoria & Albert Museum, London.
www.danielwidrig.com

Mahir M. Yavuz
Designer
Yavuz is an external Senior Researcher for Ars Electronica Futurelab. A lecturer on typography, interaction design, information design and visualization at Istanbul Bilgi University and Kunstuniversität Linz (2003–11), he is currently a PhD candidate in interface culture at Kunstuniversität Linz, and chief creative director of Newgray, a design and research company based in New York.
www.mahir.tumblr.com

Peter Zuiderwijk
Graphic designer
Zuiderwijk is based in The Hague and works in partnership with graphic designer Karen Mientjes. Recent projects include *Making Do* (2011) and *Second Hand City* (2010) for *Day of Architecture*, and *Capital Out of Culture* for *TodaysArt* (2010). Zuiderwijk has taught research by design at the Willem de Kooning Academy, Rotterdam, since 2002.
www.peterzuiderwijk.com

bibliography

Antonelli, Paola, *Design and the Elastic Mind* (New York: The Museum of Modern Art, 2008).

Bentley, Peter J, *Digital Biology: The Creation of Life Inside Computers and How it Will Affect Us* (London: Headline Review, 2001).

Beylerian, George M., and Andrew Dent, *Ultra Materials: How Materials Innovation is Changing the World* (London and New York: Thames & Hudson, 2007).

Blackley, Lachlan, *Wallpaper* (London: Laurence King Publishing, 2006).

Blais, Joline, and Jon Ippolito, *At the Edge of Art* (London and New York: Thames & Hudson, 2006).

Bolton, Andrew, *The Supermodern Wardrobe* (London: V&A Publications, 2002).

Braddock, Sarah E., and Marie O'Mahony, *Textiles and New Technology* (London: Artemis, 1994).

Brownell, Blaine, *Transmaterial: A Catalogue of Materials that Refine our Physical Environment* (New York: Princeton Architectural Press, 2006).

Clarke, Sarah E. Braddock, and Marie O'Mahony, *Techno Textiles 2: Revolutionary Fabrics for Fashion and Design* (London: Thames & Hudson, 2005).

Cubitt, Sean, *Digital Aesthetics* (London: Sage Publications, 1998).

Derrick, Robin, ed., *The Impossible Image* (London: Phaidon Press, 2000).

Evans, Caroline, *Fashion at the Edge: Spectacle, Modernity and Deathliness* (London: Yale University Press, 2003).

Evans, Caroline, et al., *Hussein Chalayan* (Rotterdam: NAi Publishers, 2005).

Fairs, Marcus, *Twenty-First Century Design: New Design Icons from Mass Market to Avant-Garde* (London: Carlton Books, 2006).

Gere, Charlie, *Digital Culture* (London: Reaktion Books, 2002).

Gibson, William, *Neuromancer* (1984; London: Voyager, 1995).

Handley, Susannah, *Nylon: The Manmade Fashion Revolution* (London: Bloomsbury Publishing, 1999).

Harris, Jane, *Surface Tension: The Aesthetic Fabrication of Digital Textiles (The Design and Construction of 3D Computer-Graphic Animation)*, PhD thesis, London, Royal College of Art, 2000.

——, 'Crafting Computer Graphics: A Convergence of Traditional and New Media', in *Textile: The Journal of Cloth and Culture* 3:1 (2005).

Hodge, Brooke, Patricia Mears and Susan Sidlauskas, *Skin + Bones: Parallel Practices in Fashion and Architecture* (London and New York: Thames & Hudson, 2006).

Honoré, Carl, *In Praise of Slow: How a Worldwide Movement is Challenging the Cult of Speed* (London: Orion, 2005).

Kamphuis, Hanneke, and Hedwig van Onna, *Atmosphere: The Shape of Things to Come: Architecture, Interior Design, Design and Art* (Amsterdam: Frame Publishers, 2007).

Kawamura, Yuniya, *The Japanese Revolution in Paris Fashion* (Oxford: Berg, 2004).

Koren, Leonard, *Wabi-Sabi for Artists, Designers, Poets and Philosophers* (Berkeley, California: Stone Bridge Press, 1994).

Kries, Mateo, and Alexander von Vegesack, eds, *A-POC Making: Issey Miyake and Dai Fujiwara* (Berlin: Vitra Design Museum, 2001).

Kronenburg, Robert, *Flexible: Architecture that Responds to Change* (London: Laurence King Publishing, 2007).

Lee, Suzanne, *Fashioning the Future: Tomorrow's Wardrobe* (London and New York: Thames & Hudson, 2005).

Lupton, Ellen, *Skin: Surface, Substance and Design* (New York: Princeton Architectural Press, 2002).

Maeda, John, *The Laws of Simplicity: Design, Technology, Business, Life* (Cambridge, Massachusetts: The MIT Press, 2006).

——, *Maeda @ Media* (London and New York: Thames & Hudson, 2000).

Manzini, Ezio, *The Material of Invention: Materials and Design* (Cambridge, Massachusetts: The MIT Press, 1989).

McCarty, Cara, and Matilda McQuaid, *Structure and Surface: Contemporary Japanese Textiles* (New York: The Museum of Modern Art, 1998).

McCullough, Malcolm, *Abstracting Craft: The Practiced Digital Hand* (Cambridge, Massachusetts: The MIT Press, 1996).

Negroponte, Nicholas, *Being Digital* (New York: Vintage, 1995).

Paik, Karen, *To Infinity and Beyond!: The Story of Pixar Animation Studios* (London: Virgin Books, 2007).

Pawley, Martin, *Buckminster Fuller* (London: Trefoil Publications, 1990).

Plant, Sadie, *Zero and Ones: Digital Women and the New Technoculture* (London: Fourth Estate, 1997).

Quinn, Bradley, *Techno Fashion* (Oxford: Berg, 2002).

Radice, Barbara, *Memphis: Research, Experiences, Results, Failures and Successes of New Design* (London and New York: Thames & Hudson, 1985).

Revill, David, *The Roaring Silence: John Cage, A Life* (New York: Arcade, 1992).

Smith, Courtenay, and Sean Topham, *Xtreme Fashion* (London: Prestel Publishing, 2005).

Swade, Doron, *The Difference Engine: Charles Babbage and the Quest to Build the First Computer* (London: Penguin, 2002).

Toffler, Alvin, *Future Shock* (New York: Bantam Books, 1971).

Troika (Conny Freyer, Sebastian Noel and Eva Rucki), *Digital by Design: Crafting Technology for Products and Environments* (London and New York: Thames & Hudson, 2008).

Youngblood, Gene, *Expanded Cinema* (London: Studio Vista, 1970).

Zellner, Peter, *Hybrid Space: New Forms in Digital Architecture* (London and New York: Thames & Hudson, 1999).

photo credits

Numbers refer to pages on which illustrations appear
(a = above; b = below; c = centre; l = left; r = right; t= top).

6a architects 57; Gerhard Richter, German, born 1932, *Woman Descending the Staircase (Frau die Treppe herabgehend)*, 1965, Oil on canvas, 198 × 128 cm (79 × 51 in.), Roy J. and Frances R. Friedman Endowment; gift of Lannan Foundation, 1997.176, The Art Institute of Chicago 17; Savithri Bartlett 137; Basso & Brooke 8, 178tr, 178bl, 179, 180; Louise Lemieux Bérubé 50b; Anuschka Blommers, Niels Schumm 65; Boredom Research 78, 79b; Daniel Brown 148; Daniel Brown and SHOWstudio, © SHOWstudio 146, 147, 149; Courtesy of Bruce Mau Design 1, 16, 30, 58, 206; Hussein Chalayan, © Hussein Chalayan and Neutral 116; Courtesy of Harold Cohen 10; Cornbreadworks 125bl,125c, 125br; Crafts Council Collection: T176. © Crafts Council / Alex Lee 193; Rory Crichton 38bl, 39; Francesca Rosella, Ryan Genz, © CuteCircuit Ltd 214r; Char Davies, © Char Davies 224; Joshua Davis 182–87; René de Wit 124; Diesel 223; Hil Driessen 123t; eBoy 76b; Eley Kishimoto 22t; Entropia Universe and Vexed Generation 226; firstVIEW. com 46, 94, 95l, 96br, 97b, 114, 115, 119, 136, 162, 163, 164r, 165, 177, 178tl, 178br, 181, 188–191, 194bl, 195r, 197; firstVIEW. com, visual effects Mesmer 221; Freedom of Creation 210; Dave Goga, background painting by Kader Attia, courtesy of de Pury & Luxembourg 54b; Mark Goulthorpe 216; Michael Hansmeyer 208, 217; Jane Harris and Textile Futures Research Centre 227; Tomoko Hayashi, Stefan Agamanolis, Matthew Karau at Media Lab Europe 207, 228; Guy Hoffmann 29c; SeungMo Hong 54t; Jason Ingram 52t; Jakob Schlaepfer 156–61; Hesam Khoshneviss 29t, 29b; Nick Knight, Trunk Archive. With Dominic Wright, digital imaging director, Createc London 66; KnoWear 67; Courtesy of Michiko Koshino 171, 172, 173l, 174l, 175l; © Ebru Kurbak, Mahir M. Yavuz 214l; Kvadrat, © Poul Ib Henriksen 92t; Tass Kyprianou 48; Jannes Linder 123b, 125tl, 125tr; Lost in Space, © Lost in Space 63; Sarah Maingot 138tr, 138br; Abraham McClurg 80; Sue McNab 84–86; Me Company 12–13, 59, 61, 62, 70, 71, 74, 117; Courtesy of Miu Miu 109; Courtesy of Issey Miyake 95r, 96l, 96tr, 97t, 98, 99; Chris Moore 23–26, 36l, 38tl, 38r, 47, 69, 164tl, 164bl, 173r, 174r, 175r, 176, 192; Sebastian Neeb 54c; Philips Design, © Philips 142t; Philips Design, © Philips. With Clive van Heerden, Jack Mama, Lucy McRae, Rachel Wingfield, Matthias Gmachl, Stijn Osserfort, Bram Osserfort, Ollie Niemi, Oliver Gondorf, Sita Fischer 143–45; Courtesy of Prada 106–8, 110–13; J. Morgan Puett and Mark Dion in collaboration with Iain Kerr 211; Radiohead, 'House of Cards' (music video), directed by James Frost, © Xurbia Xendless Ltd 212, 213; Karim Rashid 41l; Casey Reas 150–54; Casey Reas, © Robert Downs and Jay Yan 155; Vibeke Riisberg 89b, 93; Vibeke Riisberg, © Ole Akhøj 92b; Vibeke Riisberg, © Dorte Krogh 89t; Claire Robertson 194t; Ronald Grant Archive 68, 209; Ismini Samanidou 49; Shinich Sato 50t; Dianna Snape 28; Simon Schofield 6–7, 79t; Norma Starszakowna 41r; Courtesy of Peter Struycken 83, 101–5; Susumu Tachi 215; Akihide Tamura 87; Mike Thomas and Lost in Space 60; Simon Thorogood 134, 135; Simon Thorogood, © Tim Bret-Day 132, 133; Nancy Tilbury, © Perry Curties 142bl, 142 br; Nancy Tilbury, © Ellie Laycock 140, 141; Timorous Beasties 36r; Michele Turriani 138l, 139; Jan van Eijndhoven 121r; Iris van Herpen, © Petrovski & Ramone 201; Iris van Herpen, © Shamila at Eric ElenBaas 198; Iris van Herpen, © Michel Zoeter 200, 202, 203; Michiel Vijselaar 120, 121l, 122; Moritz Waldemeyer 22b, 118; Warner Textile Archive (BDMT Ltd) 19; Andrew Weatherhead 128b; Dean Wilmont 31

index